A COMPREHENSIVE ANTHOLOGY

OF AMERICAN POETRY

A COMPREHENSIVE
ANTHOLOGY OF
AMERICAN
POETRY

Edited by Conrad Aiken

THE MODERN LIBRARY
New York

THE MODERN LIBRARY
is published by RANDOM HOUSE, INC.

Manufactured in the United States of America by H. Wolff

ACKNOWLEDGMENTS

MY thanks are due to the following for permission to reprint poems contained herein:

Cameron, Blake & Co. for *Day and Dark* by George Cabot Lodge, from *Poems*.

The Century Co. for *Ecce in Deserto* by Henry Augustin Beers, from *Collected Poems,* and for *Chanson of the Bells of Oseney* by Cale Young Rice, from *Wraiths and Realities*.

Copeland & Day for *The Happiest Heart* by John Vance Cheney, from *Out of the Silence,* and for *Clover* by John Banister Tabb, from *Lyrics*.

H. D. for *Not Honey,* from *Hymen*.

The Dial Press for poems by Marianne Moore, from *Observations*.

Funk & Wagnalls Co. for *Indirection* by Richard Realf, from *Poems*.

Harcourt, Brace & Co. for *Nun Snow* by Alfred Kreymborg; *Long Feud* by Louis Untermeyer, from *Burning Bush;* and *You, Andrew Marvell* by Archibald MacLeish.

Harper & Bros. for poems by Edna St. Vincent Millay.

Henry Holt & Co. for poems by Robert Frost, from *A Boy's Will, North of Boston, Mountain Interval,* and *New Hampshire*.

Houghton Mifflin Co. for selections from Oliver Wendell Holmes, James Russell Lowell, Henry David Thoreau, Julia Ward Howe, Henry Wadsworth Longfellow, Ralph Waldo Emerson, Walt Whitman, Edward Rowland Sill, John Townsend Trowbridge, Thomas Bailey Aldrich, John Burroughs, William Vaughn Moody, Anna Hempstead Branch, Amy Lowell, H. D., John Gould Fletcher, and Archibald MacLeish.

A. A. Knopf, Inc., for *War Is Kind* by Stephen Crane; poems by Elinor Wylie, from *Trivial Breath* and *Nets to Catch the Wind;* poems by Adelaide Crapsey, from *Verse;* poems by Wallace Stevens, from *Harmonium;* poems by T. S.

14723

Eliot, from *Poems;* and poems by John Crowe Ransom, from *Chills and Fever* and *Two Gentlemen in Bonds.*

Little, Brown & Co. for poems by Emily Dickinson, from *Poems: First Series, Poems: Second Series. Poems: Third Series* and *The Single Hound;* poems by Helen Hunt Jackson, from *Collected Poems;* and for *Hic Jacet* by Louise Chandler Moulton, from *Collected Poems.*

Horace Liveright for *They Went Forth to Battle* by Shaemas O'Sheel, from *Jealous of Dead Leaves;* poems by H. D. from *A Sea Garden;* and poems by Ezra Pound, from *Personæ.*

Agnes Thompson Long for *Wild Honey* by Maurice Thompson.

The Macmillan Co. for poems by Trumbull Stickney, from *Poems;* poems by Edwin Arlington Robinson, from *Poems;* poems by Edgar Lee Masters, from *The Spoon River Anthology;* and poems by Vachel Lindsay, from *The Congo and Other Poems.*

Edwin Markham for *The Man with the Hoe,* from *Collected Poems.*

Princeton University Press for *L'Envoi* by Herman Melville, from *John Marr and Other Poems.*

Chas. Scribner's Sons for *Opposition* by Sidney Lanier, from *Collected Poems;* poems by George Santayana, from *Poems* and *The Hermit of Carmel; For a Dead Lady* by Edwin Arlington Robinson, from *The Town Down the River;* and for *Earth* by John Hall Wheelock.

Stone & Kimball for *Odes* by George Santayana, from *Sonnets and Other Verses.*

The Viking Press for *The Image of Delight* by William Ellery Leonard, from *The Vaunt of Man.*

The Whitaker & Ray-Wiggin Co. for *At the Grave of Walker* by Joaquin Miller, from *Complete Poems.*

For the right to reprint the additional copyrighted poems in the revised edition of this volume, I am indebted to the following poets, publishers and agents:

R. P. Blackmur for *Half-Tide Ledge, Scarabs for the Living I-IX* by R. P. Blackmur.

Brandt & Brandt for *Love Is More Thicker Than Forget, My Father Moved Through Dooms of Love, As Freedom Is a*

Breakfastfood, Always Before Your Voice My Soul published by Duell, Sloan & Pearce, copyright, 1939, 1940, by E. E. Cummings.

Malcolm Cowley for *The Long Voyage* by Malcolm Cowley.

Farrar and Rinehart, Inc., for *The Sea, Hide in the Heart* by Lloyd Frankenberg.

Robert Hillyer for *Letter to a Teacher of English* by Robert Hillyer.

Harcourt, Brace & Co. for *Four Preludes on Playthings of the Wind, Jazz Fantasia* by Carl Sandburg; *Portrait of a Lady, Burnt Norton, Ash Wednesday* by T. S. Eliot.

Henry Holt & Co. for *Desert Places, Bereft, For Once, Then, Something, Once by the Pacific* by Robert Frost; *Cool Tombs, Gone* by Carl Sandburg; *No Faith, His Trees, Exaggerator, The Whisperer* by Mark Van Doren.

Houghton Mifflin Co. for *Memorial Rain* by Archibald MacLeish.

A. A. Knopf, Inc., for *Domination of Black, Sea Surface Full of Clouds* by Wallace Stevens; *Spouse, Ghost, Correspondent, Ganymede, Captain's Table, Charioteer* by Witter Bynner; *This Corruptible* by Elinor Wylie.

Liveright Publishing Corporation for *The River-Merchant's Wife:A Letter, The Flame, Dance Figure, Lament of the Frontier Guard, Taking Leave of a Friend* by Ezra Pound; *Voyages II, Voyages VI, Praise for an Urn,* passages from *The Bridge* by Hart Crane.

The Macmillan Co. for *Abraham Lincoln Walks at Midnight* by Vachel Lindsay; *Islands:A Song* by John Malcolm Brinnin; *Roses Only* by Marianne Moore.

New Directions for *Song, Spring Song* by Theodore Spencer; *Sir Gawaine and the Green Knight* by Yvor Winters; *Train Ride, Fish Food* by John Wheelwright; *Bearded Oaks, Revelation* by Robert Penn Warren; *At the New Year* by Kenneth Patchen; *"Mentrechè il Vento, Comme Fa, Si Tace," Socrates' Ghost Must Haunt Me Now* by Delmore Schwartz.

Oxford University Press for *The Man Coming Toward You, The Leg in the Subway* by Oscar Williams; for *The Groundhog* by Richard Eberhart.

Random House, Inc., for *Continent's End, Apology for Bad Dreams, Love the Wild Swan* by Robinson Jeffers.

John Crowe Ransom for *Bells for John Whiteside's Daughter, Lady Lost, Here Lies a Lady* by John Crowe Ransom.

Reynal and Hitchcock, Inc., for *Poet, The Twins, Travelogue for Exiles, Nostalgia* by Karl Jay Shapiro.

Chas. Scribner's Sons for *Hasbrouck and the Rose, About Women* by H. Phelps Putnam; *Summer Wish* by Louise Bogan; *Ode to the Confederate Dead* by Allen Tate.

Mr. and Mrs. Henry A. Stickney for *Near Helikon, Fidelity, Mnemosyne, Now in the Palace Gardens* by Trumbull Stickney.

Leon Tebbetts Editions for *Confidence, Warblers, In Robin Hood Cave* by Marsden Hartley.

The Viking Press for *Be Beautiful, Noble, Like the Antique Ant, God Said, "I Made a Man," Now, If You Will Look in My Brain, My Mouth Is Very Quiet, The Way My Ideas Think Me, Saw God Dead but Laughing* by José Garcia Villa.

Edmund Wilson for *Riverton, A House of the Eighties* by Edmund Wilson.

CONRAD AIKEN

INTRODUCTION

AMERICAN POETRY has been extensively antholo-gized; but so far as I am aware there has been no attempt hitherto to present in one volume a selection which shall represent the whole range of it, from its beginnings down to the present day. In a few textbooks, it is true, one may find, along with prose selections also, a fairly adequate survey. But for some curious reason the notion of a compact and comprehensive anthology of the verse alone has not found expression. That such a thing should be useful goes without saying. That it should be difficult is obvious, too—almost as obvious as that the editor who undertakes it will inevitably make mistakes in judgment and will inevitably be reproached for them. At the very outset he faces the formidable question of proportion. How much space shall he give to "early" American poetry—the poetry of the seventeenth and eighteenth centuries? How much, in this regard, shall he allow himself to be weighed upon by purely historical considerations? Should the Connecticut wits—for example—be represented, simply on the ground that they existed, and that they enjoyed for a time a kind of popularity? Or should he frankly admit to himself that their work was almost wholly without esthetic value, and ruthlessly exclude them?

The present editor has felt that the esthetic judgment (whatever that may be, and however we may define it) is the only sound basis for procedure; and if now and then he has momentarily compromised with this principle, admitting here and there a poem merely because it has achieved an immense popularity, he has, on the whole, done this reluctantly and seldom. American poetry, if one takes it as a whole, is not yet a great or rich poetry, though it has shown not infrequently the elements of greatness and richness; it has been provincial, uneven, tentative, brilliant; but if one cannot as yet say that it takes a very high place in the poetry of the world, as the expression of a national soul or culture, one can at least say emphatically that the time has come for a firm revision of our critical attitude toward it. We are too much accustomed, I fear, to what one might term a high protective tariff in this matter. We are a little too willing to suspend or modify judgment, on the ground that too much was not to be expected of a pioneer people in a new continent. Insensibly, we have got into the habit of accepting the second-best; and by closing our eyes to the best—by which I mean the best poetry of the world— have found it not too difficult to persuade ourselves of the excellence of the native product.

It is time, I think, to give up this rather childish habit, and to regard American poetry as severely as we would re- gard Greek or Chinese or English poetry. For if American poetry is not yet great, it has at least reached that point at which one may say that it is mature. It has a history of nearly three hundred years. In sheer quantity, if one keeps in mind all the minor poets and poetasters of the eighteenth and nineteenth centuries, it is enormous: few people, un- less we except librarians, can have any idea of it. And if we admit cheerfully enough that the first two-thirds of its history is pretty barren, nevertheless one can also say with some assurance that it now comprises names of which no country need be ashamed, and that it is beginning to wear the dignity that goes with a tradition.

In view of this, it has been the present editor's intention to be somewhat severer with his material than his prede- cessors have been, in order that the process of clarification of this tradition might take a step forward. He has been rather hard on certain national favorites; it will be thought by some that he has been too drastic with Longfellow and Holmes and Whittier and Lowell and Lanier; that he has been too generous with Poe and Whitman and Dickinson; and that he has perhaps erred in proportion by giving to the poetry of the last twenty years so much more space than has been given to that of any preceding era. To such an objection he can only reply that in his opinion the poetry which begins, roughly, with Emily Dickinson has been the richest which America has produced; and that our so-called classics have been very seriously overestimated. If he can disturb prevailing notions about these things, and set in motion a revaluation of American poetry, which will find perhaps a higher place for comparatively unknown poets like Anne Bradstreet or Thomas Chivers or Trumbull Stickney than for Longfellow or Lowell or Bryant—not, be it understood, in point of range, but in point of sheer excellence or intensity—he will consider that he has been of some small service to American criticism. He has tried to eliminate, as far as possible, those things which embody the faults which so cursed American poetry in the nineteenth century—excessive sentimentality, sententiousness, easy dactylic exoticism—in order that the present movement in American poetry toward severer outline, both in idea and expression, might be more visible. If he has at all succeeded in this, he will have made one degree easier the ultimate compilation of a first-rate anthology by his successors.

Fifteen years have passed since this anthology was first published—almost a literary generation; but in now revising and amplifying it, and bringing it up to date, I have cast back even further than that. Perspective changes; the critic's eye changes; poetry changes too. One finds that one had too much of X, too little of Y, none at all of Z— nor is it even as simple as that. For there arises also the question of the relation of X with Y, and then, further, the relation of each with the whole mass and current of his day. One's own view of the mass and current, meanwhile, has been imperceptibly changing with the changing times; the shadows and lights fall now in other places; what seemed formerly only a tendency, and of the vaguest and most tentative at that, now reveals itself as a quite definite and accomplished direction; what formerly seemed to be a direction has now become vestigial, stopped off: one of Nature's little experiments which, alas, has failed.

But in adding (and to a very small extent subtracting) I believe I have only sharpened, not changed, the character of this book. The aim, as before, has been to be rid of excess baggage, particularly of the more sentimental sort, even if (such are one's bad habits) one cannot hope to be wholly successful. I have been blamed by some anthologists for being too "abstract" in my taste; if by this it is meant that I have tried to avoid the pretty, on the one hand, or the oratorical and politically tendentious, on the other, I take it as a compliment. Sentiment, whether it is for privileged classes, or for the flowers that bloom in the spring, can never excuse inadequacy of statement. For if poetry can very nearly do without meaning (witness the miracles of nonsense verse) it plainly cannot do without excellence of statement. The "greatness" of a poet will, of course, in the end, always depend, and precisely, on his range and richness of meaning: do we perceive him as an island, a peninsula, a continent? But without that *first* prerequisite of poetry, clarity and excellence of statement, he will never have been perceived by us at all, even as an islet.

It remains to add that every anthology, and this is no exception, is a collaboration, a collaboration between the anthologist, the poets and the public. It is also, however, a collaboration in experiment. Which way will taste go? Which way will poetry go? Will these yellows keep their luminosity, the reds turn gray? Even now new poets are working at this, competitively, and for survival; new ideas and fashions are competing too, if more bloodlessly, for a share in the evolving consciousness of man. The anthologist is an interpreter in all this, with perhaps a little, just a *little*, unconscious *parti pris;* and the public, the public awareness, itself grinding out its own conflicting complex of wants and fears, is the slow-working arbiter and perpetuator. The whole fascinating confusion with its involved differentials, is simply a process of communal growing. . . . And no doubt, in another twenty years, we shall know into what.

CONRAD AIKEN

Brewster, Massachusetts.
1944

CONTENTS

A COMPREHENSIVE ANTHOLOGY

OF AMERICAN POETRY

ANNE BRADSTREET

The Flesh and the Spirit

IN secret place where once I stood,
Close by the banks of lacrym flood,
I heard two sisters reason on
Things that are past and things to come.
One Flesh was called, who had her eye
On worldly wealth and vanity;
The other Spirit, who did rear
Her thoughts unto a higher sphere.
"Sister," quoth Flesh, "what livest thou on—
Nothing but meditation?
Doth contemplation feed thee, so
Regardlessly to let earth go?
Can speculation satisfy
Notion without reality?
Dost dream of things beyond the moon,
And dost thou hope to dwell there soon?
Hast treasures there laid up in store
That all in the world thou countest poor?
Art fancy sick, or turned a sot,
To catch at shadows which are not?
Come, come, I'll show unto thy sense
Industry hath its recompense.
What canst desire but thou mayst see
True substance in variety?
Dost honor like? Acquire the same,
As some to their immortal fame,
And trophies to thy name erect
Which wearing time shall ne'er deject.
For riches dost thou long full sore?
Behold enough of precious store;

3

Earth hath more silver, pearls, and gold
Than eyes can see or hands can hold.
Affectest thou pleasure? Take thy fill;
Earth hath enough of what you will.
Then let not go what thou mayst find
For things unknown, only in mind."

SPIRIT

"Be still, thou unregenerate part;
Disturb no more my settled heart,
For I have vowed, and so will do,
Thee as a foe still to pursue,
And combat with thee will and must
Until I see thee laid in the dust.
Sisters we are, yea, twins we be,
Yet deadly feud 'twixt thee and me;
For from one father are we not.
Thou by old Adam was begot,
But my arise is from above,
Whence my dear Father I do love.
Thou speakest me fair, but hatest me sore;
Thy flattering shows I'll trust no more.
How oft thy slave hast thou me made
When I believed what thou hast said,
And never had more cause of woe
Than when I did what thou bad'st do.
I'll stop mine ears at these thy charms,
And count them for my deadly harms.
Thy sinful pleasures I do hate,
Thy riches are to me no bait,
Thine honors do nor will I love,
For my ambition lies above.
My greatest honor it shall be
When I am victor over thee,
And triumph shall, with laurel head,
When thou my captive shalt be led.
How I do live thou needst not scoff,
For I have meat thou knowst not of:
The hidden manna I do eat,
The word of life it is my meat.

My thoughts do yield me more content
Than can thy hours in pleasure spent.
Nor are they shadows which I catch,
Nor fancies vain at which I snatch,
But reach at things that are so high
Beyond thy dull capacity.
Eternal substance I do see,
With which enrichéd I would be;
Mine eye doth pierce the heavens, and see
What is invisible to thee.
My garments are not silk or gold,
Nor such like trash which earth doth hold,
But royal robes I shall have on,
More glorious than the glistering sun.
My crown not diamonds, pearls, and gold,
But such as angels' heads enfold.
The city where I hope to dwell
There's none on earth can parallel:
The stately walls, both high and strong,
Are made of precious jasper stone;
The gates of pearl both rich and clear,
And angels are for porters there;
The streets thereof transparent gold,
Such as no eye did e'er behold;
A crystal river there doth run,
Which doth proceed from the Lamb's throne;
Of life there are the waters sure,
Which shall remain for ever pure;
Of sun or moon they have no need,
For glory doth from God proceed—
No candle there, nor yet torch-light,
For there shall be no darksome night.
From sickness and infirmity
For evermore they shall be free,
Nor withering age shall e'er come there,
But beauty shall be bright and clear.
This city pure is not for thee,
For things unclean there shall not be.
If I of Heaven may have my fill,
Take thou the world, and all that will."

Contemplations

SOME time now past in the Autumnal Tide,
  When *Phœbus* wanted but one hour to bed,
The trees all richly clad, yet void of pride,
Were gilded o're by his rich golden head;
Their leaves & fruits seem'd painted, but was true
Of green, of red, of yellow, mixed hew;
Rapt were my sences at this delectable view.

I wist not what to wish; "yet sure," thought I,
"If so much excellence abide below,
How excellent is he that dwells on high,
Whose power and beauty by his works we know!
Sure he is goodness, wisdome, glory, light,
That hath this under-world so richly dight."
More Heaven then Earth was here, no winter & no night.

Then on a stately Oak I cast mine Eye,
Whose ruffling top the Clouds seem'd to aspire:
"How long since thou wast in thine Infancy?
Thy strength and stature, more thy years admire.
Hath hundred winters past since thou wast born,
Or thousand since thou brakest thy shell of horn?
If so, all these as nought Eternity doth scorn."

Then higher on the glistering Sun I gaz'd,
Whose beams was shaded by the leavie Tree.
The more I look'd the more I grew amaz'd,
And softly said: "What glory 's like to thee,
Soul of this world, this Universes Eye?
No wonder some made thee a Deity:
Had I not better known, alas, the same had I.

"Thou as a Bridegroom from thy Chamber rushes,
And as a strong man joyes to run a race;
The morn doth usher thee with smiles & blushes,
The Earth reflects her glances in thy face;

Birds, insects, Animals, with Vegative,
Thy heart from death and dulness doth revive,
And in the darksome womb of fruitful nature dive.

"Thy swift Annual and diurnal Course,
Thy daily streight and yearly oblique path,
Thy pleasing fervor and thy scorching force,
All mortals here the feeling knowledg hath.
Thy presence makes it day, thy absence night;
Quaternal Seasons caused by thy might.
Hail, Creature full of sweetness, beauty, & delight!

"Art thou so full of glory that no Eye
Hath strength thy shining Rayes once to behold?
And is thy splendid Throne erect so high
As to approach it can no earthly mould?
How full of glory, then, must thy Creator be
Who gave this bright light luster unto thee:
Admir'd, ador'd for ever be that Majesty!"

Silent, alone, where none or saw or heard,
In pathless paths I lead my wandring feet,
My humble Eyes to lofty Skyes I rear'd:
To sing some Song my mazed Muse thought meet;
My great Creator I would magnifie,
That nature had thus decked liberally;
But Ah, and Ah again, my imbecility!

I heard the merry grashopper then sing,
The black-clad Cricket bear a second part;
They kept one tune and plaid on the same string
Seeming to glory in their little Art.
Shall Creatures abject thus their voices raise,
And in their kind resound their makers praise,
Whilst I as mute can warble forth no higher layes!

When present times look back to Ages past,
And men in being fancy those are dead.
It makes things gone perpetually to last,
And calls back moneths and years that long since fled;

It makes a man more aged in conceit
Then was *Methuselah* or 's grand-sire great,
While of their persons & their acts his mind doth treat.

Sometimes in *Eden* fair he seems to be;
Sees glorious *Adam* there made Lord of all;
Fancyes the Apple dangle on the Tree,
That turn'd his Sovereign to a naked thral,
Who like a miscreant's driven from that place,
To get his bread with pain and sweat of face,
A penalty impos'd on his backsliding Race.

Here sits our Grandame in retired place,
And in her lap her bloody *Cain* new born;
The weeping Imp oft looks her in the face,
Bewails his unknown hap and fate forlorn:
His Mother sighs to think of Paradise,
And how she lost her bliss to be more wise,
Believing him that was and is Father of lyes.

Here *Cain* and *Abel* come to sacrifice;
Fruits of the Earth and Fatlings each do bring:
On *Abels* gift the fire descends from Skies,
But no such sign on false *Cain's* offering.
With sullen hateful looks he goes his wayes,
Hath thousand thoughts to end his brothers dayes,
Upon whose blood his future good he hopes to raise.

There *Abel* keeps his sheep, no ill he thinks;
His brother comes, then acts his fratricide:
The Virgin Earth of blood her first draught drinks,
But since that time she often hath been cloy'd.
The wretch, with ghastly face and dreadful mind,
Thinks each he sees will serve him in his kind,
Though none on Earth but kindred near then could he find

Who fancyes not his looks now at the Barr?
His face like death, his heart with horror fraught,
Nor Male-factor ever felt like warr
When deep dispair with wish of life hath fought.

Branded with guilt and crusht with treble woes,
A Vagabond to Land of *Nod* he goes;
A City builds, that wals might him secure from foes.

Who thinks not oft upon the Fathers ages?
Their long descent; how nephews sons they saw;
The starry observations of those Sages,
And how their precepts to their sons were law;
How Adam sigh'd to see his Progeny
Cloath'd all in his black sinfull Livery,
Who neither guilt nor yet the punishment could fly.

Our Life compare we with their length of dayes;
Who to the tenth of theirs doth now arrive?
And though thus short, we shorten many wayes,
Living so little while we are alive:
In eating, drinking, sleeping, vain delight,
So unawares comes on perpetual night,
And puts all pleasures vain unto eternal flight.

When I behold the heavens as in their prime,
And then the earth, though old, stil clad in green
The stones and trees insensible of time,
Nor age nor wrinkle on their front are seen;
If winter come and greeness then do fade,
A Spring returns and they more youthfull made;
But Man grows old, lies down, remains where once he's laid.

By birth more noble then those creatures all,
Yet seems by nature and by custome curs'd:
No sooner born but grief and care makes fall,
That state obliterate he had at first;
Nor youth nor strength nor wisdom spring again,
Nor habitations long their names retain,
But in oblivion to the final day remain.

Shall I, then, praise the heavens, the trees, the earth,
Because their beauty and their strength last longer?
Shall I wish there or never to had birth,
Because they 're bigger, & their bodyes stronger?

Nay, they shall darken, perish, fade, and dye,
And when unmade so ever shall they lye;
But man was made for endless immortality.

Under the cooling shadow of a stately Elm,
Close sate I by a goodly Rivers side,
Where gliding streams the Rocks did overwhelm;
A lonely place, with pleasures dignifi'd.
I once that lov'd the shady woods so well
Now thought the rivers did the trees excel;
And if the sun would ever shine, there would I dwell.

While on the stealing stream I fixt mine eye,
Which to the long'd for Ocean held its course,
I markt nor crooks nor rubs that there did lye
Could hinder ought, but still augment its force:
"Oh happy Flood," quoth I, "that holds thy race
Till thou arrive at thy beloved place,
Nor is it rocks or shoals that can obstruct thy pace.

"Nor is 't enough that thou alone may'st slide,
But hundred brooks in thy cleer waves do meet;
So hand in hand along with thee they glide
To *Thetis* house, where all imbrace and greet:
Thou Emblem true of what I count the best,
O could I lead my Rivolets to rest,
So may we press to that vast mansion ever blest!

"Ye Fish which in this liquid Region 'bide,
That for each season have your habitation,
Now salt, now fresh, where you think best to glide
To unknown coasts to give a visitation,
In Lakes and ponds you leave your numerous fry;
So nature taught, and yet you know not why,
You watry folk that know not your felicity.

"Look how the wantons frisk to tast the air,
Then to the colder bottome streight they dive;
Eftsoon to *Neptune's* glassie Hall repair,
To see what trade they great ones there do drive,

Who forage o're the spacious sea-green field
And take the trembling prey before it yield,
Whose armour is their scales, their spreading fins
    their shield."

While musing thus, with contemplation fed,
And thousand fancies buzzing in my brain,
The sweet-tongu'd Philomel percht ore my head,
And chanted forth a most melodious strain;
Which rapt me so with wonder and delight
I judg'd my hearing better then my sight,
And wisht me wings with her a while to take my flight.

"O merry Bird," said I, "that fears no snares,
That neither toyles nor hoards up in thy barn,
Feels no sad thoughts, nor cruciating cares
To gain more good or shun what might thee harm;
Thy cloaths ne're wear, thy meat is every where,
Thy bed a bough, thy drink the water cleer;
Reminds not what is past, nor whats to come dost fear.

"The dawning morn with songs thou dost prevent,
Sets hundred notes unto thy feathered crew,
So each one tunes his pretty instrument
And, warbling out the old, begin anew;
And thus they pass their youth in summer season,
Then follow thee into a better Region,
Where winter 's never felt by that sweet airy legion."

Man at the best a creature frail and vain,
In knowledg ignorant, in strength but weak,
Subject to sorrows, losses, sickness, pain,
Each storm his state, his mind, his body break;
From some of these he never finds cessation,
But day or night, within, without, vexation,
Troubles from foes from friends, from dearest, near'st
    Relation.

And yet this sinfull creature, frail and vain,
This lump of wretchedness, of sin and sorrow,
This weather-beaten vessel wrackt with pain,

Joyes not in hope of an eternal morrow;
Nor all his losses, crosses, and vexation,
In weight, in frequency and long duration,
Can make him deeply groan for that divine Translation

The Mariner that on smooth waves doth glide
Sings merrily and steers his Barque with ease,
As if he had command of wind and tide,
And now become great Master of the seas;
But suddenly a storm spoiles all the sport,
And makes him long for a more quiet port,
Which 'gainst all adverse winds may serve for fort.

So he that saileth in this world of pleasure,
Feeding on sweets, that never bit of th' sowre,
That's full of friends, of honour, and of treasure,
Fond fool, he takes this earth ev'n for heav'ns bower.
But sad affliction comes & makes him see
Here's neither honour, wealth, nor safety:
Only above is found all with security.

O Time, the fatal wrack of mortal things,
That draws oblivions curtains over kings,
Their sumptuous monuments, men know them not,
Their names without a Record are forgot,
Their parts, their ports, their pomp's all laid in th' dust,
Nor wit nor gold nor buildings scape times rust:
But he whose name is grav'd in the white stone
Shall last and shine when all of these are gone.

A Letter to Her Husband

PHŒBUS, make haste: the day's too long; be gone;
The silent night's the fittest time for moan
But stay this once, unto my suit give ear,
And tell my griefs in either Hemisphere;
And if the whirling of thy wheels don't drown'd
The woful accents of my doleful sound,

If in thy swift Carrier thou canst make stay,
I crave this boon, this Errand by the way:
Commend me to the man more lov'd then life;
Shew him the sorrows of his widdowed wife,
My dumpish thoughts, my groans, my brakish tears
My sobs, my longing hopes, my doubting fears;
And if he love, how can he there abide?
My interest 's more then all the world beside.
He that can tell the starrs or Ocean sand,
Or all the grass that in the Meads do stand,
The leaves in th' woods, the hail or drops of rain,
Or in a corn-field number every grain,
Or every mote that in the sun-shine hops,
May count my sighs and number all my drops.
Tell him the countless steps that thou dost trace
That once a day thy Spouse thou mayst imbrace;
And when thou canst not treat by loving mouth,
Thy rayes afar salute her from the south.
But for one moneth I see no day, poor soul,
Like those far scituate under the pole,
Which day by day long wait for thy arise:
O how they joy when thou dost light the skyes.
O *Phœbus,* hadst thou but thus long from thine
Restrain'd the beams of thy beloved shine,
At thy return, if so thou could'st or durst,
Behold a Chaos blacker then the first.
Tell him here 's worse then a confused matter—
His little world 's a fathom under water;
Nought but the fervor of his ardent beams
Hath power to dry the torrent of these streams.
Tell him I would say more, but cannot well:
Oppressed minds abruptest tales do tell.
Now post with double speed, mark what I say;
By all our loves conjure him not to stay.

Longing for Heaven

AS weary pilgrim now at rest
    Hugs with delight his silent nest,
His wasted limbes now lye full soft
    That myrie steps have troden oft,
Blesses himself to think upon
    his dangers past and travailes done;
The burning sun no more shall heat,
    Nor stormy raines on him shall beat;
The bryars and thornes no more shall scratch,
    nor hungry wolves at him shall catch;
He erring pathes no more shall tread,
    nor wild fruits eate in stead of bread;
For waters cold he doth not long,
    for thirst no more shall parch his tongue;
No rugged stones his feet shall gaule,
    nor stumps nor rocks cause him to fall;
All cares and feares he bids farwell,
    and meanes in safity now to dwell:
A pilgrim I on earth perplext,
    with sinns, with cares and sorrows vext,
By age and paines brought to decay,
    and my Clay house mouldring away,
Oh how I long to be at rest
    and soare on high among the blest!
This body shall in silence sleep,
    Mine eyes no more shall ever weep,
No fainting fits shall me assaile,
    nor grinding paines my body fraile,
With cares and fears ne'r cumbred be,
    Nor losses know nor sorrowes see.
What tho my flesh shall there consume?
    it is the bed Christ did perfume;
And when a few years shall be gone,
    this mortall shall be cloth'd upon:
A Corrupt Carcasse downe it lyes,
    a glorious body it shall rise;

In weakness and dishonour sowne,
    in power 't is rais'd by Christ alone.
Then soule and body shall unite,
    and of their maker have the sight.
Such lasting joyes shall there behold
    as eare ne'r heard nor tongue e'er told.
Lord, make me ready for that day:
    then Come, deare bridgrome, Come away!

THOMAS GODFREY

The Invitation

DAMON. Haste, Sylvia, haste, my charming maid!
    Let 's leave these fashionable toys:
Let's seek the shelter of some shade,
    And revel in ne'er fading joys.
See, *Spring* in liv'ry gay appears,
    And winter's chilly blasts are fled;
Each grove its leafy honours rears,
    And meads their lovely verdure spread.

SYLVIA. Yes, Damon, glad I'll quit the town:
    It's gaieties now languid seem:
Then sweets to luxury unknown
    We 'll taste, and sip th' untainted stream.
In *Summer*'s sultry noon-tide heat
    I 'll lead thee to the shady grove,
There hush thy cares, or pleas'd repeat
    Those vows that won my soul to love.

DAMON. When o'er the mountain peeps the dawn,
    And round her ruddy beauties play,
I'll wake my love to view the lawn,
    Or hear the warblers hail the day.

But without thee the rising morn
    In vain awakes the cooling breeze;
In vain does nature's face adorn—
    Without my Sylvia nought can please.

SYLVIA. At night, when universal gloom
    Hides the bright prospects from our view,
When the gay groves give up their bloom
    And verdant meads their lovely hue,
Tho' fleeting spectres round me move,
    When in thy circling arms I 'm prest,
I 'll hush my rising fears with love,
    And sink in slumber on thy Breast.

DAMON. The new-blown rose, whilst on its leaves
    Yet the bright scented dew-drop 's found,
Pleas'd on thy bosom whilst it heaves,
    Shall shake its heav'nly fragrance round.
Then mingled sweets the sense shall raise,
    Then mingled beauties catch the eye:
What pleasure on such charms to gaze,
    What rapture 'mid such sweets to lie!

SYLVIA. How sweet thy words! But, Damon, cease,
    Nor strive to fix me ever here;
Too well you know these accents please,
    That oft have fill'd my ravish'd ear.
Come, lead me to these promis'd joys
    That dwelt so lately on thy tongue;
Direct me by thy well-known voice,
    And calm my transports with thy song!

PHILIP FRENEAU

From "The House of Night"

TREMBLING I write my dream, and recollect
A fearful vision at the midnight hour;
So late, death o'er me spreads his signal wings,
Painted with fancies of malignant power!

Such was the dream the sage Chaldean saw
Disclos'd to him that felt heaven's vengeful rod,
Such was the ghost, who through deep silence cry'd,
Shall mortal man—be juster than his God?

Let others draw from smiling skies their theme,
And tell of climes that boast unfading light,
I draw a darker scene, replete with gloom,
I sing the horrors of the *House of Night*.

Stranger, believe the truth experience tells,
Poetic dreams are of a finer cast
Than those which o'er the sober brain diffused,
Are but a repetition of some action past.

Fancy, I own thy power—when sunk in sleep
Thou play'st thy wild delusive part so well
You lift me into immortality,
Depict new heavens, or draw the scenes of hell.

By some sad means, when Reason holds no sway,
Lonely I rov'd at midnight o'er a plain
Where murmuring streams and mingling rivers flow
Far to their springs or seek the sea again.

Sweet vernal May! tho' then thy woods in bloom
Flourish'd, yet nought of this could Fancy see;
No wild pinks bless'd the meads, no green the fields,
And naked seem'd to stand each lifeless tree.

Dark was the sky, and not one friendly star
Shone from the zenith or horizon, clear;
Mist sate upon the woods, and darkness rode
In her black chariot with a wild career.

And from the woods the late-resounding note
Issued of the loquacious *Whip-poor-will;*
Hoarse, howling dogs and nightly roving wolves
Clamour'd from far-off clifts invisible.

Rude from the wide-extended *Chesapeke*
I heard the winds the dashing waves assail,
And saw from far, by picturing fancy form'd,
The black ship travelling through the noisy gale.

At last, by chance and guardian fancy led,
I reach'd a noble dome rais'd fair and high,
And saw the light from upper windows flame,
Presage of mirth and hospitality.

And by that light around the dome appear'd
A mournful garden of autumnal hue;
Its lately pleasing flowers all drooping stood
Amidst high weeds that in rank plenty grew.

The Primrose there, the violet darkly blue,
Daisies and fair Narcissus ceas'd to rise;
Gay spotted pinks their charming bloom withdrew,
And Polyanthus quench'd its thousand dyes.

No pleasant fruit or blossom gaily smil'd;
Nought but unhappy plants and trees were seen:
The yew, the myrtle, and the church-yard elm,
The cypress with its melancholy green.

There cedars dark, the osier, and the pine,
Shorn tamarisks, and weeping willows grew,
The poplar tall, the lotos, and the lime;
And pyracantha did her leaves renew.

The poppy there, companion to repose,
Display'd her blossoms that began to fall;
And here the purple amaranthus rose,
With mint strong-scented, for the funeral.

And here and there, with laurel shrubs between,
A tombstone lay, inscrib'd with strains of woe;
And stanzas sad, throughout the dismal green,
Lamented for the dead that slept below.

Peace to this awful dome!—when strait I heard
The voice of men in a secluded room;
Much did they talk of death and much of life,
Of coffins, shrouds, and horrors of a tomb. . . .

Then up three winding stairs my feet were brought
To a high chamber, hung with mourning sad;
The unsnuff'd candles glar'd with visage dim,
'Midst grief in ecstasy of woe run mad.

A wide-leaf'd table stood on either side,
Well fraught with phials, half their liquids spent;
And from a couch behind the curtain's veil
I heard a hollow voice of loud lament.

Turning to view the object whence it came,
My frighted eyes a horrid form survey'd
(*Fancy, I own thy power*): Death on the couch,
With fleshless limbs, at rueful length, was laid.

And o'er his head flew jealousies and cares,
Ghosts, imps, and half the black Tartarian crew,
Arch-angels damn'd; nor was their Prince remote,
Borne on the vaporous wings of Stygian dew.

Around his bed, by the dull flambeaux glare,
I saw pale phantoms: Rage to madness vext,
Wan, wasting grief, and ever-musing care,
Distressful pain, and poverty perplext.

Sad was his countenance—if we can call
That *countenance* where only bones were seen—
And eyes sunk in their sockets, dark and low,
And teeth that only show'd themselves to grin.

Reft was his scull of hair, and no fresh bloom
Of chearful mirth sate on his visage hoar:
Sometimes he rais'd his head, while deep-drawn groans
Were mixt with words that did his fate deplore.

Oft did he wish to see the daylight spring;
And often toward the window lean'd to hear,
Fore-runner of the scarlet-mantled morn,
The early note of wakeful *Chanticleer*. . . .

Then with a hollow voice thus went he on:
"Get up and search, and bring, when found, to me
Some cordial, potion, or some pleasant draught,
Sweet, slumb'rous poppy or the mild Bohea.

"But hark, my pitying friend!—and if you can,
Deceive the grim physician at the door—
Bring half the mountain springs—ah, hither bring
The cold rock-water from the shady bower;

"For till this night such thirst did ne'er invade,
A thirst provok'd by heav'n's avenging hand:
Hence bear me, friends, to quaff and quaff again
The cool wave bubbling from the yellow sand.

"To these dark walls with stately step I came,
Prepar'd your drugs and doses to defy;
Smit with the love of never-dying fame,
I came, alas! to conquer—not to die!"

Glad, from his side I sprang and fetch'd the draught,
Which down his greedy throat he quickly swills;
Then on a second errand sent me strait,
To search in some dark corner for his pills.

Quoth he, "These pills have long compounded been
Of dead men's bones and bitter roots, I trow;
But that I may to wonted health return
Throughout my lank veins shall their substance go."

So down they went.—He rais'd his fainting head,
And oft in feeble tone essay'd to talk:
Quoth he, "Since remedies have small avail,
Assist unhappy Death once more to walk."

Then, slowly rising from his loathsome bed,
On wasted legs the meagre monster stood,
Gap'd wide, and foam'd, and hungry seem'd to ask,
Tho' sick, an endless quantity of food.

Said he, "The sweet melodious flute prepare,
The anthem, and the organ's solemn sound,
Such as may strike my soul with ecstasy,
Such as may from yon' lofty walls rebound.

"Sweet music can the fiercest pains assuage:
She bids the soul to heav'n's blest mansions rise;
She calms despair, controuls infernal rage;
And deepest anguish, when it hears her, dies.

"And see, the mizzling, misty midnight reigns,
And no soft dews are on my eye-lids sent:
Here, stranger, lend thy hand, assist me, pray,
To walk a circuit of no large extent."

On my prest shoulders leaning, round he went,
And could have made the boldest spectre flee.
I led him up stairs, and I led him down,
But not one moment's rest from pain got he. . . .

Up rush'd a band, with compasses and scales
  To measure his slim carcase, long and lean.
"Be sure," said he, "to frame my coffin strong,
  You, master workman, and your men, I mean;

"For if the Devil, so late my trusty friend,
  Should get one hint where I am laid, from you,
Not with my soul content, he 'd seek to find
  That mouldering mass of bones, my body, too!

"Of hardest ebon let the plank be found,
  With clamps and ponderous bars secur'd around,
That if the box by Satan should be storm'd
  It may be able for resistance found."

"Yes," said the master workman, "noble Death,
  Your coffin shall be strong—that leave to me;
But who shall these your funeral dues discharge?
  Nor friends nor pence you have, that I can see."

To this said Death, "You might have ask'd me, too,
  Base caitiff, who are my executors,
Where my estate, and who the men that shall
  Partake my substance and be call'd my heirs.

"Know, then, that hell is my inheritance;
  The devil himself my funeral dues must pay:
Go—since you must be paid—go ask of him,
  For he has gold, as fabling poets say."

Strait they retir'd—when thus he gave me charge,
  Pointing from the light window to the west:
"Go three miles o'er the plain, and you shall see
  A burying-yard of sinners dead, unblest.

"Amid the graves a spiry building stands,
  Whose solemn knell resounding through the gloom
Shall call thee o'er the circumjacent lands
  To the dull mansion destin'd for my tomb.

"There, since 't is dark, I 'll plant a glimmering light
Just snatch'd from hell, by whose reflected beams
Thou shalt behold a tomb-stone, full eight feet,
Fast by a grave replete with ghosts and dreams.

"And on that stone engrave this epitaph,
Since Death, it seems, must die like mortal men;
Yes, on that stone engrave this epitaph,
Though all hell's furies aim to snatch the pen:—

"*Death in this tomb his weary bones hath laid,*
Sick of dominion o'er the human kind:
Behold what devastations he hath made;
Survey the millions by his arm confin'd.

"*Six thousand years has sovereign sway been mine;*
None but myself can real glory claim:
Great Regent of the world I reign'd alone,
And princes trembled when my mandate came.

"*Vast and unmatch'd throughout the world, my fame*
Takes place of gods, and asks no mortal date—
No, by myself and by the heavens I swear
Not Alexander's name is half so great.

"*Nor swords nor darts my prowess could withstand;*
All quit their arms and bow'd to my decree:
Even mighty JULIUS *died beneath my hand,*
For slaves and Cesars were the same to me.

"*Traveller, wouldst thou his noblest trophies seek,*
Search in no narrow spot obscure for those;
The sea profound, the surface of all land,
Is moulded with the myriads of his foes." . . .

O'er a dark field I held my dubious way,
Where Jack-a-lanthorn walk'd his lonely round;
Beneath my feet substantial darkness lay,
And screams were heard from the distemper'd ground.

Nor look'd I back, till to a far-off wood,
Trembling with fear, my weary feet had sped:
Dark was the night, but at the inchanted dome
I saw the infernal windows flaming red.

And from within the howls of Death I heard,
Cursing the dismal night that gave him birth,
Damning his ancient sire and mother sin,
Who at the gates of hell, accursed, brought him forth.

(For fancy gave to my enraptur'd soul
An eagle's eye, with keenest glance to see;
And bade those distant sounds distinctly roll,
Which, waking, never had affected me.)

Oft his pale breast with cruel hand he smote,
And, tearing from his limbs a winding-sheet,
Roar'd to the black skies, while the woods around,
As wicked as himself, his words repeat.

Thrice tow'rd the skies his meagre arms he rear'd,
Invok'd all hell and thunders on his head,
Bid light'nings fly, earth yawn, and tempests roar,
And the sea wrap him in its oozy bed.

"My life for one cool draught! O, fetch your springs!
Can one unfeeling to my woes be found?
No friendly visage comes to my relief,
But ghosts impend and spectres hover round.

"Though humbled now, dishearten'd, and distrest,
Yet, when admitted to the peaceful ground,
With heroes, kings, and conquerors I shall rest,
Shall sleep as safely and perhaps as sound."

Dim burnt the lamp; and now the phantom Death
Gave his last groans in horror and despair:
"All hell demands me hence!" he said, and threw
The red lamp hissing through the midnight air.

Trembling, across the plain my course I held,
And found the grave-yard, loitering through the gloom,
And in the midst a hell-red, wandering light,
Walking in fiery circles round the tomb. . . .

At distance far, approaching to the tomb,
By lamps and lanthorns guided through the shade,
A coal-black chariot hurried through the gloom,
Spectres attending, in black weeds array'd,

Whose woeful forms yet chill my soul with dread:
Each wore a vest in Stygian chambers wove,
Death's kindred all—Death's horses they bestrode,
And gallop'd fiercely, as the chariot drove.

Each horrid face a grizly mask conceal'd;
Their busy eyes shot terror to my soul
As now and then, by the pale lanthorn's glare,
I saw them for their parted friend condole.

Before the herse Death's chaplain seem'd to go,
Who strove to comfort, what he could, the dead;
Talk'd much of *Satan* and the land of woe,
And many a chapter from the scriptures read.

At last he rais'd the swelling anthem high;
In dismal numbers seem'd he to complain:
The captive tribes that by *Euphrates* wept,
Their song was jovial to his dreary strain.

That done, they plac'd the carcase in the tomb,
To dust and dull oblivion now resign'd;
Then turn'd the chariot tow'rd the House of Night,
Which soon flew off and left no trace behind.

The Indian Burying Ground

IN spite of all the learned have said,
　　I still my old opinion keep:
The *posture* that *we* give the dead
　　Points out the soul's eternal sleep.

Not so the ancients of these lands:
　　The Indian, when from life released,
Again is seated with his friends,
　　And shares again the joyous feast.

His imaged birds and painted bowl,
　　And venison for a journey dressed,
Bespeak the nature of the soul—
　　ACTIVITY that knows no rest.

His bow for action ready bent,
　　And arrows with a head of stone,
Can only mean that life is spent,
　　And not the old ideas gone.

Thou, stranger, that shalt come this way,
　　No fraud upon the dead commit:
Observe the swelling turf, and say,
　　"They do not *lie*, but here they *sit*."

Here still a lofty rock remains,
　　On which the curious eye may trace
(Now wasted, half, by wearing rains)
　　The fancies of a ruder race.

Here still an aged elm aspires,
　　Beneath whose far-projecting shade
(And which the shepherd still admires)
　　The children of the forest played.

There oft a restless Indian queen,
Pale *Shebah,* with her braided hair,
And many a barbarous form is seen,
To chide the man that lingers there.

By midnight moons, o'er moistening dews,
In habit for the chase arrayed,
The hunter still the deer pursues,
The hunter and the deer a shade.

And long shall timorous fancy see
The painted chief and pointed spear,
And Reason's self shall bow the knee
To shadows and delusions here.

Song of Thyrsis

THE turtle on yon withered bough,
That lately mourned her murdered mate,
Has found another comrade now—
Such changes all await!
Again her drooping plume is drest,
Again she's willing to be blest
And takes her lover to her nest.

If nature has decreed it so
With all above, and all below,
Let us like them forget our woe,
And not be killed with sorrow.
If I should quit your arms to-night
And chance to die before 't was light,
I would advise you—and you might—
Love again to-morrow.

RICHARD HENRY DANA

The Little Beach-Bird

THOU little bird, thou dweller by the sea,
 Why takest thou its melancholy voice,
  And with that boding cry
  Why o'er the waves dost fly?
O, rather, bird, with me
 Through the fair land rejoice!

Thy flitting form comes ghostly dim and pale,
 As driven by a beating storm at sea;
  Thy cry is weak and scared,
  As if thy mates had shared
The doom of us. Thy wail,—
 What doth it bring to me?

Thou call'st along the sand, and haunt'st the surge
 Restless and sad; as if, in strange accord
  With the motion and the roar
  Of waves that drive to shore,
One spirit did ye urge—
 The Mystery—the Word.

Of thousands, thou, both sepulcher and pall,
 Old Ocean! A requiem o'er the dead,
  From out thy gloomy cells,
  A tale of mourning tells,—
Tells of man's woe and fall,
 His sinless glory fled.

Then turn thee, little bird, and take thy flight
 Where the complaining sea shall sadness bring
  Thy spirit nevermore.
  Come, quit with me the shore,
For gladness and the light,
 Where birds of summer sing.

WILLIAM CULLEN BRYANT

To a Waterfowl

WHITHER, midst falling dew,
　　While glow the heavens with the last steps of day,
Far, through their rosy depths, dost thou pursue
　　Thy solitary way?

　　Vainly the fowler's eye
Might mark thy distant flight to do thee wrong,
As, darkly painted on the crimson sky,
　　Thy figure floats along.

　　Seek'st thou the plashy brink
Of weedy lake, or marge of river wide,
Or where the rocking billows rise and sink
　　On the chafed ocean-side?

　　There is a Power whose care
Teaches thy way along that pathless coast,—
The desert and illimitable air,—
　　Lone wandering, but not lost.

　　All day thy wings have fanned
At that far height, the cold, thin atmosphere,
Yet stoop not, weary, to the welcome land,
　　Though the dark night is near.

　　And soon that toil shall end;
Soon shalt thou find a summer home, and rest,
And scream among thy fellows; reeds shall bend
　　Soon, o'er thy sheltered nest.

Thou'rt gone, the abyss of heaven
Hath swallowed up thy form; yet, on my heart
Deeply hath sunk the lesson thou hast given,
And shall not soon depart.

He who, from zone to zone,
Guides through the boundless sky thy certain flight,
In the long way that I must tread alone,
Will lead my steps aright.

Thanatopsis

TO him who in the love of nature holds
Communion with her visible forms, she speaks
A various language; for his gayer hours
She has a voice of gladness, and a smile
And eloquence of beauty, and she glides
Into his darker musings, with a mild
And healing sympathy, that steals away
Their sharpness, ere he is aware. When thoughts
Of the last bitter hour come like a blight
Over thy spirit, and sad images
Of the stern agony, and shroud, and pall,
And breathless darkness, and the narrow house,
Make thee to shudder and grow sick at heart;—
Go forth, under the open sky, and list
To Nature's teachings, while from all around—
Earth and her waters, and the depths of air—
Comes a still voice:—

　　　　　　　　　　Yet a few days, and thee
The all-beholding sun shall see no more
In all his course; nor yet in the cold ground,
Where thy pale form was laid, with many tears,
Nor in the embrace of ocean, shall exist
Thy image. Earth, that nourished thee, shall claim
Thy growth, to be resolved to earth again,
And, lost each human trace, surrendering up

Thine individual being, shalt thou go
To mix forever with the elements,
To be a brother to the insensible rock
And to the sluggish clod, which the rude swain
Turns with his share, and treads upon. The oak
Shall send his roots abroad and pierce thy mold.

Yet not to thine eternal resting-place
Shalt thou retire alone, nor couldst thou wish
Couch more magnificent. Thou shalt lie down
With patriarchs of the infant world—with kings,
The powerful of the earth—the wise, the good,
Fair forms, and hoary seers of ages past,
All in one mighty sepulcher. The hills,
Rock-ribbed and ancient as the sun,—the vales
Stretching in pensive quietness between;
The venerable woods—rivers that move
In majesty, and the complaining brooks
That make the meadows green; and, poured round all,
Old Ocean's gray and melancholy waste,—
Are but the solemn decorations all
Of the great tomb of man. The golden sun,
The planets, all the infinite host of heaven,
Are shining on the sad abodes of death
Through the still lapse of ages. All that tread
The globe are but a handful to the tribes
That slumber in its bosom.—Take the wings
Of morning, pierce the Barcan wilderness,
Or lose thyself in the continuous woods
Where rolls the Oregon, and hears no sound
Save his own dashings—yet the dead are there:
And millions in those solitudes, since first
The flight of years began, have laid them down
In their last sleep—the dead reign there alone.

So shalt thou rest, and what if thou withdraw
In silence from the living, and no friend
Take note of thy departure? All that breathe
Will share thy destiny. The gay will laugh
When thou art gone, the solemn brood of care

Plod on, and each one as before will chase
His favorite phantom; yet all these shall leave
Their mirth and their employments, and shall come
And make their bed with thee. As the long train
Of ages glides away, the sons of men—
The youth in life's fresh spring, and he who goes
In the full strength of years, matron and maid,
The speechless babe, and the gray-headed man—
Shall one by one be gathered to thy side,
By those who in their turn shall follow them.

So live, that when thy summons comes to join
The innumerable caravan, which moves
To that mysterious realm, where each shall take
His chamber in the silent halls of death,
Thou go not, like the quarry-slave at night,
Scourged to his dungeon, but, sustained and soothed
By an unfaltering trust, approach thy grave
Like one who wraps the drapery of his couch
About him, and lies down to pleasant dreams.

"Oh Fairest of the Rural Maids"

OH fairest of the rural maids!
Thy birth was in the forest shades;
Green boughs, and glimpses of the sky,
Were all that met thine infant eye.

Thy sports, thy wanderings, when a child,
Were ever in the sylvan wild;
And all the beauty of the place
Is in thy heart and on thy face.

The twilight of the trees and rocks
Is in the light shade of thy locks;
Thy step is as the wind, that weaves
Its playful way among the leaves.

Thine eyes are springs, in whose serene
And silent waters heaven is seen;
Their lashes are the herbs that look
On their young figures in the brook.

The forest depths, by foot unpressed,
Are not more sinless than thy breast;
The holy peace, that fills the air
Of those calm solitudes, is there.

To the Fringed Gentian

THOU blossom bright with autumn dew,
And colored with the heaven's own blue,
That openest when the quiet light
Succeeds the keen and frosty night,

Thou comest not when violets lean
O'er wandering brooks and springs unseen,
Or columbines, in purple dressed,
Nod o'er the ground-bird's hidden nest.

Thou waitest late and com'st alone,
When woods are bare and birds are flown,
And frosts and shortening days portend
The aged year is near his end.

Then doth thy sweet and quiet eye
Look through its fringes to the sky,
Blue—blue—as if that sky let fall
A flower from its cerulean wall.

I would that thus, when I shall see
The hour of death draw near to me,
Hope, blossoming within my heart,
May look to heaven as I depart.

EDGAR ALLAN POE

Sonnet—To Science

SCIENCE, true daughter of Old Time thou art!
　　Who alterest all things with thy peering eyes.
Why preyest thou thus upon the poet's heart,
　　Vulture, whose wings are dull realities?
How should he love thee, or how deem thee wise,
　　Who wouldst not leave him in his wandering
To seek for treasure in the jewelled skies,
　　Albeit he soared with an undaunted wing?
Hast thou not dragged Diana from her car,
　　And driven the Hamadryad from the wood
To seek a shelter in some happier star?
　　Hast thou not torn the Naiad from her flood,
The Elfin from the green grass, and from me
The summer dream beneath the tamarind tree?

Song from "Al Aaraaf"

NEATH blue-bell or streamer,
　　Or tufted wild spray
That keeps from the dreamer
　　The moonbeam away,
Bright beings that ponder,
　　With half-closing eyes,
On the stars which your wonder
　　Hath drawn from the skies,
'Till they glance thro' the shade and
　　Come down to your brow
Like eyes of the maiden
　　Who calls on you now,—

Arise from your dreaming
   In violet bowers,
To duty beseeming
   These star-litten hours,
And shake from your tresses
   Encumber'd with dew
The breath of those kisses
   That cumber them too
(Oh, how, without you, Love,
   Could angels be blest?) —
Those kisses of true love
   That lull'd ye to rest!
Up! shake from your wing
   Each hindering thing:
The dew of the night —
   It would weigh down your flight;
And true-love caresses —
   O, leave them apart;
They are light on the tresses,
   But lead on the heart.
Ligeia! Ligeia!
   My beautiful one!
Whose harshest idea
   Will to melody run,
O, is it thy will
   On the breezes to toss?
Or, capriciously still,
   Like the lone Albatross,
Incumbent on night
   (As she on the air)
To keep watch with delight
   On the harmony there?
Ligeia, wherever
   Thy image may be,
No magic shall sever
   Thy music from thee!
Thou hast bound many eyes
   In a dreamy sleep;
But the strains still arise
   Which *thy* vigilance keep:

The sound of the rain
   Which leaps down to the flowe
And dances again
   In the rhythm of the shower,
The murmur that springs
   From the growing of grass,
Are the music of things—
   But are modell'd, alas!
Away, then, my dearest,
   O, hie thee away
To springs that lie clearest
   Beneath the moon-ray;
To lone lake that smiles,
   In its dream of deep rest,
At the many star-isles
   That enjewel its breast.
Where wild flowers, creeping,
   Have mingled their shade,
On its margin is sleeping
   Full many a maid;
Some have left the cool glade, and
   Have slept with the bee:
Arouse them, my maiden,
   On the moorland and lea;
Go, breathe on their slumber,
   All softly in ear,
The musical number
   They slumber'd to hear;
For what can awaken
   An angel so soon,
Whose sleep hath been taken
   Beneath the cold moon,
As the spell which no slumber
   Of witchery may test,
The rhythmical number
   Which lull'd him to rest?

To Helen

HELEN, thy beauty is to me
  Like those Nicean barks of yore,
That gently, o'er a perfumed sea,
  The weary, way-worn wanderer bore
  To his own native shore.

On desperate seas long wont to roam,
  Thy hyacinth hair, thy classic face,
Thy Naiad airs have brought me home
  To the glory that was Greece
  And the grandeur that was Rome.

Lo, in yon brilliant window-niche
  How statue-like I see thee stand,
The agate lamp within thy hand!
  Ah, Psyche, from the regions which
  Are Holy Land!

Israfel

IN Heaven a spirit doth dwell
  Whose heart-strings are a lute:
None sing so wildly well
As the angel Israfel,
And the giddy stars (so legends tell),
Ceasing their hymns, attend the spell
  Of his voice, all mute.

Tottering above
  In her highest noon,
  The enamoured moon
Blushes with love,
  While, to listen, the red levin
  (With the rapid Pleiades, even,
  Which were seven)
  Pauses in Heaven.

And they say (the starry choir
   And the other listening things)
That Israfeli's fire
Is owing to that lyre
   By which he sits and sings—
The trembling living wire
   Of those unusual strings.

But the skies that angel trod,
   Where deep thoughts are a duty,
Where Love 's a grown-up God,
   Where the Houri glances are
Imbued with all the beauty
   Which we worship in a star.

Therefore thou art not wrong,
   Israfeli, who despisest
An unimpassioned song:
To thee the laurels belong,
   Best bard because the wisest;
Merrily live, and long!

The ecstasies above
   With thy burning measures suit—
Thy grief, thy joy, thy hate, thy love,
   With the fervour of thy lute:
   Well may the stars be mute!
Yes, Heaven is thine; but this
   Is a world of sweets and sours:
   Our flowers are merely—flowers,
And the shadow of thy perfect bliss
   Is the sunshine of ours.

If I could dwell
Where Israfel
   Hath dwelt, and he where I,
He might not sing so wildly well
   A mortal melody,
While a bolder note than this might swell
   From my lyre within the sky.

The City in the Sea

LO, Death has reared himself a throne
In a strange city lying alone
Far down within the dim West,
Where the good and the bad and the worst and the best
Have gone to their eternal rest.
There shrines and palaces and towers
(Time-eaten towers that tremble not!)
Resemble nothing that is ours.
Around, by lifting winds forgot,
Resignedly beneath the sky
The melancholy waters lie.

No rays from the holy heaven come down
On the long night-time of that town;
But light from out the lurid sea
Streams up the turrets silently—
Gleams up the pinnacles far and free—
Up domes—up spires—up kingly halls—
Up fanes—up Babylon-like walls—
Up shadowy long-forgotten bowers
Of sculptured ivy and stone flowers—
Up many and many a marvellous shrine
Whose wreathèd friezes intertwine
The viol, the violet, and the vine.
Resignedly beneath the sky
The melancholy waters lie.
So blend the turrets and shadows there
That all seem pendulous in air,
While from a proud tower in the town
Death looks gigantically down.

There open fanes and gaping graves
Yawn level with the luminous waves;
But not the riches there that lie
In each idol's diamond eye,
Not the gaily-jewelled dead
Tempt the waters from their bed:
For no ripples curl, alas,

Along that wilderness of glass;
No swellings tell that winds may be
Upon some far-off happier sea;
No heavings hint that winds have been
On scenes less hideously serene.
    But, lo, a stir is in the air!
The wave—there is a movement there,
As if the towers had thrust aside,
In slightly sinking, the dull tide,
As if their tops had feebly given
A void within the filmy Heaven!
The waves have now a redder glow;
The hours are breathing faint and low;
And when, amid no earthly moans,
Down, down that town shall settle hence,
Hell, rising from a thousand thrones,
Shall do it reverence.

The Sleeper

AT midnight, in the month of June,
I stand beneath the mystic moon.
An opiate vapour, dewy, dim,
Exhales from out her golden rim,
And softly dripping, drop by drop,
Upon the quiet mountain top,
Steals drowsily and musically
Into the universal valley.
The rosemary nods upon the grave;
The lily lolls upon the wave;
Wrapping the fog about its breast,
The ruin moulders into rest;
Looking like Lethe, see, the lake
A conscious slumber seems to take,
And would not, for the world, awake.
All Beauty sleeps! And, lo, where lies
Irene, with her Destinies!

Oh, lady bright, can it be right—
This window open to the night?
The wanton airs, from the tree-top,
Laughingly through the lattice drop—
The bodiless airs, a wizard rout,
Flit through thy chamber in and out,
And wave the curtain canopy
So fitfully—so fearfully—
Above the closed and fringèd lid
'Neath which thy slumb'ring soul lies hid,
That, o'er the floor and down the wall,
Like ghosts the shadows rise and fall!
Oh, lady dear, hast thou no fear?
Why and what art thou dreaming here?
Sure thou art come o'er far-off seas,
A wonder to these garden trees!
Strange is thy pallor! strange thy dress!
Strange, above all, thy length of tress,
    And this all solemn silentness!

    The lady sleeps! Oh, may her sleep,
Which is enduring, so be deep!
Heaven have her in its sacred keep!
This chamber changed for one more holy,
This bed for one more melancholy,
I pray to God that she may lie
Forever with unopened eye,
While the pale sheeted ghosts go by!

    My love, she sleeps! Oh, may her sleep,
As it is lasting, so be deep!
Soft may the worms about her creep!
Far in the forest, dim and old,
For her may some tall vault unfold—
Some vault that oft hath flung its black
And wingèd panels fluttering back,
Triumphant, o'er the crested palls,
Of her grand family funerals—
Some sepulchre, remote, alone,
Against whose portal she hath thrown,
In childhood, many an idle stone—

Some tomb from out whose sounding door
She ne'er shall force an echo more,
Thrilling to think, poor child of sin,
It was the dead who groaned within.

To One in Paradise

THOU wast all that to me, love,
    For which my soul did pine—
A green isle in the sea, love,
    A fountain and a shrine,
All wreathed with fairy fruits and flowers,
    And all the flowers were mine.

Ah, dream too bright to last!
    Ah, starry Hope, that didst arise
But to be overcast!
    A voice from out the Future cries,
"On! on!"—but o'er the Past
    (Dim gulf!) my spirit hovering lies
Mute, motionless, aghast!

For, alas, alas, with me
    The light of Life is o'er!
"No more—no more—no more—"
    (Such language holds the solemn sea
To the sands upon the shore)
    Shall bloom the thunder-blasted tree,
Or the stricken eagle soar!

And all my days are trances,
    And all my nightly dreams
Are where thy grey eye glances,
    And where thy footstep gleams—
In what ethereal dances,
    By what eternal streams.

The Haunted Palace

IN the greenest of our valleys
  By good angels tenanted,
Once a fair and stately palace—
  Radiant palace—reared its head.
In the monarch Thought's dominion,
  It stood there;
Never seraph spread a pinion
  Over fabric half so fair!

Banners yellow, glorious, golden,
  On its roof did float and flow
(This—all this—was in the olden
  Time long ago);
And every gentle air that dallied,
  In that sweet day,
Along the ramparts plumed and pallid,
  A wingèd odor went away.

Wanderers in that happy valley,
  Through two luminous windows, saw
Spirits moving musically,
  To a lute's well-tunèd law,
Round about a throne where, sitting
  (Porphyrogene!)
In state his glory well befitting,
  The ruler of the realm was seen.

And all with pearl and ruby glowing
  Was the fair palace door,
Through which came flowing, flowing,
    flowing,
  And sparkling evermore,
A troop of Echoes, whose sweet duty
  Was but to sing,
In voices of surpassing beauty,
  The wit and wisdom of their king.

But evil things, in robes of sorrow,
    Assailed the monarch's high estate.
(Ah, let us mourn! for never morrow
    Shall dawn upon him desolate!)
And round about his home the glory
    That blushed and bloomed
Is but a dim-remembered story
    Of the old time entombed.

And travellers now, within that valley,
    Through the red-litten windows see
Vast forms, that move fantastically
    To a discordant melody;
While, like a ghastly rapid river,
    Through the pale door
A hideous throng rush out forever
    And laugh—but smile no more.

The Conqueror Worm

LO, 'tis a gala night
    Within the lonesome latter years;
An angel throng, bewinged, bedight
    In veils, and drowned in tears,
Sit in a theater, to see
    A play of hopes and fears,
While the orchestra breathes fitfully
    The music of the spheres.

Mimes, in the form of God on high,
    Mutter and mumble low,
And hither and thither fly—
    Mere puppets they, who come and go
At bidding of vast formless things
    That shift the scenery to and fro,
Flapping from out their Condor wings
    Invisible woe!

That motley drama, oh, be sure
  It shall not be forgot!
With its Phantom chased for evermore
  By a crowd that seize it not,
Through a circle that ever returneth in
  To the self-same spot,
And much of Madness, and more of Sin,
  And Horror the soul of the plot.

But see, amid the mimic rout
  A crawling shape intrude!
A blood-red thing that writhes from out
  The scenic solitude!
It writhes! it writhes! with mortal pangs
  The mimes become its food,
And seraphs sob at vermin fangs
  In human gore imbued.

Out, out are the lights—out all!
  And over each quivering form
The curtain, a funeral pall,
  Comes down with the rush of a storm;
While the angels, all pallid and wan,
  Uprising, unveiling, affirm
That the play is the tragedy "Man,"
  And its hero the Conqueror Worm.

The Raven

ONCE upon a midnight dreary, while I pondered, weak
  and weary,
Over many a quaint and curious volume of forgotten lore,
While I nodded, nearly napping, suddenly there came a
  tapping,
As of some one gently rapping, rapping at my chamber door.
" 'T is some visitor," I muttered, "tapping at my chamber
  door—
      Only this and nothing more."

Ah, distinctly I remember it was in the bleak December,
And each separate dying ember wrought its ghost upon the
floor.
Eagerly I wished the morrow; vainly I had sought to borrow
From my books surcease of sorrow—sorrow for the lost
Lenore,
For the rare and radiant maiden whom the angels name
Lenore—
Nameless *here* for evermore.

And the silken, sad, uncertain rustling of each purple curtain
Thrilled me—filled me with fantastic terrors never felt before;
So that now, to still the beating of my heart, I stood repeating,
" 'T is some visitor entreating entrance at my chamber door—
Some late visitor entreating entrance at my chamber door—
This it is and nothing more."

Presently my soul grew stronger: hesitating then no longer,
"Sir," said I, "or Madam, truly your forgiveness I implore;
But the fact is I was napping, and so gently you came rap-
ping,
And so faintly you came tapping, tapping at my chamber
door,
That I scarce was sure I heard you"—here I opened wide the
door—
Darkness there and nothing more.

Deep into that darkness, peering, long I stood there, won-
dering, fearing,
Doubting, dreaming dreams no mortal ever dared to dream
before;
But the silence was unbroken, and the stillness gave no token,
And the only word there spoken was the whispered word
"Lenore!"
This I whispered, and an echo murmured back the word
"Lenore!"
Merely this and nothing more.

Back into the chamber turning, all my soul within me
burning,

Soon again I heard a tapping, somewhat louder than before.
"Surely," said I, "surely that is something at my window
    lattice;
Let me see, then, what thereat is, and this mystery explore,—
Let my heart be still a moment and this mystery explore—
            'T is the wind and nothing more."

Open here I flung the shutter, when, with many a flirt and
    flutter,
In there stepped a stately Raven of the saintly days of yore.
Not the least obeisance made he, not a minute stopped or
    stayed he,
But with mien of lord or lady perched above my chamber
    door—
Perched upon a bust of Pallas just above my chamber door—
            Perched and sat, and nothing more.

Then, this ebony bird beguiling my sad fancy into smiling
By the grave and stern decorum of the countenance it wore,
"Though thy crest be shorn and shaven, thou," I said, "art
    sure no craven,
Ghastly, grim, and ancient Raven, wandering from the
    Nightly shore:
Tell me what thy lordly name is on the Night's Plutonian
    shore!"
          Quoth the Raven, "Nevermore."

Much I marvelled this ungainly fowl to hear discourse so
    plainly,
Though its answer little meaning, little relevancy, bore;
For we cannot help agreeing that no living human being
Ever yet was blessed with seeing bird above his chamber
    door—
Bird or beast upon the sculptured bust above his chamber
    door—
         With such name as "Nevermore."

But the Raven, sitting lonely on the placid bust, spoke only
That one word, as if his soul in that one word he did outpour.
Nothing farther then he uttered, not a feather then he flut-
    tered;

Till I scarcely more than muttered, "Other friends have
    flown before;
On the morrow *he* will leave me, as my Hopes have flown
    before."
               Then the bird said, "Nevermore."

Startled at the stillness broken by reply so aptly spoken,
"Doubtless," said I, "what it utters is its only stock and store,
    Caught from some unhappy master whom unmerciful Dis-
    aster
Followed fast and followed faster till his songs one burden
    bore,
Till the dirges of his Hope that melancholy burden bore
               Of 'Never—nevermore.' "

But the Raven still beguiling my sad fancy into smiling,
Straight I wheeled a cushioned seat in front of bird and bust
    and door;
Then, upon the velvet sinking, I betook myself to linking
Fancy unto fancy, thinking what this ominous bird of yore,
What this grim, ungainly, ghastly, gaunt, and ominous bird
    of yore,
               Meant in croaking "Nevermore."

This I sat engaged in guessing, but no syllable expressing
To the fowl whose fiery eyes now burned into my bosom's
    core;
This and more I sat divining, with my head at ease reclining
On the cushion's velvet lining that the lamp-light gloated o'er,
But whose velvet violet lining, with the lamp-light gloating
    o'er,
               She shall press, ah, nevermore!

Then, methought, the air grew denser, perfumed from an
    unseen censer
Swung by seraphim whose footfalls tinkled on the tufted floor.
"Wretch!" I cried, "thy God hath lent thee, by these angels
    he hath sent thee,
Respite—respite and nepenthe from thy memories of Lenore!
Quaff, oh quaff this kind nepenthe, and forget this lost
    Lenore!"
               Quoth the Raven, "Nevermore."

"Prophet!" said I, "thing of evil! prophet still, if bird or devil!
  Whether Tempter sent, or whether tempest tossed thee here
    ashore,
  Desolate yet all undaunted, on this desert land enchanted—
  On this home by Horror haunted—tell me truly, I implore,
  Is there—*is* there balm in Gilead?—tell me—tell me, I im-
    plore!"
                    Quoth the Raven, "Nevermore."

"Prophet!" said I, "thing of evil! prophet still, if bird or devil!
  By that Heaven that bends above us—by that God we both
    adore—
  Tell this soul with sorrow laden if, within the distant Aidenn,
  It shall clasp a sainted maiden whom the angels name
    Lenore—
  Clasp a rare and radiant maiden whom the angels name
    Lenore."
                    Quoth the Raven, "Nevermore."

"Be that word our sign of parting, bird or fiend!" I shrieked,
    upstarting;
"Get thee back into the tempest and the Night's Plutonian
    shore!
  Leave no black plume as a token of that lie thy soul hath
    spoken!
  Leave my loneliness unbroken!—quit the bust above my
    door!
  Take thy beak from out my heart, and take thy form from
    off my door!"
                    Quoth the Raven, "Nevermore."

And the Raven, never flitting, still is sitting, *still* is sitting
On the pallid bust of Pallas just above my chamber door;
And his eyes have all the seeming of a demon's that is
    dreaming,
And the lamp-light o'er him streaming throws his shadow
    on the floor;
And my soul from out that shadow that lies floating on the
    floor
                    Shall be lifted—nevermore!

Ulalume

THE skies they were ashen and sober,
   The leaves they were crispèd and sere—
The leaves they were withering and sere;
It was night in the lonesome October
   Of my most immemorial year;
It was hard by the dim lake of Auber,
   In the misty mid region of Weir—
It was down by the dank tarn of Auber,
   In the ghoul-haunted woodland of Weir.

Here once, through an alley Titanic
   Of cypress, I roamed with my Soul—
   Of cypress, with Psyche, my Soul.
These were days when my heart was volcanic
   As the scoriac rivers that roll—
   As the lavas that restlessly roll
Their sulphurous currents down Yaanek,
   In the ultimate climes of the pole—
That groan as they roll down Mount Yaanek,
   In the realms of the boreal pole.

Our talk had been serious and sober,
   But our thoughts they were palsied and sere—
   Our memories were treacherous and sere,—
For we knew not the month was October,
   And we marked not the night of the year
   (Ah, night of all nights in the year!)—
We noted not the dim lake of Auber
   (Though once we had journeyed down here)—
Remembered not the dank tarn of Auber,
   Nor the ghoul-haunted woodland of Weir.

And now, as the night was senescent
   And star-dials pointed to morn—
   As the star-dials hinted of morn,—
At the end of our path a liquescent

And nebulous lustre was born,
Out of which a miraculous crescent
    Arose with a duplicate horn—
Astarte's bediamonded crescent
    Distinct with its duplicate horn.

And I said: "She is warmer than Dian:
    She rolls through an ether of sighs—
    She revels in a region of sighs;
She has seen that the tears are not dry on
    These cheeks, where the worm never dies,
And has come past the stars of the Lion
    To point us the path to the skies—
    To the Lethean peace of the skies,—
Come up, in despite of the Lion,
    To shine on us with her bright eyes—
Come up through the lair of the Lion,
    With love in her luminous eyes."

But Psyche, uplifting her finger,
    Said: "Sadly this star I mistrust—
    Her pallor I strangely mistrust:—
Oh, hasten!—oh, let us not linger!
    Oh, fly! let us fly!—for we must."
In terror she spoke, letting sink her
    Wings until they trailed in the dust—
In agony sobbed, letting sink her
    Plumes till they trailed in the dust—
    Till they sorrowfully trailed in the dust.

I replied: "This is nothing but dreaming:
    Let us on by this tremulous light!
    Let us bathe in this crystalline light!
Its Sibyllic splendor is beaming
    With Hope and in Beauty to-night—
    See! it flickers up the sky through the night!
Ah, we safely may trust to its gleaming,
    And be sure it will lead us aright—
We safely may trust to a gleaming
    That cannot but guide us aright,
    Since it flickers up to Heaven through the night."

Thus I pacified Psyche, and kissed her,
    And tempted her out of her gloom—
    And conquered her scruples and gloom;
And we passed to the end of the vista,
    But were stopped by the door of a tomb—
    By the door of a legended tomb;
And I said: "What is written, sweet sister,
    On the door of this legended tomb?"
    She replied: "Ulalume—Ulalume—
    'T is the vault of thy lost Ulalume!"

Then my heart it grew ashen and sober
    As the leaves that were crispèd and sere—
    As the leaves that were withering and sere;
And I cried: "It was surely October
    On *this* very night of last year
    That I journeyed—I journeyed down here,—
    That I brought a dread burden down here;
    On this night of all nights in the year,
    Ah, what demon has tempted me here?
Well I know, now, this dim lake of Auber—
    This misty mid region of Weir,—
Well I know, now, this dank tarn of Auber—
    This ghoul-haunted woodland of Weir."

Annabel Lee

IT was many and many a year ago,
    In a kingdom by the sea,
That a maiden there lived whom you may know
    By the name of ANNABEL LEE;
And this maiden she lived with no other thought
    Than to love and be loved by me.

I was a child and *she* was a child,
    In this kingdom by the sea;
But we loved with a love that was more than love—
    I and my ANNABEL LEE—

With a love that the wingèd seraphs of heaven
  Coveted her and me.

And this was the reason that, long ago,
  In this kingdom by the sea,
A wind blew out of a cloud, chilling
  My beautiful ANNABEL LEE;
So that her high-born kinsmen came
  And bore her away from me,
To shut her up in a sepulchre
  In this kingdom by the sea.

The angels, not half so happy in heaven,
  Went envying her and me—
Yes! that was the reason (as all men know,
  In this kingdom by the sea)
That the wind came out of the cloud by night,
  Chilling and killing my ANNABEL LEE.

But our love it was stronger by far than the love
  Of those who were older than we—
  Of many far wiser than we;
And neither the angels in heaven above,
  Nor the demons down under the sea,
Can ever dissever my soul from the soul
  Of the beautiful ANNABEL LEE:

For the moon never beams without bringing me
    dreams
  Of the beautiful ANNABEL LEE;
And the stars never rise but I feel the bright eyes
  Of the beautiful ANNABEL LEE;
And so, all the night-tide, I lie down by the side
Of my darling—my darling—my life and my bride,
  In the sepulchre there by the sea,
  In her tomb by the sounding sea.

Eldorado

GAILY bedight,
A gallant knight,
In sunshine and in shadow,
 Had journeyed long,
 Singing a song,
In search of Eldorado.

 But he grew old—
 This knight so bold,—
And o'er his heart a shadow
 Fell as he found
 No spot of ground
That looked like Eldorado.

 And, as his strength
 Failed him at length,
He met a pilgrim shadow.
 "Shadow," said he,
 "Where can it be—
This land of Eldorado?"

 "Over the mountains
 Of the Moon,
Down the Valley of the Shadow,
 Ride, boldly ride,"
 The shade replied,
"If you seek for Eldorado!"

Romance

ROMANCE, who loves to nod and sing,
With drowsy head and folded wing,
Among the green leaves as they shake
Far down within some shadowy lake,

To me a painted paroquet
Hath been—a most familiar bird—
Taught me my alphabet to say—
To lisp my very earliest word
While in the wild wood I did lie,
A child—with a most knowing eye.

Of late, eternal Condor years
So shake the very Heaven on high
With tumult as they thunder by,
I have no time for idle cares
Through gazing on the unquiet sky.
And when an hour with calmer wings
Its down upon my spirit flings—
That little time with lyre and rhyme
To while away—forbidden things!
My heart would feel to be a crime
Unless it trembled with the strings.

A Dream Within a Dream

TAKE this kiss upon the brow!
And, in parting from you now,
Thus much let me avow—
You are not wrong, who deem
That my days have been a dream;
Yet if hope has flown away
In a night, or in a day,
In a vision, or in none,
Is it therefore the less *gone?*
All that we see or seem
Is but a dream within a dream.

I stand amid the roar
Of a surf-tormented shore,
And I hold within my hand
Grains of the golden sand—
How few! yet how they creep
Through my fingers to the deep,

While I weep—while I weep!
O God! can I not grasp
Them with a tighter clasp?
O God! can I not save
One from the pitiless wave?
Is *all* that we see or seem
But a dream within a dream?

Lenore

AH, broken is the golden bowl! the spirit flown forever!
Let the bell toll!—a saintly soul floats on the Stygian
river,
And, Guy De Vere, hast *thou* no tear?—weep now or never
more!
See! on yon drear and rigid bier low lies thy love, Lenore!
Come! let the burial rite be read—the funeral song be sung!—
An anthem for the queenliest dead that ever died so young—
A dirge for her the doubly dead in that she died so young.

"Wretches! ye loved her for her wealth and hated her for her
pride,
"And when she fell in feeble health, ye blessed her—that she
died!
"How *shall* the ritual, then, be read?—the requiem how be
sung
"By you—by yours, the evil eye,—by yours, the slanderous
tongue
"That did to death the innocence that died, and died so
young?"

Peccavimus; but rave not thus! and let a Sabbath song
Go up to God so solemnly the dead may feel no wrong!
The sweet Lenore hath "gone before," with Hope, that flew
beside,
Leaving thee wild for the dear child that should have been thy
bride—
For her, the fair and *debonair,* that now so lowly lies,
The life upon her yellow hair but not within her eyes—
The life still there. upon her hair—the death upon her eyes.

"Avaunt! to-night my heart is light. No dirge will I upraise.
"But waft the angel on her flight with a pæan of old days!
"Let *no* bell toll!—lest her sweet soul, amid its hallowed mirth,
"Should catch the note, as it doth float up from the damnèd
    Earth.
"To friends above, from fiends below, the indignant ghost is
    riven—
"From Hell unto a high estate far up within the Heaven—
"From grief and groan, to a golden throne, beside the King
    of Heaven."

Dream-Land

BY a route obscure and lonely,
Haunted by ill angels only,
Where an Eidolon, named NIGHT,
On a black throne reigns upright,
I have reached these lands but newly
From an ultimate dim Thule—
From a wild weird clime that lieth, sublime,
        Out of SPACE—out of TIME.

Bottomless vales and boundless floods,
And chasms, and caves, and Titan woods,
With forms that no man can discover
For the tears that drip all over;
Mountains toppling evermore
Into seas without a shore;
Seas that restlessly aspire,
Surging, unto skies of fire;
Lakes that endlessly outspread
Their lone waters—lone and dead,—
Their still waters—still and chilly
With the snows of the lolling lily.

By the lakes that thus outspread
Their lone waters, lone and dead,—
Their sad waters, sad and chilly
With the snows of the lolling lily,—

By the mountains—near the river
Murmuring lowly, murmuring ever,—
By the grey woods,—by the swamp
Where the toad and the newt encamp,—
By the dismal tarns and pools
    Where dwell the Ghouls,—
By each spot the most unholy—
In each nook most melancholy,—
There the traveller meets, aghast,
Sheeted Memories of the Past—
Shrouded forms that start and sigh
As they pass the wanderer by—
White-robed forms of friends long given,
In agony, to the Earth—and Heaven.

For the heart whose woes are legion
 Tis a peaceful, soothing region—
For the spirit that walks in shadow
'Tis—oh 'tis an Eldorado!
But the traveller, travelling through it,
May not—dare not openly view it;
Never its mysteries are exposed
To the weak human eye unclosed;
So wills its King, who hath forbid
The uplifting of the fringèd lid;
And thus the sad Soul that here passes
Beholds it but through darkened glasses.

By a route obscure and lonely,
Haunted by ill angels only,
Where an Eidolon, named NIGHT,
On a black throne reigns upright,
I have wandered home but newly
From this ultimate dim Thule.

For Annie

THANK Heaven! the crisis—
   The danger is past,
And the lingering illness
   Is over at last—
And the fever called "Living"
   Is conquered at last.

Sadly, I know
   I am shorn of my strength,
And no muscle I move
   As I lie at full length—
But no matter!—I feel
   I am better at length.

And I rest so composedly
   Now, in my bed,
That any beholder
   Might fancy me dead—
Might start at beholding me,
   Thinking me dead.

The moaning and groaning,
   The sighing and sobbing,
Are quieted now,
   With that horrible throbbing
At heart:—ah that horrible,
   Horrible throbbing!

The sickness—the nausea—
   The pitiless pain—
Have ceased with the fever
   That maddened my brain—
With the fever called "Living"
   That burned in my brain.

And oh! of all tortures
   That torture the worst
Has abated—the terrible
   Torture of thirst
For the napthaline river
   Of Passion accurst:—
I have drunk of a water
   That quenches all thirst:—

Of a water that flows,
   With a lullaby sound,
From a spring but a very few
   Feet under ground—
From a cavern not very far
   Down under ground.

And ah! let it never
   Be foolishly said
That my room it is gloomy
   And narrow my bed;
For a man never slept
   In a different bed—
And, to sleep, you must slumber
   In just such a bed.

My tantalized spirit
   Here blandly reposes,
Forgetting, or never
   Regretting, its roses—
Its old agitations
   Of myrtles and roses:

For now, while so quietly
   Lying, it fancies
A holier odor
   About it, of pansies—
A rosemary odor,
   Commingled with pansies—
With rue and the beautiful
   Puritan pansies.

And so it lies happily,
    Bathing in many
A dream of the truth
    And the beauty of Annie—
Drowned in a bath
    Of the tresses of Annie.

She tenderly kissed me,
    She fondly caressed,
And then I fell gently
    To sleep on her breast—
Deeply to sleep
    From the heaven of her breast.

When the light was extinguished,
    She covered me warm,
And she prayed to the angels
    To keep me from harm—
To the queen of the angels
    To shield me from harm.

And I lie so composedly,
    Now, in my bed,
(Knowing her love)
    That you fancy me dead—
And I rest so contentedly,
    Now, in my bed,
(With her love at my breast)
    That you fancy me dead—
That you shudder to look at me,
    Thinking me dead:—

But my heart it is brighter
    Than all of the many
Stars of the sky,
    For it sparkles with Annie--
It glows with the light
    Of the love of my Annie—
With the thought of the light
    Of the eyes of my Annie.

EDWARD COATE PINKNEY

A Serenade

LOOK out upon the stars, my love,
    And shame them with thine eyes,
On which, than on the lights above,
    There hang more destinies.
Night's beauty is the harmony
    Of blending shades and light;
Then, lady, up,—look out, and be
    A sister to the night!

Sleep not! thine image wakes for aye
    Within my watching breast:
Sleep not! from her soft sleep should fly
    Who robs all hearts of rest.
Nay, lady, from thy slumbers break,
    And make this darkness gay
With looks, whose brightness well might make
    Of darker nights a day.

Votive Song

I BURN no incense, hang no wreath,
    On this thine early tomb:
Such cannot cheer the place of death,
    But only mock its gloom.
Here odorous smoke and breathing flower
    No grateful influence shed;
They lose their perfume and their power,
    When offered to the dead.

And if, as is the Afghan's creed,
  The spirit may return,
A disembodied sense to feed,
  On fragrance, near its urn,—
It is enough that she, whom thou
  Didst love in living years,
Sits desolate beside it now,
  And fall these heavy tears.

———— • ◦ • ————

T. H. CHIVERS

———— • ◦ • ————

Avalon

DEATH'S pale cold orb has turned to an eclipse
  My Son of Love!
The worms are feeding on thy lily-lips,
  My milk-white Dove!
Pale purple tinges thy soft finger-tips!
While nectar thy pure soul in glory sips,
As Death's cold frost mine own forever nips!
    Where thou art lying
    Beside the beautiful undying
In the Valley of the pausing of the Moon,
Oh! Avalon! my son! my son!

Wake up, oh! Avalon! my son! my son!
  And come from Death!
Heave off the clod that lies so heavy on
  Thy breast beneath
In that cold grave, my more than Precious One!
And come to me! for I am here alone—
With none to comfort me!—my hopes are gone
    Where thou art lying
    Beside the beautiful undying
In the Valley of the pausing of the Moon,
Oh! Avalon! my son! my son!

Forever more must I, on this damp sod,
    Renew and keep
My Covenant of Sorrows with my God,
    And weep, weep, weep!
Writhing in pain beneath Death's iron rod!
Till I shall go to that Divine Abode—
Treading the path that thy dear feet have trod—
      Where thou art lying
      Beside the beautiful undying
In the Valley of the pausing of the Moon,
Oh! Avalon! my son! my son!

Oh! precious Saviour! gracious heavenly Lord!
    Refresh my soul!
Here, with the healings of thy heavenly Word,
    Make my heart whole!
My little Lambs are scattered now abroad
In Death's dark Valley, where they bleat unheard!
Dear Shepherd! give their Shepherd his reward
      Where they are lying
      Beside the beautiful undying
In the Valley of the pausing of the Moon,
With Avalon! my son! my son!

For thou didst tread with fire-ensandaled feet,
    Star-crowned, forgiven,
The burning diapason of the stars so sweet,
    To God in Heaven!
And, walking on the sapphire-paven street,
Didst take upon the highest Sill thy seat—
Waiting in glory there my soul to meet,
      When I am lying
      Beside the beautiful undying
In the Valley of the pausing of the Moon,
Oh! Avalon! my son! my son!

Thou wert my Micro-Uranos below—
    My Little Heaven!
My Micro-Cosmos in this world of wo,
    From morn till even!

A living Lyre of God who charmed me so
With thy sweet songs, that I did seem to go
Out of this world where thou art shining now,
  But without lying
   Beside the beautiful undying
In the Valley of the pausing of the Moon,
Oh! Avalon! my son! my son!

Thou wert my son of Melody alway,
  Oh! Child Divine!
Whose golden radiance filled the world with Day!
  For thou didst shine
A lustrous Diadem of Song for aye,
Whose Divertisements, through Heaven's Holyday,
Now ravish Angel's ears—as well they may—
  While I am crying
   Beside the beautiful undying
In the Valley of the pausing of the Moon,
Oh! Avalon! my son! my son!

Thy soul did soar up to the Gates of God,
  Oh! Lark-like Child!
And through Heaven's Bowers of Bliss, by Angels trod,
  Poured Wood-notes wild!
In emulation of that Bird, which stood,
In solemn silence, listening to thy flood
Of golden Melody deluge the wood
  Where thou art lying
   Beside the beautiful undying
In the Valley of the pausing of the Moon,
Oh! Avalon! my son! my son!

The redolent quintessence of thy tongue,
  Oh! Avalon!
Embowered by Angels Heaven's sweet Bowers among—
  Many in one—
Is gathered from the choicest of the throng,
In an Æonian Hymn forever young,
Thou Philomelian Eclecticist of Song!
  While I am sighing

Beside the beautiful undying
In the Valley of the pausing of the Moon,
For Avalon! my son! my son!

Thou wert like Taleisin, "full of eyes,"
    Bardling of Love!
My beautiful Divine Eumenides!
    My gentle Dove!
Thou silver Swan of Golden Elegies!
Whose Mendelssohnian Songs now fill the skies!
While I am weeping where my Lily lies!
        Where thou art lying
        Beside the beautiful undying
In the Valley of the pausing of the Moon,
Oh! Avalon! my son! my son!

Kindling the high-uplifted stars at even
    With thy sweet song,
The Angels, on the Sapphire Sills of Heaven,
    In Rapturous throng,
Melted to milder meekness, with the Seven
Bright Lamps of God to glory given,
Leant down to hear thy voice roll up the leven,
        Where thou art lying
        Beside the beautiful undying
In the Valley of the pausing of the Moon,
Oh! Avalon! my son! my son!

Can any thing that Christ has ever said,
    Make my heart whole?
Can less than bringing back the early dead,
    Restore my soul?
No! this alone can make my Heavenly bread—
Christ's Bread of Life brought down from Heaven, in-
        stead
Of this sad Song, on which my soul has fed,
        Where thou art lying
        Beside the beautiful undying
In the Valley of the pausing of the Moon,
Oh! Avalon! my son! my son!

Have I not need to weep from Morn till Even
    Far bitterer tears
Than cruel Earth, the unforgiven,
    Through his long years—
Inquisitorial Hell, or strictest Heaven,
Wrung from Christ's bleeding heart when riven?
Thus from one grief unto another driven,
      Where thou art lying
      Beside the beautiful undying
In the Valley of the pausing of the Moon,
Oh! Avalon! my son! my son!

JOHN GREENLEAF WHITTIER

The Eternal Goodness

O FRIENDS! with whom my feet have trod
    The quiet aisles of prayer,
Glad witness to your zeal for God
    And love of man I bear.

I trace your lines of argument;
    Your logic linked and strong
I weigh as one who dreads dissent,
    And fears a doubt as wrong.

But still my human hands are weak
    To hold your iron creeds:
Against the words ye bid me speak
    My heart within me pleads.

Who fathoms the Eternal Thought?
    Who talks of scheme and plan?
The Lord is God! He needeth not
    The poor device of man.

I walk with bare, hushed feet the ground
    Ye tread with boldness shod;
I dare not fix with mete and bound
    The love and power of God.

Ye praise His justice; even such
    His pitying love I deem:
Ye seek a king; I fain would touch
    The robe that hath no seam.

Ye see the curse which overbroods
    A world of pain and loss;
I hear our Lord's beatitudes
    And prayer upon the cross.

More than your schoolmen teach, within
    Myself, alas! I know:
Too dark ye cannot paint the sin,
    Too small the merit show.

I bow my forehead to the dust,
    I veil mine eyes for shame,
And urge, in trembling self-distrust,
    A prayer without a claim.

I see the wrong that round me lies,
    I feel the guilt within;
I hear, with groan and travail-cries,
    The world confess its sin.

Yet, in the maddening maze of things,
    And tossed by storm and flood,
To one fixed trust my spirit clings;
    I know that God is good!

Not mine to look where cherubim
    And seraphs may not see,
But nothing can be good in Him
    Which evil is in me.

The wrong that pains my soul below
    I dare not throne above,
I know not of His hate,—I know
    His goodness and His love.

I dimly guess from blessings known
    Of greater out of sight,
And, with the chastened Psalmist, own
    His judgments too are right.

I long for household voices gone,
    For vanished smiles I long,
But God hath led my dear ones on,
    And He can do no wrong.

I know not what the future hath
    Of marvel or surprise,
Assured alone that life and death
    His mercy underlies.

And if my heart and flesh are weak
    To bear an untried pain,
The bruisëd reed He will not break,
    But strengthen and sustain.

No offering of my own I have,
    Nor works my faith to prove;
I can but give the gifts He gave,
    And plead His love for love.

And so beside the Silent Sea
    I wait the muffled oar;
No harm from Him can come to me
    On ocean or on shore.

I know not where His islands lift
    Their fronded palms in air;
I only know I cannot drift
    Beyond His love and care.

O brothers! if my faith is vain,
    If hopes like these betray,
Pray for me that my feet may gain
    The sure and safer way.

And Thou, O Lord! by whom are seen
    Thy creatures as they be,
Forgive me if too close I lean
    My human heart on Thee!

Ichabod

SO fallen, so lost! the light withdrawn
    Which once he wore!
The glory from his gray hairs gone
    Forevermore!

Revile him not—the Tempter hath
    A snare for all;
And pitying tears, not scorn and wrath,
    Befit his fall.

Oh dumb be passion's stormy rage
    When he who might
Have lighted up and led his age
    Falls back in night.

Scorn? would the angels laugh to mark
    A bright soul driven,
Fiend-goaded, down the endless dark,
    From hope and heaven?

Let not the land once proud of him
    Insult him now,
Nor brand with deeper shame his dim,
    Dishonored brow.

But let its humbled sons, instead,
    From sea to lake,

A long lament as for the dead
    In sadness make.

Of all we loved and honored, nought
    Save power remains —
A fallen angel's pride of thought,
    Still strong in chains.

All else is gone; from those great eyes
    The soul has fled:
When faith is lost, when honor dies,
    The man is dead.

Then pay the reverence of old days
    To his dead fame;
Walk backward, with averted gaze,
    And hide the shame.

My Playmate

THE pines were dark on Ramoth hill,
    Their song was soft and low;
The blossoms in the sweet May wind
    Were falling like the snow.

The blossoms drifted at our feet,
    The orchard birds sang clear;
The sweetest and the saddest day
    It seemed of all the year.

For, more to me than birds or flowers,
    My playmate left her home,
And took with her the laughing spring,
    The music and the bloom.

She kissed the lips of kith and kin,
    She laid her hand in mine:
What more could ask the bashful boy,
    Who fed her father's kine?

She left us in the bloom of May:
    The constant years told o'er
Their seasons with as sweet May morns,
    But she came back no more.

I walk. with noiseless feet, the round
    Of uneventful years;
Still o'er and o'er I sow the spring
    And reap the autumn ears.

She lives where all the golden year
    Her summer roses blow;
The dusky children of the sun
    Before her come and go.

There haply with her jewelled hands
    She smooths her silken gown—
No more the homespun lap wherein
    I shook the walnuts down.

The wild grapes wait us by the brook,
    The brown nuts on the hill,
And still the May-day flowers make sweet
    The woods of Follymill.

The lilies blossom in the pond,
    The bird builds in the tree,
The dark pines sing on Ramoth hill
    The slow song of the sea.

I wonder if she thinks of them,
    And how the old time seems;
If ever the pines of Ramoth wood
    Are sounding in her dreams.

I see her face, I hear her voice:
    Does she remember mine?
And what to her is now the boy
    Who fed her father's kine?

What cares she that the orioles build
 For other eyes than ours;
That other hands with nuts are filled,
 And other laps with flowers?

O playmate in the golden time,
 Our mossy seat is green,
Its fringing violets blossom yet,
 The old trees o'er it lean.

The winds so sweet with birch and fern
 A sweeter memory blow;
And there in spring the veeries sing
 The song of long ago.

And still the pines of Ramoth wood
 Are moaning like the sea—
The moaning of the sea of change
 Between myself and thee!

OLIVER WENDELL HOLMES

The Last Leaf

I SAW him once before,
 As he passed by the door,
   And again
The pavement stones resound,
As he totters o'er the ground
   With his cane.

They say that in his prime,
Ere the pruning-knife of Time
   Cut him down,
Not a better man was found
By the Crier on his round
   Through the town.

But now he walks the streets,
And he looks at all he meets
   Sad and wan,
And he shakes his feeble head,
That it seems as if he said,
   "They are gone."

The mossy marbles rest
On the lips that he has prest
   In their bloom,
And the names he loved to hear
Have been carved for many a year
   On the tomb.

My grandmama has said,—
Poor old lady, she is dead
   Long ago,—
That he had a Roman nose,
And his cheek was like a rose
   In the snow;

But now his nose is thin,
And it rests upon his chin
   Like a staff,
And a crook is in his back,
And a melancholy crack
   In his laugh.

I know it is a sin
For me to sit and grin
   At him here;
But the old three-cornered hat,
And the breeches, and all that,
   Are so queer!

And if I should live to be
The last leaf upon the tree,
   In the spring,
Let them smile, as I do now,
At the old forsaken bough
   Where I cling.

JAMES RUSSELL LOWELL

Hebe

I SAW the twinkle of white feet,
  I saw the flash of robes descending;
Before her ran an influence fleet,
  That bow'd my heart like barley bending.

As, in bare fields, the searching bees
  Pilot to blooms beyond our finding,
It led me on,—by sweet degrees,
  Joy's simple honey-cells unbinding.

Those graces were that seem'd grim fates;
  With nearer love the sky lean'd o'er me;
The long-sought secret's golden gates
  On musical hinges swung before me.

I saw the brimm'd bowl in her grasp
  Thrilling with godhood; like a lover,
I sprang the proffer'd life to clasp:
  The beaker fell, the luck was over.

The earth has drunk the vintage up;
  What boots it patch the goblet's splinters?
Can Summer fill the icy cup
  Whose treacherous crystal is but Winter's?

O spendthrift haste! Await the gods;
  Their nectar crowns the lips of Patience.
Haste scatters on unthankful sods
  The immortal gift in vain libations.

Coy Hebe flies from those that woo,
  And shuns the hands would seize upon her;
Follow thy life, and she will sue
  To pour for thee the cup of honour!

Auspex

MY heart, I cannot still it,
Nest that had song-birds in it;
And when the last shall go,
The dreary days to fill it,
Instead of lark or linnet,
Shall whirl dead leaves and snow.

Had they been swallows only,
Without the passion stronger
That skyward longs and sings,—
Woe 's me, I shall be lonely
When I can feel no longer
The impatience of their wings!

A moment, sweet delusion,
Like birds the brown leaves hover;
But it will not be long
Before their wild confusion
Fall wavering down to cover
The poet and his song.

St. Michael the Weigher

STOOD the tall Archangel weighing
All man's dreaming, doing, saying,
All the failure and the pain,
All the triumph and the gain,
In the unimagined years,
Full of hopes, more full of tears,
Since old Adam's hopeless eyes
Backward searched for Paradise,
And, instead, the flame-blade saw
Of inexorable Law.

Waking, I beheld him there,
With his fire-gold, flickering hair,
In his blinding armor stand,
And the scales were in his hand:
Mighty were they, and full well
They could poise both heaven and hell.

"Angel," asked I humbly then,
"Weighest thou the souls of men?
That thine office is, I know."
"Nay," he answered me, "not so;
But I weigh the hope of Man
Since the power of choice began,
In the world, of good or ill."
Then I waited and was still.

In one scale I saw him place
All the glories of our race,
Cups that lit Belshazzar's feast,
Gems, the lightning of the East,
Kublai's sceptre, Cæsar's sword,
Many a poet's golden word,
Many a skill of science, vain
To make men as gods again.

In the other scale he threw
Things regardless, outcast, few,
Martyr-ash, arena sand,
Of St. Francis' cord a strand,
Beechen cups of men whose need
Fasted that the poor might feed,
Disillusions and despairs
Of young saints with grief-grayed hairs,
Broken hearts that brake for Man.

Marvel through my pulses ran
Seeing then the beam divine
Swiftly on this hand decline,
While Earth's splendor and renown
Mounted light as thistle-down.

MARIA WHITE LOWELL

An Opium Fantasy

SOFT hangs the opiate in the brain,
   And lulling soothes the edge of pain,
Till harshest sound, far off or near,
Sings floating in its mellow sphere.

What wakes me from my heavy dream?
   Or am I still asleep?
Those long and soft vibrations seem
   A slumberous charm to keep.

The graceful play, a moment stopt,
   Distance again unrolls,
Like silver balls, that, softly dropt,
   Ring into golden bowls.

I question of the poppies red,
   The fairy flaunting band,
While I, a weed with drooping head,
   Within their phalanx stand: —

"Some airy one, with scarlet cap,
   The name unfold to me
Of this new minstrel who can lap
   Sleep in his melody!"

Bright grew their scarlet-kerchief'd heads,
   As freshening winds had blown,
And from their gently-swaying beds
   They sang in undertone: —

"Oh he is but a little owl,
   The smallest of his kin,

Who sits beneath the midnight's cowl
And makes this airy din."

"Deceitful tongues of fiery tints!
    Far more than this ye know,
That he is your enchanted prince
    Doom'd as an owl to go;—

"Nor his fond play for years hath stopt,
    But nightly he unrolls
His silver balls, that, softly dropt,
    Ring into golden bowls."

RALPH WALDO EMERSON

The Rhodora:

ON BEING ASKED, WHENCE IS THE FLOWER?

IN May, when sea-winds pierced our solitudes,
I found the fresh Rhodora in the woods,
Spreading its leafless blooms in a damp nook,
To please the desert and the sluggish brook.
The purple petals, fallen in the pool,
Made the black water with their beauty gay;
Here might the red-bird come his plumes to cool,
And court the flower that cheapens his array.
Rhodora! if the sages ask thee why
This charm is wasted on the earth and sky,
Tell them, dear, that if eyes were made for seeing,
Then Beauty is its own excuse for being:
Why thou wert there, O rival of the rose!
I never thought to ask, I never knew;
But, in my simple ignorance, suppose
The self-same Power that brought me there brought you.

Compensation

WHY should I keep holiday
　　When other men have none?
Why but because, when these are gay,
　　I sit and mourn alone?

And why, when mirth unseals all tongues,
　　Should mine alone be dumb?
Ah! late I spoke to silent throngs,
　　And now their hour is come.

Give All to Love

GIVE all to love;
　　Obey thy heart;
Friends, kindred, days,
Estate, good-fame,
Plans, credit, and the Muse,—
Nothing refuse.

'Tis a brave master;
Let it have scope:
Follow it utterly,
Hope beyond hope:
High and more high
It dives into noon,
With wing unspent,
Untold intent;
But it is a god,
Knows its own path,
And the outlets of the sky.

It was never for the mean.
It requireth courage stout,
Souls above doubt,
Valor unbending;

It will reward,—
They shall return
More than they were,
And ever ascending

Leave all for love;
Yet, hear me, yet,
One word more thy heart behoved,
One pulse more of firm endeavor,—
Keep thee to-day
To-morrow, forever,
Free as an Arab
Of thy beloved.

Cling with life to the maid;
But when the surprise,
First vague shadow of surmise
Flits across her bosom young
Of a joy apart from thee,
Free be she, fancy-free;
Nor thou detain her vesture's hem,
Nor the palest rose she flung
From her summer diadem.

Though thou loved her as thyself,
As a self of purer clay,
Though her parting dims the day,
Stealing grace from all alive;
Heartily know,
When half-gods go,
The gods arrive.

Bacchus

BRING me wine, but wine which never grew
In the belly of the grape,
Or grew on vine whose tap-roots, reaching through
Under the Andes to the Cape,
Suffer no savor of the earth to scape.

Let its grapes the morn salute
From a nocturnal root,
Which feels the acrid juice
Of Styx and Erebus;
And turns the woe of Night,
By its own craft, to a more rich delight.

We buy ashes for bread;
We buy diluted wine;
Give me of the true,—
Whose ample leaves and tendrils curled
Among the silver hills of heaven,
Draw everlasting dew;
Wine of wine,
Blood of the world,
Form of forms, and mould of statures,
That I intoxicated,
And by the draught assimilated,
May float at pleasure through all natures;
The bird-language rightly spell,
And that which roses say so well.

Wine that is shed
Like the torrents of the sun
Up the horizon walls,
Or like the Atlantic streams, which run
When the South Sea calls.

Water and bread,
Food which needs no transmuting,
Rainbow-flowering, wisdom-fruiting,
Wine which is already man,
Food which teach and reason can.

Wine which Music is,—
Music and wine are one,—
That I, drinking this,
Shall hear far Chaos talk with me;
Kings unborn shall walk with me;
And the poor grass shall plot and plan

What it will do when it is man.
Quickened so, will I unlock
Every crypt of every rock.

I thank the joyful juice
For all I know;—
Winds of remembering
Of the ancient being blow,
And seeming-solid walls of use
Open and flow.

Pour, Bacchus! the remembering wine;
Retrieve the loss of me and mine!
Vine for vine be antidote,
And the grape requite the lote!
Haste to cure the old despair,—
Reason in Nature's lotus drenched,
The memory of ages quenched;
Give them again to shine;
Let wine repair what this undid;
And where the infection slid,
A dazzling memory revive;
Refresh the faded tints,
Recut the aged prints,
And write my old adventures with the pen
Which on the first day drew,
Upon the tablets blue,
The dancing Pleiads and eternal men.

Brahma

IF the red slayer think he slays,
   Or if the slain think he is slain,
They know not well the subtle ways
   I keep, and pass, and turn again.

Far or forgot to me is near;
   Shadow and sunlight are the same;
The vanquished gods to me appear;
   And one to me are shame and fame.

They reckon ill who leave me out;
  When me they fly, I am the wings;
I am the doubter and the doubt,
  And I the hymn the Brahmin sings.

The strong gods pine for my abode,
  And pine in vain the sacred Seven;
But thou, meek lover of the good!
  Find me, and turn thy back on heaven.

Merops

WHAT care I, so they stand the same,—
    Things of the heavenly mind,—
How long the power to give them name
    Tarries yet behind?

Thus far to-day your favors reach,
  O fair, appeasing presences!
Ye taught my lips a single speech,
  And a thousand silences.

Space grants beyond his fated road
  No inch to the god of day;
And copious language still bestowed
  One word, no more, to say.

Uriel

IT fell in the ancient periods
    Which the brooding soul surveys,
Or ever the wild Time coined itself
    Into calendar months and days.

This was the lapse of Uriel,
Which in Paradise befell.
Once, among the Pleiads walking,

Seyd overhead the young gods talking;
And the treason, too long pent,
To his ears was evident.
The young deities discussed
Laws of form, and metre just,
Orb, quintessence, and sunbeams,
What subsisteth, and what seems.
One, with low tones that decide,
And doubt and reverend use defied,
With a look that solved the sphere,
And stirred the devils everywhere,
Gave his sentiment divine
Against the being of a line.
'Line in nature is not found;
Unit and universe are round;
In vain produced, all rays return;
Evil will bless, and ice will burn.'
As Uriel spoke with piercing eye,
A shudder ran around the sky;
The stern old war-gods shook their heads,
The seraphs frowned from myrtle-beds;
Seemed to the holy festival
The rash word boded ill to all;
The balance-beam of Fate was bent;
The bounds of good and ill were rent;
Strong Hades could not keep his own,
But all slid to confusion.

A sad self-knowledge, withering, fell
On the beauty of Uriel;
In heaven once eminent, the god
Withdrew, that hour, into his cloud;
Whether doomed to long gyration
In the sea of generation,
Or by knowledge grown too bright
To hit the nerve of feebler sight.
Straightway, a forgetting wind
Stole over the celestial kind,
And their lips the secret kept,
If in ashes and fire-seed slept.

But now and then, truth-speaking things
Shamed the angels' veiling wings;
And, shrilling from the solar course,
Or from fruit of chemic force,
Procession of a soul in matter,
Or the speeding change of water,
Or out of the good of evil born,
Came Uriel's voice of cherub scorn,
And a blush tinged the upper sky,
And the gods shook, they knew not why.

Days

DAUGHTERS of Time, the hypocritic Days,
Muffled and dumb like barefoot dervishes,
And marching single in an endless file,
Bring diadems and fagots in their hands.
To each they offer gifts after his will,
Bread, kingdoms, stars, and sky that holds them all.
I, in my pleached garden, watched the pomp,
Forgot my morning wishes, hastily
Took a few herbs and apples, and the Day
Turned and departed silent. I, too late,
Under her solemn fillet saw the scorn.

Character

THE sun set, but set not his hope:
Stars rose; his faith was earlier up:
Fixed on the enormous galaxy,
Deeper and older seemed his eye;
And matched his sufferance sublime
The taciturnity of time.
He spoke, and words more soft than rain
Brought the Age of Gold again:
His action won such reverence sweet
As hid all measure of the feat.

HENRY DAVID THOREAU

Inspiration

IF with light head erect I sing,
Though all the Muses lend their force,
From my poor love of anything,
The verse is weak and shallow as its source.

But if with bended neck I grope
Listening behind me for my wit,
With faith superior to hope,
More anxious to keep back than forward it,—

Making my soul accomplice there
Unto the flame my heart hath lit,
Then will the verse forever wear,—
Time cannot bend the line which God has writ.

I hearing get, who had but ears,
And sight, who had but eyes before;
I moments live, who lived but years,
And truth discern, who knew but learning's lore.

Now chiefly is my natal hour,
And only now my prime of life;
Of manhood's strength it is the flower,
'T is peace's end, and war's beginning strife.

It comes in summer's broadest noon,
By a gray wall, or some chance place,
Unseasoning time, insulting June,
And vexing day with its presuming face.

I will not doubt the love untold
Which not my worth nor want hath bought,
Which wooed me young, and woos me old,
And to this evening hath me brought.

Smoke

LIGHT-WINGED Smoke! Icarian bird,
　　Melting thy pinions in thy upward flight,
Lark without song, and messenger of dawn,
Circling above the hamlets as thy nest;
Or else, departing dream, and shadowy form
Of midnight vision, gathering up thy skirts;
By night star-veiling, and by day
Darkening the light and blotting out the sun;
Go thou my incense upward from this hearth,
And ask the gods to pardon this clear flame.

JULIA WARD HOWE

The Battle-Hymn of the Republic

MINE eyes have seen the glory of the coming of the Lord;
　　He is trampling out the vintage where the grapes of wrath
　　　　are stored;
He hath loosed the fateful lightning of His terrible swift sword;
　　　　His truth is marching on.

I have seen Him in the watch-fires of a hundred circling camps;
They have builded Him an altar in the evening dews and
　　　　damps;
I can read His righteous sentence by the dim and flaring lamps;
　　　　His day is marching on.

I have read a fiery gospel, writ in burnished rows of steel:
"As ye deal with my contemners, so with you my grace shall
　　　　deal;
Let the Hero, born of woman, crush the serpent with his heel,
　　　　Since God is marching on."

He has sounded forth the trumpet that shall never call retreat;
He is sifting out the hearts of men before His judgment-seat:
Oh, be swift, my soul, to answer Him! be jubilant, my feet!
    Our God is marching on.

In the beauty of the lilies Christ was born across the sea,
With a glory in His bosom that transfigures you and me:
As He died to make men holy, let us die to make men free,
    While God is marching on.

HENRY WADSWORTH LONGFELLOW

Hymn to the Night

Ἀσπασίη, τρίλλιστος

I HEARD the trailing garments of the Night
    Sweep through her marble halls;
I saw her sable skirts all fringed with light
    From the celestial walls.

I felt her presence, by its spell of might,
    Stoop o'er me from above—
The calm, majestic presence of the Night,
    As of the one I love.

I heard the sounds of sorrow and delight,
    The manifold, soft chimes,
That fill the haunted chambers of the Night,
    Like some old poet's rhymes.

From the cool cisterns of the midnight air
    My spirit drank repose;
The fountain of perpetual peace flows there,
    From those deep cisterns flows.

O holy Night! from thee I learn to bear
    What man has borne before;
Thou layest thy finger on the lips of Care,
    And they complain no more.

Peace! Peace! Orestes-like I breathe this prayer;
    Descend with broad-winged flight,
The welcome, the thrice-prayed for, the most fair,
    The best-beloved Night!

My Lost Youth

OFTEN I think of the beautiful town
    That is seated by the sea,
Often in thought go up and down
The pleasant streets of that dear old town,
    And my youth comes back to me.
        And a verse of a Lapland song
        Is haunting my memory still:
"A boy's will is the wind's will,
And the thoughts of youth are long, long thoughts."

I can see the shadowy lines of its trees,
    And catch, in sudden gleams,
The sheen of the far-surrounding seas,
And islands that were the Hesperides
    Of all my boyish dreams.
        And the burden of that old song,
        It murmurs and whispers still:
"A boy's will is the wind's will,
And the thoughts of youth are long, long thoughts."

I remember the black wharves and the slips,
    And the sea-tides tossing free,
And Spanish sailors with bearded lips,
And the beauty and mystery of the ships,
    And the magic of the sea.
        And the voice of that wayward song

Is singing and saying still:
"A boy's will is the wind's will,
And the thoughts of youth are long, long thoughts."

I remember the bulwarks by the shore,
   And the fort upon the hill;
The sunrise gun, with its hollow roar,
The drum-beat repeated o'er and o'er,
   And the bugle wild and shrill.
      And the music of that old song
      Throbs in my memory still:
"A boy's will is the wind's will,
And the thoughts of youth are long, long, thoughts."

I remember the sea-fight far away,
   How it thundered o'er the tide!
And the dead captains, as they lay
In their graves, o'erlooking the tranquil bay,
   Where they in battle died.
      And the sound of that mournful song
      Goes through me with a thrill:
"A boy's will is the wind's will,
And the thoughts of youth are long, long thoughts."

I can see the breezy dome of groves,
   The shadows of Deering's Woods;
And the friendships old and the early loves
Come back with a sabbath sound, as of doves
   In quiet neighborhoods.
      And the verse of that sweet old song,
      It flutters and murmurs still:
"A boy's will is the wind's will,
And the thoughts of youth are long, long thoughts."

I remember the gleams and glooms that dart
   Across the school-boy's brain;
The song and the silence in the heart,
That in part are prophecies and in part
   Are longings wild and vain.
      And the voice of that fitful song

Sings on, and is never still:
"A boy's will is the wind's will,
And the thoughts of youth are long, long thoughts."

There are things of which I may not speak;
    There are dreams that cannot die;
There are thoughts that make the strong heart weak,
And bring a pallor into the cheek
        And a mist before the eye.
            And the words of that fatal song
            Come over me like a chill:
"A boy's will is the wind's will,
And the thoughts of youth are long, long thoughts."

Strange to me now are the forms I meet
    When I visit the dear old town;
But the native air is pure and sweet,
And the trees that o'ershadow each well-known street,
    As they balance up and down,
        Are singing the beautiful song,
        Are sighing and whispering still:
"A boy's will is the wind's will,
And the thoughts of youth are long, long thoughts."

And Deering's Woods are fresh and fair;
    And with joy that is almost pain
My heart goes back to wander there,
And among the dreams of the days that were
    I find my lost youth again.
        And the strange and beautiful song,
        The groves are repeating it still:
"A boy's will is the wind's will,
And the thoughts of youth are long, long thoughts."

The Three Silences of Molinos

TO JOHN GREENLEAF WHITTIER

THREE Silences there are: the first of speech,
The second of desire, the third of thought;
This is the lore a Spanish monk, distraught
With dreams and visions, was the first to teach.
These Silences, commingling each with each,
Made up the perfect Silence that he sought
And prayed for, and wherein at times he caught
Mysterious sounds from realms beyond our reach.
O thou, whose daily life anticipates
The life to come, and in whose thought and word
The spiritual world preponderates,
Hermit of Amesbury! thou too hast heard
Voices and melodies from beyond the gates,
And speakest only when thy soul is stirred!

The Sound of the Sea

THE sea awoke at midnight from its sleep,
And round the pebbly beaches far and wide
I heard the first wave of the rising tide
Rush onward with uninterrupted sweep;
A voice out of the silence of the deep,
A sound mysteriously multiplied
As of a cataract from the mountain's side,
Or roar of winds upon a wooded steep.
So comes to us at times, from the unknown
And inaccessible solitudes of being,
The rushing of the sea-tides of the soul;
And inspirations, that we deem our own,
Are some divine foreshadowing and foreseeing
Of things beyond our reason or control.

Divina Commedia

I

OFT have I seen at some cathedral door
    A laborer, pausing in the dust and heat,
    Lay down his burden, and with reverent feet
    Enter, and cross himself, and on the floor
Kneel to repeat his paternoster o'er;
    Far off the noises of the world retreat;
    The loud vociferations of the street
    Become an undistinguishable roar.
So, as I enter here from day to day,
    And leave my burden at this minster gate,
    Kneeling in prayer, and not ashamed to pray,
The tumult of the time disconsolate
    To inarticulate murmurs dies away,
    While the eternal ages watch and wait.

II

How strange the sculptures that adorn these towers!
    This crowd of statues, in whose folded sleeves
    Birds build their nests; while canopied with leaves
    Parvis and portal bloom like trellised bowers,
And the vast minster seems a cross of flowers!
    But fiends and dragons of the gargoyled eaves
    Watch the dead Christ between the living thieves,
    And, underneath, the traitor Judas lowers!
Ah! from what agonies of heart and brain,
    What exultations trampling on despair,
    What tenderness, what tears, what hate of wrong.
What passionate outcry of a soul in pain,
    Uprose this poem of the earth and air,
    This mediæval miracle of song!

III

I enter, and I see thee in the gloom
    Of the long aisles, O poet saturnine!
    And strive to make my steps keep pace with thine.

The air is filled with some unknown perfume;
The congregation of the dead make room
    For thee to pass; the votive tapers shine;
    Like rooks that haunt Ravenna's groves of pine
    The hovering echoes fly from tomb to tomb.
From the confessionals I hear arise
    Rehearsals of forgotten tragedies,
    And lamentations from the crypts below;
And then a voice celestial that begins
    With the pathetic words, "Although your sins
As scarlet be," and ends with "as the snow."

IV

With snow-white veil and garments as of flame,
    She stands before thee, who so long ago
    Filled thy young heart with passion and the woe
    From which thy song and all its splendors came;
And while with stern rebuke she speaks thy name,
    The ice about thy heart melts as the snow
    On the mountain heights, and in swift overflow
    Comes gushing from thy lips in sobs of shame.
Thou makest full confession; and a gleam,
    As of the dawn on some dark forest cast,
    Seems on thy lifted forehead to increase;
Lethe and Eunoë—the remembered dream
    And the forgotten sorrow—bring at last
    That perfect pardon which is perfect peace.

V

I lift mine eyes, and all the windows blaze
    With forms of Saints and holy men who died,
    Here martyred and hereafter glorified;
    And the great Rose upon its leaves displays
Christ's Triumph, and the angelic roundelays,
    With splendor upon splendor multiplied;
    And Beatrice again at Dante's side
    No more rebukes, but smiles her words of praise.
And then the organ sounds, and unseen choirs
    Sing the old Latin hymns of peace and love
    And benedictions of the Holy Ghost;

And the melodious bells among the spires
    O'er all the house-tops and through heaven above
    Proclaim the elevation of the Host!

VI

O star of morning and of liberty!
    O bringer of the light, whose splendor shines
    Above the darkness of the Apennines,
    Forerunner of the day that is to be!
The voices of the city and the sea,
    The voices of the mountains and the pines,
    Repeat thy song, till the familiar lines
    Are footpaths for the thought of Italy!
Thy flame is blown abroad from all the heights,
    Through all the nations, and a sound is heard,
    As of a mighty wind, and men devout,
Strangers of Rome, and the new proselytes,
    In their own language hear thy wondrous word,
    And many are amazed and many doubt.

HERMAN MELVILLE

L'Envoi

THE RETURN OF THE SIRE DE NESLE
A.D. 16—

MY towers at last! These rovings end,
    Their thirst is slaked in larger dearth:
The yearning infinite recoils,
    For terrible is earth.

Kaf thrusts his snouted crags through fog:
Araxes swells beyond his span,
And knowledge poured by pilgrimage
    Overflows the banks of man.

But thou, my stay, thy lasting love
One lonely good, let this but be!
Weary to view the wide world's swarm,
    But blest to fold but thee.

Southern Cross

EMBLAZONED bleak in austral skies—
A heaven remote, whose starry swarm
Like Science lights but cannot warm—
Translated Cross, hast thou withdrawn,
Dim paling too at every dawn,
With symbols vain once counted wise,
And gods declined to heraldries?

Estranged, estranged: can friend prove so?
Aloft, aloof, a frigid sign:
How far removed, thou Tree divine,
Whose tender fruit did reach so low—
Love apples of New-Paradise!
About the wide Australian sea
The planted nations yet to be—

When, ages hence, they lift their eyes,
Tell, what shall they retain of thee?
But class thee with Orion's sword?
In constellations unadored,
Christ and the Giant equal prize?
The atheist cycles—*must* they be?
Fomentors as forefathers we?

Monody

TO have known him, to have loved him
    After loneness long;
And then to be estranged in life,
    And neither in the wrong;

And now for death to set his seal—
    Ease me, a little ease, my song!

By wintry hills his hermit-mound
    The sheeted snow-drifts drape,
And houseless there the snow-bird flits
    Beneath the fir-trees crape:
Glazed now with ice the cloistral vine
    That hid the shyest grape.

Of Rama

THAT Rama whom the Indian sung—
    A god he was, but knew it not;
Hence vainly puzzled at the wrong
Misplacing him in human lot.
Curtailment of his right he bare
Rather than wrangle; but no less
Was taunted for his tameness there.
A fugitive without redress,
He never the Holy Spirit grieved,
Nor the divine in him bereaved,
Though what that was he might not guess.

    Live they who, like to Rama, led
Unspotted from the world aside,
Like Rama are discredited—
Like him, in outlawry abide?
May life and fable so agree?—
    The innocent if lawless elf,
Ethereal in virginity,
Retains the consciousness of self.
Though black frost nip, though white frost chill,
Nor white frost nor the black may kill
The patient root, the vernal sense
Surviving hard experience
As grass the winter. Even that curse
Which is the wormwood mixed with gall—
Better dependent on the worse—

Divine upon the animal—
That can not make such natures fall.
  Though yielding easy rein, indeed,
To impulse which the fibers breed,
Nor quarreling with indolence;
Shall these the cup of grief dispense
Deliberate to any heart?
Not craft they know, nor envy's smart.
Theirs be the thoughts that dive and skim,
Theirs the spiced tears that overbrim,
And theirs the dimple and the lightsome whim.

The Night-March

WITH banners furled, the clarions mute,
    An army passes in the night;
And beaming spears and helms salute
    The dark with bright.

In silence deep the legions stream,
    With open ranks, in order true;
Over boundless plains they stream and gleam—
    No chief in view!

Afar, in twinkling distance lost,
    (So legends tell) he lonely wends
And back through all that shining host
    His mandate sends.

Lone Founts

THOUGH fast youth's glorious fable flies,
    View not the world with worldling's eyes;
Nor turn with weather of the time.
Foreclose the coming of surprise:
Stand where Posterity shall stand;
Stand where the Ancients stood before,

And, dipping in lone founts thy hand,
Drink of the never-varying lore:
Wise once, and wise thence evermore.

WALT WHITMAN

The Last Invocation

AT the last, tenderly,
From the walls of the powerful, fortressed house,
From the clasp of the knitted locks—from the keep of the well-
closed doors,
Let me be wafted.

Let me glide noiselessly forth;
With the key of softness unlock the locks—with a whisper
Set ope the doors, O Soul!

    Tenderly! be not impatient!
    (Strong is your hold, O mortal flesh!
    Strong is your hold, O love.)

Out of the Cradle Endlessly Rocking

OUT of the cradle endlessly rocking,
Out of the mocking-bird's throat, the musical shuttle,
Out of the Ninth-month midnight,
Over the sterile sands and the fields beyond, where the child
    leaving his bed wandered alone, bareheaded, barefoot,
Down from the showered halo,
Up from the mystic play of shadows twining and twisting as
    if they were alive,
Out from the patches of briers and blackberries,
From the memories of the bird that chanted to me,

From your memories, sad brother, from the fitful risings and
   fallings I heard,
From under that yellow half-moon late-risen and swollen as if
   with tears,
From those beginning notes of yearning and love there in the
   mist,
From the thousand responses of my heart never to cease.
From the myriad thence-aroused words,
From the word stronger and more delicious than any,
From such as now they start the scene revisiting,
As a flock, twittering, rising, or overhead passing,
Borne hither, ere all eludes me, hurriedly,
A man, yet by these tears a little boy again,
Throwing myself on the sand, confronting the waves,
I, chanter of pains and joys, uniter of here and hereafter,
Taking all hints to use them, but swiftly leaping beyond them,
A reminiscence sing.
Once Paumanok,
When the lilac-scent was in the air and Fifth-month grass
   was growing,
Up this seashore in some briers,
Two feathered guests from Alabama, two together,
And their nest, and four light-green eggs spotted with brown,
And every day the he-bird to and fro near at hand,
And every day the she-bird crouched on her nest, silent, with
   bright eyes,
And every day I, a curious boy, never too close, never disturb-
   ing them,
Cautiously peering, absorbing, translating.

Shine! shine! shine!
Pour down your warmth, great sun!
While we bask, we two together.

Two together!
Winds blow south, or winds blow north,
Day come white, or night come black,
Home, or rivers and mountains from home,
Singing all time, minding no time,
While we two keep together.

Till of a sudden,
Maybe killed, unknown to her mate,
One forenoon the she-bird crouched not on the nest,
Nor returned that afternoon, nor the next,
Nor ever appeared again.

And thenceforward all summer in the sound of the sea,
And at night under the full of the moon in calmer weather,
Over the hoarse surging of the sea,
Or flitting from brier to brier by day,
I saw, I heard at intervals the remaining one, the he-bird,
The solitary guest from Alabama.

Blow! blow! blow!
Blow up sea-winds along Paumanok's shore;
I wait and I wait till you blow my mate to me.

Yes, when the stars glistened,
All night long on the prong of a moss-scalloped stake,
Down almost amid the slapping waves,
Sat the lone singer, wonderful, causing tears.

He called on his mate,
He poured forth the meanings which I of all men know.

Yes, my brother, I know,—
The rest might not, but I have treasured every note,
For more than once dimly down to the beach gliding,
Silent, avoiding the moonbeams, blending myself with the
    shadows,
Recalling now the obscure shapes, the echoes, the sounds and
    sights after their sorts,
The white arms out in the breakers tirelessly tossing,
I, with bare feet, a child, the wind wafting my hair,
Listened long and long.

Listened to keep, to sing, now translating the notes,
Following you, my brother.

Soothe! soothe! soothe!
Close on its wave soothes the wave behind,
And again another behind embracing and lapping, every one
* close,*
But my love soothes not me, not me.

Low hangs the moon, it rose late,
It is lagging—O I think it is heavy with love, with love.

O madly the sea pushes upon the land,
With love, with love.

O night! do I not see my love fluttering out among the
* breakers?*
What is that little black thing I see there in the white?

Loud! loud! loud!
Loud I call to you, my love!

High and clear I shoot my voice over the waves,
Surely you must know who is here, is here,
You must know who I am, my love.

Low-hanging moon!
What is that dusky spot in your brown yellow?
O it is the shape, the shape of my mate!
O moon, do not keep her from me any longer.

Land! land! O land!
Whichever way I turn, O, I think you could give me my mate
* back again if you only would,*
For I am almost sure I see her dimly whichever way I look.

O rising stars!
Perhaps the one I want so much will rise, will rise with some
* of you.*

O throat! O trembling throat!
Sound clearer through the atmosphere!
Pierce the woods, the earth,
Somewhere listening to catch you must be the one I want.

Shake out carols!
Solitary here, the night's carols!
Carols of lonesome love! death's carols!
Carols under that lagging, yellow, waning moon!
O under that moon where she droops almost down into the sea!
O reckless despairing carols!

But soft! sink low!
Soft! let me just murmur,
And do you wait a moment, you husky-noised sea,
For somewhere I believe I heard my mate responding to me,
So faint, I must be still, be still to listen,
But not altogether still, for then she might not come imme-
    diately to me.

Hither, my love!
Here I am! here!
With this just-sustained note I announce myself to you,
This gentle call is for you, my love, for you.

Do not be decoyed elsewhere:
That is the whistle of the wind, it is not my voice,
That is the fluttering, the fluttering of the spray,
Those are the shadows of leaves.

O darkness! O in vain!
O I am very sick and sorrowful.
O brown halo in the sky near the moon, drooping upon the sea!
O troubled reflection in the sea!
O throat! O throbbing heart!
And I singing uselessly! uselessly all the night.

O past! O happy life; O songs of joy!
In the air, in the woods, over fields,
Loved! loved! loved! loved! loved!
But my mate no more, no more with me!
We two together no more.

The aria sinking,
All else continuing, the stars shining,
The winds blowing, the notes of the bird continuous echoing.

With angry moans the fierce old mother incessantly moaning,
On the sands of Paumanok's shore gray and rustling,
The yellow half-moon enlarged, sagging down, drooping, the
    face of the sea almost touching,
The boy ecstatic, with his bare feet the waves, with his hair
    the atmosphere dallying,
The love in the heart long pent, now loose, now at last tumultu-
    ously bursting,
The aria's meaning, the ears, the soul, swiftly depositing,
The strange tears down the cheeks coursing,
The colloquy there, the trio, each uttering,
The undertone, the savage old mother incessantly crying,
To the boy's soul's questions sullenly timing, some drown'd
    secret hissing,
To the outsetting bard.
Demon or bird! (said the boy's soul)
Is it indeed toward your mate you sing? or is it really to me?
For I, that was a child, my tongue's use sleeping, now I have
    heard you,
Now in a moment I know what I am for, I awake,
And already a thousand singers, a thousand songs, clearer,
    louder and more sorrowful than yours,
A thousand warbling echoes have started to life within me,
    never to die.

O you singers solitary, singing by yourself, projecting me,
O solitary me listening, never more shall I cease perpetuating
    you,
Never more shall I escape, never more the reverberations,
Never more the cries of unsatisfied love be absent from me,
Never again leave me to be the peaceful child I was before
    what there in the night,
By the sea under yellow and sagging moon,
The messenger there aroused, the fire, the sweet hell within,
The unknown want, the destiny of me.
O give me the clew! (it lurks in the night here somewhere)
O if I am to have so much, let me have more!

A word then, (for I will conquer it)
The word final, superior to all,

Subtle, sent up—what is it?—I listen;
Are you whispering it, and have been all the time, you sea-
    waves?
Is that it from your liquid rims and wet sands?
Whereto answering, the sea,
Delaying not, hurrying not,
Whispered me through the night, and very plainly before day-
    break,
Lisped to me the low and delicious word death,
And again death, death, death, death,
Hissing melodious, neither like the bird nor like my aroused
    child's heart,
But edging near as privately for me, rustling at my feet,
Creeping thence steadily up to my ears and laving me softly
    all over,
Death, death, death, death, death.

Which I do not forget,
But fuse the song of my dusky demon and brother,
That he sang to me in the moonlight on Paumanok's gray
    beach,
With the thousand responsive songs at random,
My own songs awaked from that hour,
And with them the key, the word up from the waves,
The word of the sweetest song and all songs,
That strong and delicious word which, creeping to my feet,
(Or like some old crone rocking the cradle, swathed in sweet
    garments, bending aside)
The sea whispered me.

Death Carol

(FROM "WHEN LILACS LAST IN THE DOOR-YARD BLOOMED")

COME, lovely and soothing Death,
    Undulate round the world, serenely arriving, arriving,
In the day, in the night, to all, to each,
Sooner or later, delicate Death.

Praised be the fathomless universe,
For life and joy, and for objects and knowledge curious;
And for love, sweet love—But praise! praise! praise!
For the sure-enwinding arms of cool-enfolding Death.

Dark Mother, always gliding near, with soft feet,
Have none chanted for thee a chant of fullest welcome?
Then I chant it for thee—I glorify thee above all;
I bring thee a song that when thou must indeed come, come
    unfalteringly.

Approach, strong deliveress!
When it is so—when thou hast taken them, I joyously sing the
    dead,
Lost in the loving, floating ocean of thee,
Laved in the flood of thy bliss, O Death.

From me to thee glad serenades,
Dances for thee I propose, saluting thee—adornments and
    feastings for thee;
And the sights of the open landscape, and the high-spread sky,
    are fitting,
And life and the fields, and the huge and thoughtful night.

The night, in silence, under many a star;
The ocean shore, and the husky whispering wave, whose voice
    I know;
And the soul turning to thee, O vast and well-veiled Death,
And the body gratefully nestling close to thee.

Over the tree-tops I float thee a song!
Over the rising and sinking waves—over the myriad fields, and
    the prairies wide;
Over the dense-packed cities all, and the teeming wharves and
    ways,
I float this carol with joy, with joy to thee, O Death!

A Noiseless, Patient Spider

A NOISELESS, patient spider,
    I marked, where, on a little promontory, it stood isolated;
Marked how, to explore the vacant, vast surrounding,
It launched forth filament, filament, filament, out of itself;
Ever unreeling them—ever tirelessly speeding them.

And you, O my Soul, where you stand,
Surrounded, surrounded, in measureless oceans of space.
Ceaselessly musing, venturing, throwing,—seeking the spheres,
    to connect them;
Till the bridge you will need, be formed—till the ductile anchor
    hold;
Till the gossamer thread you fling, catch somewhere, O my
    Soul.

Song of Myself

1

I CELEBRATE myself, and I sing myself,
    And what I assume you shall assume,
For every atom belonging to me as good belongs to you.

I loafe and invite my soul,
I lean and loafe at my ease observing a spear of summer grass.

My tongue, every atom of my blood, form'd from this soil, this
    air,
Born here of parents born here from parents the same, and
    their parents the same,
I, now thirty-seven years old in perfect health begin,
Hoping to cease not till death.

Creeds and schools in abeyance,
Retiring back a while sufficed at what they are, but never for-
    gotten,

I harbor for good or bad, I permit to speak at every hazard,
Nature without check with original energy.

2

Houses and rooms are full of perfumes, the shelves are crowded
    with perfumes,
I breathe the fragrance myself and know it and like it,
The distillation would intoxicate me also, but I shall not let it.

The atmosphere is not a perfume, it has no taste of the distilla-
    tion, it is odorless,
It is for my mouth forever, I am in love with it,
I will go to the bank by the wood and become undisguised and
    naked,
I am mad for it to be in contact with me.

The smoke of my own breath,
Echoes, ripples, buzz'd whispers, love-root, silk-thread, crotch
    and vine,
My respiration and inspiration, the beating of my heart, the
    passing of blood and air through my lungs,
The sniff of green leaves and dry leaves, and of the shore and
    dark-color'd sea-rocks, and of hay in the barn,
The sound of the belch'd words of my voice loos'd to the eddies
    of the wind,
A few light kisses, a few embraces, a reaching around of
    arms,
The play of shine and shade on the trees as the supple boughs
    wag,
The delight alone or in the rush of the streets, or along the
    fields and hill-sides,
The feeling of health, the full-moon trill, the song of me
    rising from bed and meeting the sun.

Have you reckon'd a thousand acres much? have you reckon'd
    the earth much?
Have you practis'd so long to learn to read?
Have you felt so proud to get at the meaning of poems?

Stop this day and night with me and you shall possess the
    origin of all poems.

You shall possess the good of the earth and sun, (there are
    millions of suns left,)
You shall no longer take things at second or third hand, nor
    look through the eyes of the dead, nor feed on the spectres
    in books,
You shall not look through my eyes either, nor take things
    from me,
You shall listen to all sides and filter them from your self.

3

I have heard what the talkers were talking, the talk of the
    beginning and the end,
But I do not talk of the beginning or the end.

There was never any more inception than there is now,
Nor any more youth or age than there is now,
And will never be any more perfection than there is now,
Nor any more heaven or hell than there is now.

Urge and urge and urge,
Always the procreant urge of the world.
Out of the dimness opposite equals advance, always substance
    and increase, always sex,
Always a knit of identity, always distinction, always a breed
    of iife.

To elaborate is no avail, learn'd and unlearn'd feel that it is so.

Sure as the most certain sure, plumb in the uprights, wel'
    entretied, braced in the beams,
Stout as a horse, affectionate, haughty, electrical,
I and this mystery here we stand.

Clear and sweet is my soul, and clear and sweet is all that is
    not my soul.

Lack one lacks both, and the unseen is proved by the seen,
Till that becomes unseen and receives proof in its turn.

Showing the best and dividing it from the worst age vexes age,
Knowing the perfect fitness and equanimity of things, while
    they discuss I am silent, and go bathe and admire myself.

Welcome is every organ and attribute of me, and of any man
    hearty and clean,
Not an inch nor a particle of an inch is vile, and none shall be
    less familiar than the rest.

I am satisfied—I see, dance, laugh, sing;
As the hugging and loving bed-fellow sleeps at my side through
    the night, and withdraws at the peep of the day with
    stealthy tread,
Leaving me baskets cover'd with white towels swelling the
    house with their plenty,
Shall I postpone my acceptation and realization and scream
    at my eyes,
That they turn from gazing after and down the road,
And forthwith cipher and show me to a cent,
Exactly the value of one and exactly the value of two, and
    which is ahead?

4

Trippers and askers surround me,
People I meet, the effect upon me of my early life or the ward
    and city I live in, or the nation,
The latest dates, discoveries, inventions, societies, authors old
    and new,
My dinner, dress, associates, looks, compliments, dues,
The real or fancied indifference of some man or woman I love,
The sickness of one of my folks or of myself, or ill-doing or
    loss or lack of money, or depressions or exaltations,
Battles, the horrors of fratricidal war, the fever of doubtful
    news, the fitful events;
These come to me days and nights and go from me again,
But they are not the Me myself.

Apart from the pulling and hauling stands what I am,
Stands amused, complacent, compassionating, idle, unitary,

Looks down, is erect, or bends an arm on an impalpable
    certain rest,
Looking with side-curved head curious what will come next,
Both in and out of the game and watching and wondering
    at it.

Backward I see in my own days where I sweated through
    fog with linguists and contenders,
I have no mockings or arguments, I witness and wait.

5

I believe in you my soul, the other I am must not abase itself
    to you,
And you must not be abased to the other.

Loafe with me on the grass, loose the stop from your throat,
Not words, not music or rhyme I want, not custom or lecture,
    not even the best,
Only the lull I like, the hum of your valvèd voice.
I mind how once we lay such a transparent summer morning,
How you settled your head athwart my hips and gently turn'd
    over upon me,
And parted the shirt from my bosom-bone, and plunged your
    tongue to my bare-stript heart,
And reach'd till you felt my beard, and reach'd till you held
    my feet.

Swiftly arose and spread around me the peace and knowledge
    that pass all the argument of the earth,
And I know that the hand of God is the promise of my own,
And I know that the spirit of God is the brother of my own,
And that all the men ever born are also my brothers, and the
    women my sisters and lovers,
And that a kelson of the creation is love,
And limitless are leaves stiff or drooping in the fields,
And brown ants in the little wells beneath them,
And mossy scabs of the worm fence, heap'd stones, elder,
    mullein and poke-weed.

6

A child said *What is the grass?* fetching it to me with full
    hands,
How could I answer the child? I do not know what it is any
    more than he.

I guess it must be the flag of my disposition, out of hopeful
    green stuff woven.

Or I guess it is the handkerchief of the Lord,
A scented gift and remembrancer designedly dropt,
Bearing the owner's name some way in the corners, that we
    may see and remark, and say *Whose?*

Or I guess the grass is itself a child, the produced babe of the
    vegetation.

Or I guess it is a uniform hieroglyphic,
And it means, Sprouting alike in broad zones and narrow
    zones,
Growing among black folks as among white,
Kanuck, Tuckahoe, Congressman, Cuff, I give them the same,
    I receive them the same.

And now it seems to me the beautiful uncut hair of graves.

Tenderly will I use you curling grass,
It may be you transpire from the breasts of young men,
It may be if I had known them I would have loved them,
It may be you are from old people, or from offspring taken
    soon out of their mothers' laps,
And here you are the mothers' laps.

This grass is very dark to be from the white heads of old
    mothers,
Darker than the colorless beards of old men,
Dark to come from under the faint red roofs of mouths.

O I perceive after all so many uttering tongues,
And I perceive they do not come from the roofs of mouths
for nothing.

I wish I could translate the hints about the dead young men
and women,
And the hints about old men and mothers, and the offspring
taken soon out of their laps.

What do you think has become of the young and old men?
And what do you think has become of the women and
children?

They are alive and well somewhere,
The smallest sprout shows there is really no death,
And if ever there was it led forward life, and does not wait
at the end to arrest it,
And ceas'd the moment life appear'd.

All goes onward and outward, nothing collapses,
And to die is different from what any one supposed, and
luckier.

7

Has any one supposed it lucky to be born?
I hasten to inform him or her it is just as lucky to die, and
I know it.

I pass death with the dying and birth with the new-wash'd
babe, and am not contain'd between my hat and boots,
And peruse manifold objects, no two alike and every one
good,
The earth good and the stars good, and their adjuncts all good.

I am not an earth nor an adjunct of an earth,
I am the mate and companion of people, all just as immortal
and fathomless as myself,
(They do not know how immortal, but I know.)

Every kind for itself and its own, for me mine male and
female,

For me those that have been boys and that love women,
For me the man that is proud and feels how it stings to be
   slighted,
For me the sweet-heart and the old maid, for me mothers and
   the mothers of mothers,
For me lips that have smiled, eyes that have shed tears,
For me children and the begetters of children.

Undrape! you are not guilty to me, nor stale nor discarded,
I see through the broadcloth and gingham whether or no,
And am around, tenacious, acquisitive, tireless, and cannot be
   shaken away.

8

The little one sleeps in its cradle,
I lift the gauze and look a long time, and silently brush away
   flies with my hand.

The youngster and the red-faced girl turn aside up the bushy
   hill,
I peeringly view them from the top.

The suicide sprawls on the bloody floor of the bedroom,
I witness the corpse with its dabbled hair, I note where the
   pistol has fallen.

The blab of the pave, tires of carts, sluff of boot-soles, talk of
   the promenaders,
The heavy omnibus, the driver with his interrogating thumb,
   the clank of the shod horses on the granite floor,
The snow-sleighs, clinking, shouted jokes, pelts of snow-balls,
The hurrahs for popular favorites, the fury of rous'd mobs,
The flap of the curtain'd litter, a sick man inside borne to the
   hospital,
The meeting of enemies, the sudden oath, the blows and fall,
The excited crowd, the policeman with his star quickly work-
   ing his passage to the centre of the crowd,
The impassive stones that receive and return so many echoes,
What groans of over-fed or half-starv'd who fall sunstruck or
   in fits,

What exclamations of women taken suddenly who hurry home
    and give birth to babes,
What living and buried speech is always vibrating here, what
    howls restrain'd by decorum,
Arrests of criminals, slights, adulterous offers made, accept-
    ances, rejections with convex lips,
I mind them or the show or resonance of them--I come and
    I depart.

9

The doors of the country barn stand open and ready,
The dried grass of the harvest-time loads the slow-drawn
    wagon,
The clear light plays on the brown gray and green intertinged,
The armfuls are pack'd to the sagging mow.

I am there, I help, I came stretch'd atop of the load,
I felt its soft jolts, one leg reclined on the other,
I jump from the cross-beams and seize the clover and timothy,
And roll head over heels and tangle my hair full of wisps.

10

Alone far in the wilds and mountains I hunt,
Wandering amazed at my own lightness and glee,
In the late afternoon choosing a safe spot to pass the night,
Kindling a fire and broiling the fresh-kill'd game,
Falling asleep on the gather'd leaves with my dog and gun
    by my side.

The Yankee clipper is under her sky-sails, she cuts the sparkle
    and scud,
My eyes settle the land, I bend at her prow or shout joyously
    from the deck.

The boatmen and clam-diggers arose early and stopt for me,
I tuck'd my trowser-ends in my boots and went and had a
    good time;
You should have been with us that day round the chowder-
    kettle.

I saw the marriage of the trapper in the open air in the far
    west, the bride was a red girl,
Her father and his friends sat near cross-legged and dumbly
    smoking, they had moccasins to their feet and large thick
    blankets hanging from their shoulders,
On a bank lounged the trapper, he was drest mostly in skins,
    his luxuriant beard and curls protected his neck, he held
    his bride by the hand,
She had long eyelashes, her head was bare, her coarse straight
    locks descended upon her voluptuous limbs and reach'd
    to her feet.

The runaway slave came to my house and stopt outside,
I heard his motions crackling the twigs of the woodpile,
Through the swung half-door of the kitchen I saw him limpsy
    and weak,
And went where he sat on a log and led him in and assured
    him,
And brought water and fill'd a tub for his sweated body and
    bruis'd feet,
And gave him a room that enter'd from my own, and gave
    him some coarse clean clothes,
And remember perfectly well his revolving eyes and his awk-
    wardness,
And remember putting plasters on the galls of his neck and
    ankles;
He staid with me a week before he was recuperated and pass'd
    north,
I had him sit next to me at table, my fire-lock lean'd in the
    corner.

11

Twenty-eight young men bathe by the shore,
Twenty-eight young men and all so friendly;
Twenty-eight years of womanly life and all so lonesome.

She owns the fine house by the rise of the bank,
She hides handsome and richly drest aft the blinds of the win-
    dow.

Which of the young men does she like the best?
Ah the homeliest of them is beautiful to her.

Where are you off to, lady? for I see you,
You splash in the water there, yet stay stock still in your room.

Dancing and laughing along the beach came the twenty-ninth
  bather,
The rest did not see her, but she saw them and loved them.

The beards of the young men glisten'd with wet, it ran from
  their long hair,
Little streams pass'd all over their bodies.

An unseen hand also pass'd over their bodies,
It descended tremblingly from their temples and ribs.

The young men float on their backs, their white bellies bulge
  to the sun, they do not ask who seizes fast to them,

They do not know who puffs and declines with pendant and
  bending arch,
They do not think whom they souse with spray.

12

The butcher-boy puts off his killing-clothes, or sharpens his
  knife at the stall in the market,
I loiter enjoying his repartee and his shuffle and break-down.

Blacksmiths with grimed and hairy chests environ the anvil,
Each has his main-sledge, they are all out, here is a great heat
  in the fire.

From the cinder-strew'd threshold I follow their movements,
The lithe sheer of their waists plays even with their massive
  arms,
Overhand the hammers swing, overhand so slow, overhand so
  sure,
They do not hasten, each man hits in his place.

13

The Negro holds firmly the reins of his four horses, the block
    swags underneath on its tied-over chain,
The Negro that drives the long dray of the stone-yard, steady
    and tall he stands pois'd on one leg on the string-piece,
His blue shirt exposes his ample neck and breast and loosens
    over his hip-band,
His glance is calm and commanding, he tosses the slouch of
    his hat away from his forehead,
The sun falls on his crispy hair and mustache, falls on the black
    of his polish'd and perfect limbs.

I behold the picturesque giant and love him, and I do not stop
    there,
I go with the team also.

In me the caresser of life wherever moving, backward as well
    as forward sluing,
To niches aside and junior bending, not a person or object
    missing,
Absorbing all to myself and for this song.

Oxen that rattle the yoke and chain or halt in the leafy shade,
    what is that you express in your eyes?
It seems to me more than all the print I have read in my life.

My tread scares the wood-drake and wood-duck on my distant
    and day-long ramble,
They rise together, they slowly circle around.

I believe in those wing'd purposes,
And acknowledge red, yellow, white, playing within me,
And consider green and violet and the tufted crown intentional,
And do not call the tortoise unworthy because she is not some-
    thing else,
And the jay in the woods never studied the gamut, yet trills
    pretty well to me,
And the look of the bay mare shames silliness out of me.

14

The wild gander leads his flock through the cool night,
Ya-honk he says, and sounds it down to me like an invitation,
The pert may suppose it meaningless, but I listening close,
Find its purpose and place up there toward the wintry sky.

The sharp-hoof'd moose of the north, the cat on the house-sill,
    the chickadee, the prairie-dog,
The litter of the grunting sow as they tug at her teats,
The brood of the turkey-hen and she with her half-spread
    wings.
I see in them and myself the same old law.

The press of my foot to the earth springs a hundred affections,
They scorn the best I can do to relate them.

I am enamour'd of growing out-doors,
Of men that live among cattle or taste of the ocean or woods,
Of the builders and steerers of ships and the wielders of axes
    and mauls, and the drivers of horses,
I can eat and sleep with them week in and week out.

What is commonest, cheapest, nearest, easiest, is Me,
Me going in for my chances, spending for vast returns,
Adorning myself to bestow myself on the first that will take
    me,
Not asking the sky to come down to my good will,
Scattering it freely forever.

15

The pure contralto sings in the organ loft,
The carpenter dresses his plank, the tongue of his foreplane
    whistles its wild ascending lisp,
The married and unmarried children ride home to their
    Thanksgiving dinner,
The pilot seizes the king-pin, he heaves down with a strong
    arm,
The mate stands braced in the whale-boat, lance and harpoon
    are ready,

The duck-shooter walks by silent and cautious stretches,

The deacons are ordain'd with cross'd hands at the altar,

The spinning-girl retreats and advances to the hum of the big wheel,

The farmer stops by the bars as he walks on a First-day loafe and looks at the oats and rye,

The lunatic is carried at last to the asylum a confirm'd case,

(He will never sleep any more as he did in the cot in his mother's bed-room;)

The jour printer with gray head and gaunt jaws works at his case,

He turns his quid of tobacco while his eyes blurr with the manuscript;

The malform'd limbs are tied to the surgeon's table,

What is removed drops horribly in a pail;

The quadroon girl is sold at the auction-stand, the drunkard nods by the bar-room stove,

The machinist rolls up his sleeves, the policeman travels his beat, the gate-keeper marks who pass,

The young fellow drives the express wagon, (I love him, though I do not know him;)

The half-breed straps on his light boots to compete in the race,

The western turkey-shooting draws old and young, some lean on their rifles, some sit on logs,

Out from the crowds steps the marksman, takes his position, levels his piece;

The groups of newly-come immigrants cover the wharf or levee,

As the woolly-pates hoe in the sugar-field, the overseer views them from his saddle,

The bugle calls in the ball-room, the gentlemen run for their partners, the dancers bow to each other,

The youth lies awake in the cedar-roof'd garret and harks to the musical rain,

The Wolverine sets traps on the creek that helps fill the Huron,

The squaw wrapt in her yellow-hemm'd cloth is offering moccasins and bead-bags for sale,

The connoisseur peers along the exhibition-gallery with half-shut eyes bent sideways,

As the deck-hands make fast the steamboat the plank is thrown for the shore-going passengers,

The young sister holds out the skein while the elder sister winds it off in a ball, and stops now and then for the knots,

The one-year wife is recovering and happy having a week ago borne her first child,

The clean-hair'd Yankee girl works with her sewing-machine or in the factory or mill,

The paving man leans on his two-handed rammer, the reporter's lead flies swiftly over the note-book, the sign-painter is lettering with blue and gold,

The canal boy trots on the tow-path, the book-keeper counts at his desk, the shoemaker waxes his thread,

The conductor beats time for the band and all the performers follow him,

The child is baptized, the convert is making his first professions,

The regatta is spread on the bay, the race is begun, (how the white sails sparkle!)

The drover watching his drove sings out to them that would stray,

The peddler sweats with his pack on his back, (the purchaser higgling about the odd cent;)

The bride unrumples her white dress, the minute-hand of the clock moves slowly,

The opium-eater reclines with rigid head and just-open'd lips,

The prostitute draggles her shawl, her bonnet bobs on her tipsy and pimpled neck,

The crowd laugh at her blackguard oaths, the men jeer and wink to each other,

(Miserable! I do not laugh at your oaths nor jeer you;)

The President holding a cabinet council is surrounded by the great Secretaries,

On the piazza walk three matrons stately and friendly with twined arms,

The crew of the fish-smack pack repeated layers of halibut in the hold,

The Missourian crosses the plains toting his wares and his cattle,

As the fare-collector goes through the train he gives notice by the jingling of loose change,

The floor-men are laying the floor, the tinners are tinning the roof, the masons are calling for mortar,

In single file each shouldering his hod pass onward the laborers;
Seasons pursuing each other the indescribable crowd is gather'd,
    it is the fourth of Seventh-month, (what salutes of cannon
    and small arms!)
Seasons pursuing each other the plougher ploughs, the mower
    mows, and the winter-grain falls in the ground;
Off on the lakes the pike-fisher watches and waits by the hole
    in the frozen surface,
The stumps stand thick round the clearing, the squatter strikes
    deep with his axe,
Flatboatmen make fast towards dusk near the cotton-wood or
    pecan-trees,
Coon-seekers go through the regions of the Red river or through
    those drain'd by the Tennessee, or through those of the
    Arkansas,
Torches shine in the dark that hangs on the Chattahooche or
    Altamahaw,
Patriarchs sit at supper with sons and grandsons and great
    grandsons around them,
In walls of adobe, in canvas tents, rest hunters and trappers
    after their day's sport,
The city sleeps and the country sleeps,
The living sleep for their time, the dead sleep for their time,
The old husband sleeps by his wife and the young husband
    sleeps by his wife;
And these tend inward to me, and I tend outward to them,
And such as it is to be of these more or less I am,
And of these one and all I weave the song of myself.

16

I am of old and young, of the foolish as much as the wise,
Regardless of others, ever regardful of others,
Maternal as well as paternal, a child as well as a man,
Stuff'd with the stuff that is coarse and stuff'd with the stuff
    that is fine,
One of the Nation of many nations, the smallest the same and
    the largest the same,
A Southerner soon as a Northerner, a planter nonchalant and
    hospitable down by the Oconee I live,

A Yankee bound my own way ready for trade, my joints the
  limberest joints on earth and the sternest joints on earth,
A Kentuckian walking the vale of the Elkhorn in my deer-
  skin leggings, a Louisianian or Georgian,
A boatman over lakes or bays or along coasts, a Hoosier,
  Badger, Buckeye;
At home on Kanadian snow-shoes or up in the bush, or with
  fishermen off Newfoundland,
At home in the fleet of ice-boats, sailing with the rest and
  tacking,
At home on the hills of Vermont or in the woods of Maine,
  or the Texan ranch,
Comrade of Californians, comrade of free North-Westerners,
  (loving their big proportions,)
Comrade of raftsmen and coalmen, comrade of all who shake
  hands and welcome to drink and meat,
A learner with the simplest, a teacher of the thoughtfullest,
A novice beginning yet experient of myriads of seasons,
Of every hue and caste am I, of every rank and religion,
A farmer, mechanic, artist, gentleman, sailor, quaker,
Prisoner, fancy-man, rowdy, lawyer, physician, priest.

I resist any thing better than my own diversity,
Breathe the air but leave plenty after me,
And am not stuck up, and am in my place.

(The moth and the fish-eggs are in their place,
The bright suns I see and the dark suns I cannot see are in
  their place,
The palpable is in its place and the impalpable is in its place.)

17

These are really the thoughts of all men in all ages and lands,
  they are not original with me,
If they are not yours as much as mine they are nothing, or next
  to nothing,
If they are not the riddle and the untying of the riddle they
  are nothing,
If they are not just as close as they are distant they are nothing.

This is the grass that grows wherever the land is and the
     water is,
This is the common air that bathes the globe.

18

With music strong I come, with my cornets and my drums,
I play not marches for accepted victors only, I play marches for
     conquer'd and slain persons.
Have you heard that it was good to gain the day?
I also say it is good to fall, battles are lost in the same spirit
     in which they are won.

I beat and pound for the dead,
I blow through my embouchures my loudest and gayest for
     them.

Vivas to those who have fail'd!
And to those whose war-vessels sank in the sea!
And to those themselves who sank in the sea!
And to all generals that lost engagements, and all overcome
     heroes!
And the numberless unknown heroes equal to the greatest
     heroes known!

19

This is the meal equally set, this the meat for natural hunger,
It is for the wicked just the same as the righteous, I make
     appointments with all,
I will not have a single person slighted or left away,
The kept-woman, sponger, thief, are hereby invited,
The heavy-lipp'd slave is invited, the venerealee is invited;
There shall be no difference between them and the rest.

This is the press of a bashful hand, this the float and odor of
     hair,
This is the touch of my lips to yours, this the murmur of
     yearning,
This the far-off depth and height reflecting my own face,
This the thoughful merge of myself, and the outlet again.

Do you guess I have some intricate purpose?
Well I have, for the Fourth-month showers have, and the mica
   on the side of a rock has.

Do you take it I would astonish?
Does the daylight astonish? does the early redstart twittering
   through the woods?
Do I astonish more than they?

This hour I tell things in confidence,
I might not tell everybody, but I will tell you.

20

Who goes there? hankering, gross, mystical, nude;
How is it I extract strength from the beef I eat?

What is a man anyhow? what am I? what are you?

All I mark as my own you shall offset it with your own,
Else it were time lost listening to me.

I do not snivel that snivel the world over,
That months are vacuums and the ground but wallow and
   filth.

Whimpering and truckling fold with powders for invalids,
   conformity goes to the fourth-remov'd,
I wear my hat as I please indoors or out.

Why should I pray? why should I venerate and be cere-
   monious?

Having pried through the strata, analyzed to a hair, counsel'd
   with doctors and calculated close,
I find no sweeter fat than sticks to my own bones.

In all people I see myself, none more and not one a barley-
   corn less,
And the good or bad I say of myself I say of them.

I know I am solid and sound,
To me the converging objects of the universe perpetually flow,
All are written to me, and I must get what the writing means.

I know I am deathless,
I know this orbit of mine cannot be swept by a carpenter's
    compass,
I know I shall not pass like a child's carlacue cut with a burnt
    stick at night.

I know I am august,
I do not trouble my spirit to vindicate itself or be understood,
I see that the elementary laws never apologize,
(I reckon I behave no prouder than the level I plant my house
    by, after all.)

I exist as I am, that is enough,
If no other in the world be aware I sit content,
And if each and all be aware I sit content.

One world is aware and by far the largest to me, and that is
    myself,
And whether I come to my own to-day or in ten thousand or
    ten million years,
I can cheerfully take it now, or with equal cheerfulness I can
    wait.

My foothold is tenon'd and mortis'd in granite,
I laugh at what you call dissolution,
And I know the amplitude of time.

21

I am the poet of the Body and I am the poet of the Soul,
The pleasures of heaven are with me and the pains of hell are
    with me,
The first I graft and increase upon myself, the latter I trans-
    late into a new tongue.

I am the poet of the woman the same as the man,
And I say it is as great to be a woman as to be a man,
And I say there is nothing greater than the mother of men.

I chant the chant of dilation or pride,
We have had ducking and deprecating about enough,
I show that size is only development.

Have you outstript the rest? are you the President?
It is a trifle, they will more than arrive there every one, and
    still pass on.
I am he that walks with the tender and growing night,
I call to the earth and sea half-held by the night.

Press close bare-bosom'd night—press close magnetic nourishing
    night!
Night of south winds—night of the large few stars!
Still nodding night—mad naked summer night.

Smile O voluptuous cool-breath'd earth!
Earth of the slumbering and liquid trees!

Earth of departed sunset—earth of the mountains misty-topt!
Earth of the vitreous pour of the full moon just tinged with
    blue!
Earth of shine and dark mottling the tide of the river!
Earth of the limpid gray of clouds brighter and clearer for my
    sake!
Far-swooping elbow'd earth—rich apple-blossom'd earth!
Smile, for your lover comes.

Prodigal, you have given me love—therefore I to you give love!
O unspeakable passionate love.

22

You sea! I resign myself to you also—I guess what you mean,
I behold from the beach your crooked inviting fingers,
I believe you refuse to go back without feeling of me,
We must have a turn together, I undress, hurry me out of sight
    of the land,
Cushion me soft, rock me in billowy drowse,
Dash me with amorous wet, I can repay you.

Sea of stretch'd ground-swells,
Sea breathing broad and convulsive breaths,
Sea of the brine of life and of unshovell'd yet always-ready
    graves,
Howler and scooper of storms, capricious and dainty sea,
I am integral with you, I too am of one phase and of all phases.

Partaker of influx and efflux, I, extoller of hate and conciliation,
Extoller of amies and those that sleep in each others' arms.

I am he attesting sympathy,
(Shall I make my list of things in the house and skip the house
    that supports them?)

I am not the poet of goodness only, I do not decline to be the
    poet of wickedness also.

What blurt is this about virtue and about vice?
Evil propels me and reform of evil propels me, I stand indif-
    ferent,
My gait is no fault-finder's or rejector's gait,
I moisten the roots of all that has grown.

Did you fear some scrofula out of the unflagging pregnancy?
Did you guess the celestial laws are yet to be work'd over and
    rectified?

I find one side a balance and the antipodal side a balance,
Soft doctrine as steady help as stable doctrine,
Thoughts and deeds of the present our rouse and early start.

This minute that comes to me over the past decillions,
There is no better than it and now.

What behaved well in the past or behaves well to-day is not
    such a wonder,
The wonder is always and always how there can be a mean
    man or an infidel.

23

Endless unfolding of words of ages!
And mine a word of the modern, the word En-Masse.

A word of the faith that never balks,
Here or henceforward it is all the same to me, I accept Time
absolutely.
It alone is without flaw, it alone rounds and completes all,
That mystic baffling wonder alone completes all.

I accept Reality and dare not question it,
Materialism first and last imbuing.

Hurrah for positive science! long live exact demonstration!
Fetch stonecrop mixt with cedar and branches of lilac,
This is the lexicographer, this the chemist, this made a gram-
mar of the old cartouches,
These mariners put the ship through dangerous unknown seas,
This is the geologist, this works with the scalpel, and this is a
mathematician.

Gentlemen, to you the first honors always!
Your facts are useful, and yet they are not my dwelling,
I but enter by them to an area of my dwelling.

Less the reminders of properties told my words,
And more the reminders they of life untold, and of freedom
and extrication,
And make short account of neuters and geldings, and favor
men and women fully equipt,
And beat the gong of revolt, and stop with fugitives and them
that plot and conspire.

24

Walt Whitman, a kosmos, of Manhattan the son,
Turbulent, fleshy, sensual, eating, drinking and breeding,
No sentimentalist, no stander above men and women or apart
from them,
No more modest than immodest.

Unscrew the locks from the doors!
Unscrew the doors themselves from their jambs!

Whoever degrades another degrades me,
And whatever is done or said returns at last to me.
Through me the afflatus surging and surging, through me the
    current and index.

I speak the pass-word primeval, I give the sign of democracy,
By God! I will accept nothing which all cannot have their
    counterpart of on the same terms.

Through me many long dumb voices,
Voices of the interminable generations of prisoners and slaves
Voices of the diseas'd and despairing and of thieves and dwarfs,
Voices of cycles of preparation and accretion,
And of the threads that connect the stars, and of wombs and
    of the father-stuff,
And of the rights of them the others are down upon,
Of the deform'd, trivial, flat, foolish, despised,
Fog in the air, beetles rolling balls of dung.

Through me forbidden voices,
Voices of sexes and lusts, voices veil'd and I remove the veil,
Voices indecent by me clarified and transfigur'd.

I do not press my fingers across my mouth,
I keep as delicate around the bowels as around the head and
    heart,
Copulation is no more rank to me than death is.
I believe in the flesh and the appetites,
Seeing, hearing, feeling, are miracles, and each part and tag of
    me is a miracle.

Divine am I inside and out, and I make holy whatever I touch
    or am touch'd from,
The scent of these arm-pits aroma finer than prayer,
This head more than churches, bibles, and all the creeds.

If I worship one thing more than another it shall be the spread
    of my own body, or any part of it,
Translucent mould of me it shall be you!
Shaded ledges and rests it shall be you!
Firm masculine colter it shall be you!
Whatever goes to the tilth of me it shall be you!
You my rich blood! your milky stream pale strippings of my
    life!
Breast that presses against other breasts it shall be you!
My brain it shall be your occult convolutions!
Root of wash'd sweet-flag! timorous pond-snipe! nest of guarded
    duplicate eggs! it shall be you!
Mix'd tussled hay of head, beard, brawn, it shall be you!
Trickling sap of maple, fibre of manly wheat, it shall be you!
Sun so generous it shall be you!
Vapors lighting and shading my face it shall be you!
You sweaty brooks and dews it shall be you!
Winds whose soft-tickling genitals rub against me it shall be
    you!
Broad muscular fields, branches of live oak loving lounger in
    my winding paths, it shall be you!
Hands I have taken, face I have kiss'd, mortal I have ever
    touch'd, it shall be you.

I dote on myself, there is that lot of me and all so luscious,
Each moment and whatever happens thrills me with joy,
I cannot tell how my ankles bend, nor whence the cause of my
    faintest wish,
Nor the cause of the friendship I emit, nor the cause of the
    friendship I take again.

That I walk up my stoop, I pause to consider if it really be,
A morning-glory at my window satisfies me more than the
    metaphysics of books.

To behold the day-break!
The little light fades the immense and diaphanous shadows,
The air tastes good to my palate.

Hefts of the moving world at innocent gambols silently rising,
    freshly exuding,
Scooting obliquely high and low.
Something I cannot see puts upward libidinous prongs,
Seas of bright juice suffuse heaven.

The earth by the sky staid with, the daily close of their junction,
The heav'd challenge from the east that moment over my head,
The mocking taunt, See then whether you shall be master!

25

Dazzling and tremendous how quick the sun-rise would kill
    me,
If I could not now and always send sun-rise out of me.

We also ascend dazzling and tremendous as the sun,
We found our own O my soul in the calm and cool of the
    daybreak.

My voice goes after what my eyes cannot reach,
With the twirl of my tongue I encompass worlds and volumes
    of worlds.

Speech is the twin of my vision, it is unequal to measure itself,
It provokes me forever, it says sarcastically,
Walt you contain enough, why don't you let it out then?

Come now I will not be tantalized, you conceive too much of
    articulation,
Do you not know O speech how the buds beneath you are
    folded?
Waiting in gloom, protected by frost,
The dirt receding before my prophetical screams,
I underlying causes to balance them at last,
My knowledge my live parts, it keeping tally with the meaning
    of all things,
Happiness, (which whoever hears me let him or her set out in
    search of this day.)

My final merit I refuse you, I refuse putting from me what I
    really am,

Encompass worlds, but never try to encompass me,
I crowd your sleekest and best by simply looking toward you.

Writing and talk do not prove me,
I carry the plenum of proof and every thing else in my face,
With the hush of my lips I wholly confound the skeptic.

26

Now I will do nothing but listen,
To accrue what I hear into this song, to let sounds contribute
   toward it.

I hear bravuras of birds, bustle of growing wheat, gossip of
   flames, clack of sticks cooking my meals,
I hear the sound I love, the sound of the human voice,
I hear all sounds running together, combined, fused or fol-
   lowing,
Sounds of the city and sounds out of the city, sounds of the day
   and night,
Talkative young ones to those that like them, the loud laugh
   of work-people at their meals,
The angry base of disjointed friendship, the faint tones of the
   sick,
The judge with hands tight to the desk, his pallid lips pro-
   nouncing a death-sentence,
The heave'e'yo of stevedores unlading ships by the wharves,
   the refrain of the anchor-lifters,
The ring of alarm-bells, the cry of fire, the whir of swift-streak-
   ing engines and hose-carts with premonitory tinkles and
   color'd lights,
The steam-whistle, the solid roll of the train of approaching
   cars,
The slow march play'd at the head of the association marching
   two and two,
(They go to guard some corpse, the flag-tops are draped with
   black muslin.)

I hear the violoncello, ('tis the young man's heart's complaint,)
I hear the key'd cornet, it glides quickly in through my ears,
It shakes mad-sweet pangs through my belly and breast.

I hear the chorus, it is a grand opera,
Ah this indeed is music—this suits me.

A tenor large and fresh as the creation fills me,
The orbic flex of his mouth is pouring and filling me full.

I hear the train'd soprano (what work with hers is this?)
The orchestra whirls me wider than Uranus flies,
It wrenches such ardors from me I did not know I possess'd
    them,
It sails me, I dab with bare feet, they are lick'd by the indolent
    waves,
I am cut by bitter and angry hail, I lose my breath,
Steep'd amid honey'd morphine, my windpipe throttled in
    fakes of death,
At length let up again to feel the puzzle of puzzles,
And that we call Being.

27

To be in any form, what is that?
(Round and round we go, all of us, and ever come back
    thither,)
If nothing lay more develop'd the quahaug in its callous shell
    were enough.

Mine is no callous shell,
I have instant conductors all over me whether I pass or stop,
They seize every object and lead it harmlessly through me.

I merely stir, press, feel with my fingers, and am happy,
To touch my person to some one else's is about as much as I
    can stand.

28

Is this then a touch? quivering me to a new identity,
Flames and ether making a rush for my veins,
Treacherous tip of me reaching and crowding to help them,
My flesh and blood playing out lightning to strike what is
    hardly different from myself,
On all sides prurient provokers stiffening my limbs,

Straining the udder of my heart for its withheld drip,
Behaving licentious toward me, taking no denial,
Depriving me of my best as for a purpose,
Unbuttoning my clothes, holding me by the bare waist,
Deluding my confusion with the calm of the sunlight **and**
    pasture-fields,
Immodestly sliding the fellow-senses away,
They bribed to swap off with touch and go and graze at the
    edges of me,
No consideration, no regard for my draining strength or my
    anger,
Fetching the rest of the herd around to enjoy them a while,
Then all uniting to stand on a headland and worry me.

The sentries desert every other part of me,
They have left me helpless to a red marauder,
They all come to the headland to witness and assist against me.

I am given up by traitors,
I talk wildly, I have lost my wits, I and nobody else am the
    greatest traitor,
I went myself first to the headland, my own hands carried me
    there.
You villain touch! what are you doing? my breath is tight in
    its throat,
Unclench your floodgates, you are too much for me.

29

Blind loving wrestling touch, sheath'd hooded sharp-**tooth'd**
    touch!
Did it make you ache so, leaving me?

Parting track'd by arriving, perpetual payment of perpetual
    loan,
Rich showering rain, and recompense richer afterward.

Sprouts take and accumulate, stand by the curb prolific and
    vital,
Landscapes projected masculine, full-sized and golden.

30

All truths wait in all things,
They neither hasten their own delivery nor resist it,
They do not need the obstetric forceps of the surgeon,
The insignificant is as big to me as any,
(What is less or more than a touch?)

Logic and sermons never convince,
The damp of the night drives deeper into my soul.

(Only what proves itself to every man and woman is so,
Only what nobody denies is so.)

A minute and a drop of me settle my brain,
I believe the soggy clods shall become lovers and lamps,
And a compend of compends is the meat of a man or woman.
And a summit and flower there is the feeling they have for each
    other,
And they are to branch boundlessly out of that lesson until it
    becomes omnific,
And until one and all shall delight us, and we them.

31

I believe a leaf of grass is no less than the journey-work of the
    stars,
And the pismire is equally perfect, and a grain of sand, and
    the egg of the wren,
And the tree-toad is a chef-d'œuvre for the highest,
And the running blackberry would adorn the parlors of heaven,
And the narrowest hinge in my hand puts to scorn all ma-
    chinery,
And the cow crunching with depress'd head surpasses any
    statue,
And a mouse is miracle enough to stagger sextillions of infidels.

I find I incorporate gneiss, coal, long-threaded moss, fruits,
    grains, esculent roots,
And am stucco'd with quadrupeds and birds all over,

And have distanced what is behind me for good reasons,
But call any thing back again when I desire it.

In vain the speeding or shyness,
In vain the plutonic rocks send their old heat against my approach,
In vain the mastodon retreats beneath its own powder'd bones,
In vain objects stand leagues off and assume manifold shapes,
In vain the ocean settling in hollows and the great monsters
    lying low,
In vain the buzzard houses herself with the sky,
In vain the snake slides through the creepers and logs,
In vain the elk takes to the inner passes of the woods,
In vain the razor-bill'd auk sails far north to Labrador,
I follow quickly, I ascend to the nest in the fissure of the cliff.

32

I think I could turn and live with animals, they are so placid
    and self-contain'd,
I stand and look at them long and long.

They do not sweat and whine about their condition,
They do not lie awake in the dark and weep for their sins,
They do not make me sick discussing their duty to God,
Not one is dissatisfied, not one is demented with the mania of
    owning things,
Not one kneels to another, nor to his kind that lived thousands
    of years ago,
Not one is respectable or unhappy over the whole earth.

So they show their relations to me and I accept them,
They bring me tokens of myself, they evince them plainly in
    their possession.

I wonder where they get those tokens,
Did I pass that way huge times ago and negligently drop
    them?
Myself moving forward then and now and forever,
Gathering and showing more always and with velocity,
Infinite and omnigenous, and the like of these among them.

Not too exclusive toward the reachers of my remembrancers,
Picking out here one that I love, and now go with him on
    brotherly terms.

A gigantic beauty of a stallion, fresh and responsive to my
    caresses,
Head high in the forehead, wide between the ears,
Limbs glossy and supple, tail dusting the ground,
Eyes full of sparkling wickedness, ears finely cut, flexibly
    moving.

His nostrils dilate as my heels embrace him,
His well-built limbs tremble with pleasure as we race around
    and return.
I but use you a minute, then I resign you, stallion,
Why do I need your paces when I myself out-gallop them?
Even as I stand or sit passing faster than you.

33

Space and Time! now I see it is true, what I guess'd at,
What I guess'd when I loaf'd on the grass,
What I guess'd while I lay alone in my bed,
And again as I walk'd the beach under the paling stars of the
    morning.

My ties and ballasts leave me, my elbows rest in sea-gaps,
I skirt sierras, my palms cover continents,
I am afoot with my vision.

By the city's quadrangular houses—in log huts, camping with
    lumbermen,
Along the ruts of the turnpike, along the dry gulch and rivulet
    bed,
Weeding my onion-patch or hoeing rows of carrots and pars-
    nips, crossing savannas, trailing in forests,
Prospecting, gold-digging, girdling the trees of a new purchase,
Scorch'd ankle-deep by the hot sand, hauling my boat down
    the shallow river,
Where the panther walks to and fro on a limb overhead,
    where the buck turns furiously at the hunter,

Where the rattlesnake suns his flabby length on a rock, where
the otter is feeding on fish,

Where the alligator in his tough pimples sleeps by the bayou,

Where the black bear is searching for roots or honey, where
the beaver pats the mud with his paddle-shaped tail;

Over the growing sugar, over the yellow-flower'd cotton plant,
over the rice in its low moist field,

Over the sharp-peak'd farm house, with its scallop'd scum and
slender shoots from the gutters,

Over the western persimmon, over the long-leav'd corn, over
the delicate blue-flower flax,

Over the white and brown buckwheat, a hummer and buzzer
there with the rest,

Over the dusky green of the rye as it ripples and shades in
the breeze;

Scaling mountains, pulling myself cautiously up, holding on
by low scragged limbs,

Walking the path worn in the grass and beat through the
leaves of the brush,

Where the quail is whistling betwixt the woods and the wheat-
lot,

Where the bat flies in the Seventh-month eve, where the great
gold-bug drops through the dark,

Where the brook puts out of the roots of the old tree and flows
to the meadow,

Where cattle stand and shake away flies with the tremulous
shuddering of their hides,

Where the cheese-cloth hangs in the kitchen, where andirons
straddle the hearth-slab, where cobwebs fall in festoons
from the rafters;

Where trip-hammers crash, where the press is whirling its
cylinders,

Wherever the human heart beats with terrible throes under its
ribs,

Where the pear-shaped bailoon is floating aloft, (floating in it
myself and looking composedly down,)

Where the life-car is drawn on the slip-noose, where the heat
hatches pale-green eggs in the dented sand,

Where the she-whale swims with her calf and never forsakes it,

Where the steam-ship trails hind-ways its long pennant of
    smoke,
Where the fin of the shark cuts like a black chip out of the
    water,
Where the half-burn'd brig is riding on unknown currents,
Where shells grow to her slimy deck, where the dead are
    corrupting below;
Where the dense-starr'd flag is borne at the head of the regi-
    ments,
Approaching Manhattan up by the long-stretching island,
Under Niagara, the cataract falling like a veil over my counte-
    nance,
Upon a door-step, upon the horse-block of hard wood outside,
Upon the race-course, or enjoying picnics or jigs or a good
    game of base-ball,
At he-festivals, with blackguard gibes, ironical license, bull-
    dances, drinking, laughter,
At the cider-mill tasting the sweets of the brown mash, sucking
    the juice through a straw,
At apple-peelings wanting kisses for all the red fruit I find,
At musters, beach-parties, friendly bees, huskings, house-
    raisings;
Where the mocking-bird sounds his delicious gurgles, cackles,
    screams, weeps,
Where the hay-rick stands in the barn-yard, where the dry
    stalks are scatter'd, where the brood-cow waits in the hovel,
Where the bull advances to do his masculine work, where the
    stud to the mare, where the cock is treading the hen,
Where the heifers browse, where geese nip their food with
    short jerks,
Where sun-down shadows lengthen over the limitless and
    lonesome prairie,
Where herds of buffalo make a crawling spread of the square
    miles far and near,
Where the humming-bird shimmers, where the neck of the
    long-lived swan is curving and winding,
Where the laughing-gull scoots by the shore, where she laughs
    her near-human laugh,
Where bee-hives range on a gray bench in the garden half hid
    by the high weeds,

Where band-neck'd partridges roost in a ring on the ground with their heads out,

Where burial coaches enter the arch'd gates of a cemetery,

Where winter wolves bark amid wastes of snow and icicled trees,

Where the yellow-crown'd heron comes to the edge of the marsh at night and feeds upon small crabs,

Where the splash of swimmers and divers cools the warm moon,

Where the katy-did works her chromatic reed on the walnut-tree over the well,

Through patches of citrons and cucumbers with silver-wired leaves,

Through the salt-lick or orange glade, or under conical firs,

Through the gymnasium, through the curtain'd saloon, through the office or public hall;

Pleas'd with the native and pleas'd with the foreign, pleas'd with the new and old,

Pleas'd with the homely woman as well as the handsome,

Pleas'd with the quakeress as she puts off her bonnet and talks melodiously,

Pleas'd with the tune of the choir of the whitewash'd church,

Pleas'd with the earnest words of the sweating Methodist preacher, impress'd seriously at the camp-meeting;

Looking in at the shop-windows of Broadway the whole forenoon, flatting the flesh of my nose on the thick plate glass,

Wandering the same afternoon with my face turn'd up to the clouds, or down a lane or along the beach,

My right and left arms around the sides of two friends, and I in the middle;

Coming home with the silent and dark-cheek'd bush-boy, (behind me he rides at the drape of the day,)

Far from the settlements studying the print of animals' feet, or the moccasin print,

By the cot in the hospital reaching lemonade to a feverish patient,

Nigh the coffin'd corpse when all is still, examining with a candle;

Voyaging to every port to dicker and adventure,

Hurrying with the modern crowd as eager and fickle as any,
Hot toward one I hate, ready in my madness to knife him,
Solitary at midnight in my back yard, my thoughts gone from
    me a long while,
Walking the old hills of Judæa with the beautiful gentle God
    by my side,
Speeding through space, speeding through heaven and the
    stars,
Speeding amid the seven satellites and the broad ring, and the
    diameter of eighty thousand miles,
Speeding with tail'd meteors, throwing fire-balls like the rest,
Carrying the crescent child that carries its own full mother in
    its belly,
Storming, enjoying, planning, loving, cautioning,
Backing and filling, appearing and disappearing,
I tread day and night such roads.

I visit the orchards of spheres and look at the product,
And look at quintillions ripen'd and look at quintillions green.

I fly those flights of a fluid and swallowing soul,
My course runs below the soundings of plummets.

I help myself to material and immaterial,
No guard can shut me off, no law prevent me.

I anchor my ship for a little while only,
My messengers continually cruise away or bring their returns
    to me.

I go hunting polar furs and the seal, leaping chasms with a
    pike-pointed staff, clinging to topples of brittle and blue.
I ascend to the foretruck,
I take my place at night in the crow's-nest,
We sail the arctic sea, it is plenty light enough,
Through the clear atmosphere I stretch around on the won-
    derful beauty,
The enormous masses of ice pass me and I pass them, the
    scenery is plain in all directions,

The white-topt mountains show in the distance, I fling out my
    fancies toward them,
We are approaching some great battle-field in which we are
    soon to be engaged,
We pass the colossal outposts of the encampment, we pass
    with still feet and caution,
Or we are entering by the suburbs some vast and ruin'd city,
The blocks and fallen architecture more than all the living
    cities of the globe.

I am a free companion, I bivouac by invading watchfires,
I turn the bridegroom out of bed and stay with the bride
    myself,
I tighten her all night to my thighs and lips.

My voice is the wife's voice, the screech by the rail of the stairs,
They fetch my man's body up dripping and drown'd.

I understand the large hearts of heroes,
The courage of present times and all times,
How the skipper saw the crowded and rudderless wreck of the
    steam-ship, and Death chasing it up and down the storm,
How he knuckled tight and gave not an inch, and was faith-
    ful of days and faithful of nights,
And chalk'd in large letters on a board, *Be of good cheer, we
    will not desert you;*
How he follow'd with them and tack'd with them three days
    and would not give it up,
How he saved the drifting company at last,
How the lank loose-gown'd women look'd when boated from
    the side of their prepared graves,
How the silent old-faced infants and the lifted sick, and the
    sharp-lipp'd unshaven men;
All this I swallow, it tastes good, I like it well, it becomes
    mine,
I am the man, I suffer'd, I was there.

The disdain and calmness of martyrs,
The mother of old, condemn'd for a witch, burnt with dry
    wood, her children gazing on,

The hounded slave that flags in the race, leans by the fence,
blowing, cover'd with sweat.
The twinges that sting like needles his legs and neck, the mur-
derous buckshot and the bullets,
All these I feel or am.

I am the hounded slave, I wince at the bite of the dogs,
Hell and despair are upon me, crack and again crack the
marksmen,
I clutch the rails of the fence, my gore dribs, thinn'd with the
ooze of my skin,
I fall on the weeds and stones,
The riders spur their unwilling horses, haul close,
Taunt my dizzy ears and beat me violently over the head with
whip-stocks.

Agonies are one of my changes of garments,
I do not ask the wounded person how he feels, I myself become
the wounded person,
My hurts turn livid upon me as I lean on a cane and observe.

I am the mash'd fireman with breast-bone broken,
Tumbling walls buried me in their debris,
Heat and smoke I inspired, I heard the yelling shouts of my
comrades,
I heard the distant click of their picks and shovels,
They have clear'd the beams away, they tenderly lift me forth.

I lie in the night air in my red shirt, the pervading hush is
for my sake,
Painless after all I lie exhausted but not so unhappy,
White and beautiful are the faces around me, the heads are
bared of their fire-caps,
The kneeling crowd fades with the light of the torches.

Distant and dead resuscitate,
They show as the dial or move as the hands of me, I am the
clock myself.

I am an old artillerist, I tell of my fort's bombardment,
I am there again.

Again the long roll of the drummers,
Again the attacking cannon, mortars,
Again to my listening ears the cannon responsive.

I take part, I see and hear the whole,
The cries, curses, roar, the plaudits for well-aim'd shots,
The ambulanza slowly passing trailing its red drip,
Workmen searching after damages, making indispensable repairs,
The fall of grenades through the rent roof, the fan-shaped explosion,
The whizz of limbs, heads, stone, wood, iron, high in the air.

Again gurgles the mouth of my dying general, he furiously waves with his hand,
He gasps through the clot *Mind not me—mind—the entrenchments.*

34

Now I tell what I knew in Texas in my early youth,
(I tell not the fall of Alamo,
Not one escaped to tell the fall of Alamo,
The hundred and fifty are dumb yet at Alamo,)
'Tis the tale of the murder in cold blood of four hundred and twelve young men.

Retreating they had form'd in a hollow square with their baggage for breastworks,
Nine hundred lives out of the surrounding enemy's, nine times their number, was the price they took in advance,
Their colonel was wounded and their ammunition gone,
They treated for an honorable capitulation, receiv'd writing and seal, gave up their arms and march'd back prisoners of war.

They were the glory of the race of rangers,
Matchless with horse, rifle, song, supper, courtship,
Large, turbulent, generous, handsome, proud, and affectionate,
Bearded, sunburnt, drest in the free costume of hunters,
Not a single one over thirty years of age.

The second First-day morning they were brought out in squads
and massacred, it was beautiful early summer,
The work commenced about five o'clock and was over by
eight.

None obey'd the command to kneel,
Some made a mad and helpless rush, some stood stark and
straight,
A few fell at once, shot in the temple or heart, the living and
dead lay together,
The maim'd and mangled dug in the dirt, the new-comers
saw them there,
Some half-kill'd attempted to crawl away,
These were despatch'd with bayonets or batter'd with the
blunts of muskets,
A youth not seventeen years old seiz'd his assassin till two
more came to release him,
The three were all torn and cover'd with the boy's blood.

At eleven o'clock began the burning of the bodies;
That is the tale of the murder of the four hundred and twelve
young men.

35

Would you hear of an old-time sea-fight?
Would you learn who won by the light of the moon and
stars?
List to the yarn, as my grandmother's father the sailor told
it to me.

Our foe was no skulk in his ship I tell you, (said he,)
His was the surly English pluck, and there is no tougher or
truer, and never was, and never will be;
Along the lower'd eve he came horribly raking us.

We closed with him, the yards entangled, the cannon touch'd,
My captain lash'd fast with his own hands.

We had receiv'd some eighteen pound shots under the water,
On our lower-gun-deck two large pieces had burst at the first
fire, killing all around and blowing up overhead.

Fighting at sun-down, fighting at dark,
Ten o'clock at night, the full moon well up, our leaks on the
gain, and five feet of water reported,
The master-at-arms loosing the prisoners confined in the after-
hold to give them a chance for themselves.

The transit to and from the magazine is now stopt by the
sentinels,
They see so many strange faces they do not know whom to
trust.

Our frigate takes fire,
The other asks if we demand quarter?
If our colors are struck and the fighting done?

Now I laugh content, for I hear the voice of my little captain,
We have not struck, he composedly cries, *we have just begun
our part of the fighting.*

Only three guns are in use,
One is directed by the captain himself against the enemy's
main-mast,
Two well serv'd with grape and canister silence his musketry
and clear his decks.

The tops alone second the fire of this little battery, especially
the main-top,
They hold out bravely during the whole of the action.

Not a moment's cease,
The leaks gain fast on the pumps, the fire eats toward the
powder-magazine.

One of the pumps has been shot away, it is generally thought
we are sinking.

Serene stands the little captain,
He is not hurried, his voice is neither high nor low,
His eyes give more light to us than our battle-lanterns.

Toward twelve there in the beams of the moon they surrender
    to us.

36

Stretch'd and still lies the midnight,
Two great hulls motionless on the breast of the darkness,
Our vessel riddled and slowly sinking, preparations to pass to
    the one we have conquer'd,
The captain on the quarter-deck coldly giving his orders
    through a countenance white as a sheet,
Near by the corpse of the child that serv'd in the cabin,
The dead face of an old salt with long white hair and carefully
    curl'd whiskers,
The flames spite of all that can be done flickering aloft and
    below,
The husky voices of the two or three officers yet fit for duty,
Formless stacks of bodies and bodies by themselves, dabs of
    flesh upon the masts and spars,
Cut of cordage, dangle of rigging, slight shock of the soothe of
    waves,
Black and impassive guns, litter of powder parcels, strong
    scent,
A few large stars overhead, silent and mournful shining,
Delicate sniffs of sea-breeze, smells of sedgy grass and fields
    by the shore, death-messages given in charge to survivors.
The hiss of the surgeon's knife, the gnawing teeth of his saw,
Wheeze, cluck, swash of falling blood, short wild scream, and
    long, dull, tapering groan,
These so, these irretrievable.

37

You laggards there on guard! look to your arms!
In at the conquer'd doors they crowd! I am possess'd!
Embody all presences outlaw'd or suffering,
See myself in prison shaped like another man,
And feel the dull unintermitted pain.

For me the keepers of convicts shoulder their carbines and
keep watch,
It is I let out in the morning and barr'd at night.

Not a mutineer walks handcuff'd to jail but I am handcuff'd to
him and walk by his side,
(I am less the jolly one there, and more the silent one with
sweat on my twitching lips.)

Not a youngster is taken for larceny but I go up too, and am
tried and sentenced.

Not a cholera patient lies at the last gasp but I also lie at the
last gasp,
My face is ash-color'd, my sinews gnarl, away from me people
retreat.

Askers embody themselves in me and I am embodied in them,
I project my hat, sit shame-faced, and beg.

38

Enough! enough! enough!
Somehow I have been stunn'd. Stand back!
Give me a little time beyond my cuff'd head, slumbers, dreams,
gaping,
I discover myself on the verge of a usual mistake.
That I could forget the mockers and insults!
That I could forget the trickling tears and the blows of the
bludgeons and hammers!
That I could look with a separate look on my own crucifixion
and bloody crowning.

I remember now,
I resume the overstaid fraction,
The grave of rock multiplies what has been confided to it, or to
any graves,
Corpses rise, gashes heal, fastenings roll from me.

I troop forth replenish'd with supreme power, one of an average
unending procession,

Inland and sea-coast we go, and pass all boundary lines,
Our swift ordinances on their way over the whole earth,
The blossoms we wear in our hats the growth of thousands of
    years.

Eleves, I salute you! come forward!
Continue your annotations, continue your questionings.

39

The friendly and flowing savage, who is he?
Is he waiting for civilization, or past it and mastering it?

Is he some Southwesterner rais'd out-doors? is he Kanadian?
Is he from the Mississippi country? Iowa, Oregon, California?
The mountains? prairie-life, bush-life? or sailor from the sea?

Wherever he goes men and women accept and desire him,
They desire he should like them, touch them, speak to them,
    stay with them.

Behavior lawless as snow-flakes, words simple as grass, un-
    comb'd head, laughter, and naiveté,
Slow-stepping feet, common features, common modes and
    emanations,
They descend in new forms from the tips of his fingers,
They are wafted with the odor of his body or breath, they fly
    out of the glance of his eyes.

40

Flaunt of the sunshine I need not your bask—lie over!
You light surfaces only, I force surfaces and depths also.

Earth! you seem to look for something at my hands,
Say, old top-knot, what do you want?

Man or woman, I might tell how I like you, but cannot,
And might tell what it is in me and what it is in you, but
    cannot,
And might tell that pining I have, that pulse of my nights and
    days.

Behold, I do not give lectures or a little charity,
When I give I give myself.

You there, impotent, loose in the knees,
Open your scarf'd chops till I blow grit within you,
Spread your palms and lift the flaps of your pockets,
I am not to be denied, I compel, I have stores plenty and to
　　spare,
And any thing I have I bestow.

I do not ask who you are, that is not important to me,
You can do nothing and be nothing but what I will infold you.

To cotton-field drudge or cleaner of privies I lean,
On his right cheek I put the family kiss,
And in my soul I swear I never will deny him.

On women fit for conception I start bigger and nimbler babes,
(This day I am jetting the stuff of far more arrogant republics.)

To any one dying, thither I speed and twist the knob of the
　　door,
Turn the bed-clothes toward the foot of the bed,
Let the physician and the priest go home.

I seize the descending man and raise him with resistless will,
O despairer, here is my neck,
By God, you shall not go down! hang your whole weight
　　upon me.

I dilate you with tremendous breath, I buoy you up,
Every room of the house do I fill with an arm'd force,
Lovers of me, bafflers of graves.

Sleep—I and they keep guard all night,
Not doubt, not decease shall dare to lay finger upon you,
I have embraced you, and henceforth possess you to myself,
And when you rise in the morning you will find what I tell
　　you is so.

41

I am he bringing help for the sick as they pant on their backs,
And for strong upright men I bring yet more needed help.

I heard what was said of the universe,
Heard it and heard it of several thousand years;
It is middling well as far as it goes—but is that all?

Magnifying and applying come I,
Outbidding at the start the old cautious hucksters,
Taking myself the exact dimensions of Jehovah,
Lithographing Kronos, Zeus his son, and Hercules his grand-
        son,
Buying drafts of Osiris, Isis, Belus, Brahma, Buddha,
In my portfolio placing Manito loose, Allah on a leaf, the cruci-
        fix engraved,
With Odin and the hideous-faced Mexitli and every idol and
        image,
Taking them all for what they are worth and not a cent more,
Admitting they were alive and did the work of their days,
(They bore mites as for unfledg'd birds who have now to rise
        and fly and sing for themselves,)
Accepting the rough deific sketches to fill out better in myself,
        bestowing them freely on each man and woman I see,
Discovering as much or more in a framer framing a house,
Putting higher claims for him there with his roll'd-up sleeves
        driving the mallet and chisel,
Not objecting to special revelations, considering a curl of smoke
        or a hair on the back of my hand just as curious as any
        revelation,
Lads ahold of fire-engines and hook-and-ladder ropes no less to
        me than the gods of the antique wars,
Minding their voices' peal through the crash of destruction,
Their brawny limbs passing safe over charr'd laths, their white
        foreheads whole and unhurt out of the flames;
By the mechanic's wife with her babe at her nipple interceding
        for every person born,
Three scythes at harvest whizzing in a row from three lusty
        angels with shirts bagg'd out at their waists,

The snag-tooth'd hostler with red hair redeeming sins past and
    to come,
Selling all he possesses, travelling on foot to fee lawyers for his
    brother and sit by him while he is tried for forgery;
What was strewn in the amplest strewing the square rod about
    me, and not filling the square rod then,
The bull and the bug never worshipp'd half enough,
Dung and dirt more admirable than was dream'd,
The supernatural of no account, myself waiting my time to be
    one of the supremes,
The day getting ready for me when I shall do as much good
    as the best, and be as prodigious;
By my life-lumps! becoming already a creator,
Putting myself here and now to the ambush'd womb of the
    shadows.

42

A call in the midst of the crowd,
My own voice, orotund, sweeping and final.

Come my children,
Come my boys and girls, my women, household and intimates,
Now the performer launches his nerve, he has pass'd his prel-
    ude on the reeds within.

Easily written loose-finger'd chords—I feel the thrum of your
    climax and close.

My head slues round on my neck,
Music rolls, but not from the organ,
Folks are around me, but they are no household of mine.

Ever the hard unsunk ground,
Ever the eaters and drinkers, ever the upward and downward
    sun, ever the air and the ceaseless tides,
Ever myself and my neighbors, refreshing, wicked, real,
Ever the old inexplicable query, ever that thorn'd thumb, that
    breath of itches and thirsts,
Ever the vexer's *hoot! hoot!* till we find where the sly one hides
    and bring him forth,

Ever love, ever the sobbing liquid of life,
Ever the bandage under the chin, ever the trestles of death.

Here and there with dimes on the eyes walking,
To feed the greed of the belly the brains liberally spooning,
Tickets buying, taking, selling, but in to the feast never once
    going,
Many sweating, ploughing, thrashing, and then the chaff for
    payment receiving,
A few idly owning, and they the wheat continually claiming.

This is the city and I am one of the citizens,
Whatever interests the rest interests me, politics, wars, markets,
    newspapers, schools,
The mayor and councils, banks, tariffs, steamships, factories,
    stocks, stores, real estate and personal estate.

The little plentiful manikins skipping around in collars and
    tail'd coats,
I am aware who they are, (they are positively not worms or
    fleas,)
I acknowledge the duplicates of myself, the weakest and shal-
    lowest is deathless with me,
What I do and say the same waits for them,
Every thought that flounders in me the same flounders in them.

I know perfectly well my own egotism,
Know my omnivorous lines and must not write any less,
And would fetch you whoever you are flush with myself.

Not words of routine this song of mine,
But abruptly to question, to leap beyond yet nearer bring;
This printed and bound book—but the printer and the print-
    ing-office boy?
The well-taken photographs—but your wife or friend close and
    solid in your arms?
The black ship mail'd with iron, her mighty guns in her tur-
    rets—but the pluck of the captain and engineers?
In the houses the dishes and fare and furniture—but the host
    and hostess, and the look out of their eyes?

The sky up there—yet here or next door, or across the way?
The saints and sages in history—but you yourself?
Sermons, creeds, theology—but the fathomless human brain,
And what is reason? and what is love? and what is life?

43

I do not despise you priests, all time, the world over,
My faith is the greatest of faiths and the least of faiths,
Enclosing worship ancient and modern and all between ancient
and modern,
Believing I shall come again upon the earth after five thousand
years,
Waiting responses from oracles, honoring the gods, saluting the
sun,
Making a fetich of the first rock or stump, powowing with
sticks in the circle of obis,
Helping the lama or brahmin as he trims the lamps of the
idols,
Dancing yet through the streets in a phallic procession, rapt
and austere in the woods a gymnosophist,
Drinking mead from the skull-cup, to Shastas and Vedas ad-
mirant, minding the Koran,
Walking the Teokallis, spotted with gore from the stone and
knife, beating the serpent-skin drum,
Accepting the Gospels, accepting him that was crucified, know-
ing assuredly that he is divine,
To the mass kneeling or the puritan's prayer rising, or sitting
patiently in a pew,
Ranting and frothing in my insane crisis, or waiting dead-like
till my spirit arouses me,
Looking forth on pavement and land, or outside of pavement
and land,
Belonging to the winders of the circuit of circuits.

One of that centripetal and centrifugal gang I turn and talk
like a man leaving charges before a journey.

Down-hearted doubters dull and excluded,
Frivolous, sullen, moping, angry, affected, dishearten'd, atheis-
tical,

I know every one of you, I know the sea of torment, doubt, de-
   spair and unbelief.

How the flukes splash!
How they contort rapid as lightning, with spasms and spouts
   of blood!

Be at peace bloody flukes of doubters and sullen mopers,
I take my place among you as much as among any,
The past is the push of you, me, all, precisely the same,
And what is yet untried and afterward is for you, me, all,
   precisely the same.

I do not know what is untried and afterward,
But I know it will in its turn prove sufficient, and cannot fail.

Each who passes is consider'd, each who stops is consider'd,
   not a single one can it fail.

It cannot fail the young man who died and was buried,
Nor the young woman who died and was put by his side,
Nor the little child that peep'd in at the door, and then drew
   back and was never seen again,
Nor the old man who has lived without purpose, and feels it
   with bitterness worse than gall,
Nor him in the poor house tubercled by rum and the bad dis-
   order,
Nor the numberless slaughter'd and wreck'd, nor the brutish
   koboo call'd the ordure of humanity,
Nor the sacs merely floating with open mouths for food to
   slip in,
Nor any thing in the earth, or down in the oldest graves of the
   earth,
Nor any thing in the myriads of spheres, nor the myriads of
   myriads that inhabit them,
Nor the present, nor the least wisp that is known.

44

It is time to explain myself—let us stand up.

What is known I strip away,
I launch all men and women forward with me into the Unknown.

The clock indicates the moment—but what does eternity indicate?

We have thus far exhausted trillions of winters and summers,
There are trillions ahead, and trillions ahead of them.

Births have brought us richness and variety,
And other births will bring us richness and variety.

I do not call one greater and one smaller,
That which fills its period and place is equal to any.

Were mankind murderous or jealous upon you, my brother, my sister?
I am sorry for you, they are not murderous or jealous upon me,
All has been gentle with me, I keep no account with lamentation,
(What have I to do with lamentation?)

I am an acme of things accomplish'd, and I an encloser of things to be.

My feet strike an apex of the apices of the stairs,
On every step bunches of ages, and larger bunches between the steps,
All below duly travel'd, and still I mount and mount.

Rise after rise bow the phantoms behind me,
Afar down I see the huge first Nothing, I know I was even there,
I waited unseen and always, and slept through the lethargic mist,
And took my time, and took no hurt from the fetid carbon.

Long I was hugg'd close—long and long.

Immense have been the preparations for me,
Faithful and friendly the arms that have help'd me.

Cycles ferried my cradle, rowing and rowing like cheerful boat-
    men,
For room to me stars kept aside in their own rings,
They sent influences to look after what was to hold me.

Before I was born out of my mother generations guided me,
My embryo has never been torpid, nothing could overlay it.

For it the nebula cohered to an orb,
The long slow strata piled to rest it on,
Vast vegetables gave it sustenance,
Monstrous sauroids transported it in their mouths and depos-
    ited it with care.

All forces have been steadily employ'd to complete and delight
    me,
Now on this spot I stand with my robust soul.

45

O span of youth! ever-push'd elasticity.
O manhood, balanced, florid and full.

My lovers suffocate me,
Crowding my lips, thick in the pores of my skin,
Jostling me through streets and public halls, coming naked to
    me at night,
Crying by day *Ahoy!* from the rocks of the river, swinging and
    chirping over my head,
Calling my name from flower-beds, vines, tangled underbrush,
Lighting on every moment of my life,
Bussing my body with soft balsamic busses,
Noiselessly passing handfuls out of their hearts and giving them
    to be mine.

Old age superbly rising! O welcome, ineffable grace of dying
    days!

Every condition promulges not only itself, it promulges what
    grows after and out of itself,
And the dark hush promulges as much as any.

I open my scuttle at night and see the far-sprinkled systems,
And all I see multiplied as high as I can cipher edge but the
    rim of the farther systems.

Wider and wider they spread, expanding, always expanding,
Outward and outward and forever outward.

My sun has his sun and round him obediently wheels,
He joins with his partners a group of superior circuit,
And greater sets follow, making specks of the greatest inside
    them.

There is no stoppage and never can be stoppage,
If I, you, and the worlds, and all beneath or upon their sur-
    faces, were this moment reduced back to a pallid float, it
    would not avail in the long run,
We should surely bring up again where we now stand,
And surely go as much farther, and then farther and farther.

A few quadrillions of eras, a few octillions of cubic leagues, do
    not hazard the span or make it impatient,
They are but parts, any thing is but a part.

See ever so far, there is limitless space outside of that,
Count ever so much, there is limitless time around that.

My rendezvous is appointed, it is certain,
The Lord will be there and wait till I come on perfect terms,
The great Camerado, the lover true for whom I pine will be
    there.

46

I know I have the best of time and space, and was never meas-
    ured and never will be measured.

I tramp a perpetual journey, (come listen all!)
My signs are a rain-proof coat, good shoes, and a staff cut from
    the woods,

No friend of mine takes his ease in my chair,
I have no chair, no church, no philosophy,
I lead no man to a dinner-table, library, exchange,
But each man and each woman of you I lead upon a knoll,
My left hand hooking you round the waist,
My right hand pointing to landscapes of continents and the
    public road.

Not I, not any one else can travel that road for you,
You must travel it for yourself.

It is not far, it is within reach,
Perhaps you have been on it since you were born and did not
    know,
Perhaps it is everywhere on water and on land.

Shoulder your duds dear son, and I will mine, and let us hasten
    forth,
Wonderful cities and free nations we shall fetch as we go.

If you tire, give me both burdens, and rest the chuff of your
    hand on my hip,
And in due time you shall repay the same service to me,
For after we start we never lie by again.

This day before dawn I ascended a hill and look'd at the
    crowded heaven,
And I said to my spirit *When we become the enfolders of
those orbs, and the pleasure and knowledge of every thing
in them, shall we be fill'd and satisfied then?*
And my spirit said *No, we but level that lift to pass and con-
tinue beyond.*

You are also asking me questions and I hear you,
I answer that I cannot answer, you must find out for yourself.

Sit a while dear son,
Here are biscuits to eat and here is milk to drink,
But as soon as you sleep and renew yourself in sweet clothes,
    I kiss you with a good-by kiss and open the gate for your
    egress hence.

Long enough have you dream'd contemptible dreams,
Now I wash the gum from your eyes,
You must habit yourself to the dazzle of the light and of every
    moment of your life.

Long have you timidly waded holding a plank by the shore,
Now I will you to be a bold swimmer,
To jump off in the midst of the sea, rise again, nod to me,
    shout, and laughingly dash with your hair.

47

I am the teacher of athletes,
He that by me spreads a wider breast than my own proves the
    width of my own,
He most honors my style who learns under it to destroy the
    teacher.

The boy I love, the same becomes a man not through derived
    power, but in his own right,
Wicked rather than virtuous out of conformity or fear,
Fond of his sweetheart, relishing well his steak,
Unrequited love or a slight cutting him worse than sharp steel
    cuts,
First-rate to ride, to fight, to hit the bull's eye, to sail a skiff,
    to sing a song or play on the banjo,
Preferring scars and the beard and faces pitted with small-pox
    over all latherers,
And those well-tann'd to those that keep out of the sun.

I teach straying from me, yet who can stray from me?
I follow you whoever you are from the present hour,
My words itch at your ears till you understand them.

I do not say these things for a dollar or to fill up the time while
    I wait for a boat,
(It is you talking just as much as myself, I act as the tongue
    of you,
Tied in your mouth, in mine it begins to be loosen'd.)

I swear I will never again mention love or death inside a house,
And I swear I will never translate myself at all, only to him
   or her who privately stays with me in the open air.

If you would understand me go to the heights or water-shore,
The nearest gnat is an explanation, and a drop or motion of
   waves a key,
The maul, the oar, the hand-saw, second my words.

No shutter'd room or school can commune with me,
But roughs and little children better than they.

The young mechanic is closest to me, he knows me well,
The woodman that takes his axe and jug with him shall take
   me with him all day,
The farm-boy ploughing in the field feels good· at the sound of
   my voice,
In vessels that sail my words sail, I go with fishermen and
   seamen and love them.

The soldier camp'd or upon the march is mine,
On the night ere the pending battle many seek me, and I do
   not fail them,
On that solemn night (it may be their last) those that know
   me seek me.

My face rubs to the hunter's face when he lies down alone in
   his blanket,
The driver thinking of me does not mind the jolt of his wagon,
The young mother and old mother comprehend me,
The girl and the wife rest the needle a moment and forget
   where they are,
They and· all would resume what I have told them.

48

I have said that the soul is not more than the body,
And I have said that the body is not more than the soul,
And nothing, not God, is greater to one than one's self is,
And whoever walks a furlong without sympathy walks to his
   own funeral drest in his shroud,

And I or you pocketless of a dime may purchase the pick of
the earth,
And to glance with an eye or show a bean in its pod confounds
the learning of all times,
And there is no trade or employment but the young man fol-
lowing it may become a hero,
And there is no object so soft but it makes a hub for the
wheel'd universe,
And I say to any man or woman, Let your soul stand cool and
composed before a million universes.

And I say to mankind, Be not curious about God,
For I who am curious about each am not curious about God,
(No array of terms can say how much I am at peace about God
and about death.)

I hear and behold God in every object, yet understand God not
in the least,
Nor do I understand who there can be more wonderful than
myself.

Why should I wish to see God better than this day?
I see something of God each hour of the twenty-four, and each
moment then,
In the faces of men and women I see God, and in my own
face in the glass,
I find letters from God dropt in the street, and every one is
sign'd by God's name,
And I leave them where they are, for I know that wheresoe'er
I go,
Others will punctually come for ever and ever.

49

And as to you Death, and you bitter hug of mortality, it is
idle to try to alarm me.

To his work without flinching the accoucheur comes
I see the elder-hand pressing receiving supporting,
I recline by the sills of the exquisite flexible doors,
And mark the outlet, and mark the relief and escape.

And as to you Corpse I think you are good manure, but that
    does not offend me,
I smell the white roses sweet-scented and growing,
I reach to the leafy lips, I reach to the polish'd breasts of
    melons.

And as to you Life I reckon you are the leavings of many
    deaths,
(No doubt I have died myself ten thousand times before.)
I hear you whispering there O stars of heaven,
O suns—O grass of graves—O perpetual transfers and pro-
    motions,
If you do not say any thing how can I say any thing?

Of the turbid pool that lies in the autumn forest,
Of the moon that descends the steeps of the soughing twilight,
Toss, sparkles of day and dusk—toss on the black stems that
    decay in the muck,
Toss to the moaning gibberish of the dry limbs.

I ascend from the moon, I ascend from the night,
I perceive that the ghastly glimmer is noonday sunbeams re-
    flected,
And debouch to the steady and central from the offspring
    great or small.

50

There is that in me—I do not know what it is—but I know it
    is in me.

Wrench'd and sweaty—calm and cool then my body becomes,
I sleep—I sleep long.

I do not know it—it is without name—it is a word unsaid,
It is not in any dictionary, utterance, symbol.

Something it swings on more than the earth I swing on,
To it the creation is the friend whose embracing awakes me.

Perhaps I might tell more. Outlines! I plead for my brothers
    and sisters.

Do you not see O my brothers and sisters?
It is not chaos or death—it is form, union, plan—it is eternal
life—it is Happiness.

51

The past and present wilt—I have fill'd them, emptied them,
And proceed to fill my next fold of the future.

Listener up there! what have you to confide to me?
Look in my face while I snuff the sidle of evening,
(Talk honestly, no one else hears you, and I stay only a minute
longer.)

Do I contradict myself?
Very well then I contradict myself,
(I am large, I contain multitudes.)

I concentrate toward them that are nigh, I wait on the door-
slab.

Who has done his day's work? who will soonest be through
with his supper?
Who wishes to walk with me?

Will you speak before I am gone? will you prove already too
late?

52

The spotted hawk swoops by and accuses me, he complains of
my gab and my loitering.

I too am not a bit tamed, I too am untranslatable,
I sound my barbaric yawp over the roofs of the world.

The last scud of day holds back for me,
It flings my likeness after the rest and true as any on the
shadow'd wilds,
It coaxes me to the vapor and the dusk.

I depart as air, I shake my white locks at the runaway sun,
I effuse my flesh in eddies, and drift it in lacy jags.

I bequeath myself to the dirt to grow from the grass I love,
If you want me again look for me under your boot-soles.

You will hardly know who I am or what I mean,
But I shall be good health to you nevertheless,
And filter and fibre your blood.

Failing to fetch me at first keep encouraged,
Missing me one place search another,
I stop somewhere waiting for you.

To Think of Time
(1855, 1881)

1

TO think of time—of all that retrospection,
  To think of to-day, and the ages continued henceforward.

Have you guess'd you yourself would not continue?
Have you dreaded these earth-beetles?
Have you fear'd the future would be nothing to you?

Is to-day nothing? is the beginningless past nothing?
If the future is nothing they are just as surely nothing.

To think that the sun rose in the east—that men and women
    were flexible, real, alive—that every thing was alive,
To think that you and I did not see, feel, think, nor bear our
    part,
To think that we are now here and bear our part.

2

Not a day passes, not a minute or second without an accouche-
    ment,
Not a day passes, not a minute or second without a corpse.

The dull nights go over and the dull days also,
The soreness of lying so much in bed goes over,

The physician after long putting off gives the silent and terrible look for an answer,
The children come hurried and weeping, and the brothers and sisters are sent for,
Medicines stand unused on the shelf, (the camphor-smell has long pervaded the rooms,)
The faithful hand of the living does not desert the hand of the dying,
The twitching lips press lightly on the forehead of the dying,
The breath ceases and the pulse of the heart ceases,
The corpse stretches on the bed and the living look upon it,
It is palpable as the living are palpable.

The living look upon the corpse with their eyesight,
But without eyesight lingers a different living and looks curiously on the corpse.

3

To think the thought of death merged in the thought of materials,
To think of all these wonders of city and country, and others taking great interest in them, and we taking no interest in them.

To think how eager we are in building our houses,
To think others shall be just as eager, and we quite indifferent.

(I see one building the house that serves him a few years, or seventy or eighty years at most,
I see one building the house that serves him longer than that.)

Slow-moving and black lines creep over the whole earth—they never cease—they are the burial lines,
He that was President was buried, and he that is now President shall surely be buried.

4

A reminiscence of the vulgar fate,
A frequent sample of the life and death of workmen,
Each after his kind.
Cold dash of waves at the ferry-wharf, posh and ice in the river, half-frozen mud in the streets,

A gray discouraged sky overhead, the short last daylight of
    December,
A hearse and stages, the funeral of an old Broadway stage-
    driver, the cortege mostly drivers.

Steady the trot to the cemetery, duly rattles the death-bell,
The gate is pass'd, the new-dug grave is halted at, the living
    alight, the hearse uncloses,
The coffin is pass'd out, lower'd and settled, the whip is laid
    on the coffin, the earth is swiftly shovel'd in,
The mound above is flatted with the spades—silence,
A minute—no one moves or speaks—it is done,
He is decently put away—is there any thing more?

He was a good fellow, free-mouth'd, quick-temper'd, not bad-
    looking,
Ready with life or death for a friend, fond of women, gambled,
    ate hearty, drank hearty,
Had known what it was to be flush, grew low-spirited toward
    the last, sicken'd, was help'd by a contribution,
Died, aged forty-one years—and that was his funeral.

Thumb extended, finger uplifted, apron, cape, gloves, strap,
    wet-weather clothes, whip carefully chosen,
Boss, spotter, starter, hostler, somebody loafing on you, you
    loafing on somebody, headway, man before and man be-
    hind,
Good day's work, bad day's work, pet stock, mean stock, first
    out, last out, turning-in at night,
To think that these are so much and so nigh to other drivers,
    and he there takes no interest in them.

Good-Bye, My Fancy

GOOD-BYE, my Fancy!
    Farewell, dear mate, dear love!
      I'm going away, I know not where,
Or to what fortune, or whether I may ever see you again,
So Good-bye, my Fancy.

Now for my last—let me look back a moment;
The slower fainter ticking of the clock is in me,
Exit, nightfall, and soon the heart-thud stopping.
Long have we lived, joy'd, caress'd together;
Delightful!—now separation—Good-bye, my Fancy.

Yet let me not be too hasty:
Long indeed have we lived, slept, filter'd, become really
    blended into one;
Then if we die we die together (yes, we'll remain one),
If we go anywhere we 'll go together to meet what happens,
May-be we'll be better off and blither, and learn something,
May-be it is yourself now really ushering me to the true songs
    (who knows?),
May-be it is you the mortal knob really undoing, turning—so
    now finally,
Good-bye—and hail! my Fancy.

Whispers of Heavenly Death

WHISPERS of heavenly death murmur'd I hear,
    Labial gossip of night, sibilant chorals,
Footsteps gently ascending, mystical breezes wafted soft and
    low,
Ripples of unseen rivers, tides of a current flowing, forever
    flowing
(Or is it the plashing of tears? the measureless waters of hu-
    man tears?)

I see, just see skyward, great cloud-masses;
Mournfully, slowly they roll, silently swelling and mixing,
With at times a half-dimm'd sadden'd far-off star,
Appearing and disappearing.

(Some parturition rather, some solemn immortal birth;
On the frontiers to eyes impenetrable,
Some soul is passing over.)

O Captain! My Captain!

O CAPTAIN! my Captain! our fearful trip is done,
  The ship has weathered every rack, the prize we sought
    is won,
The port is near, the bells I hear, the people all exulting,
While follow eyes the steady keel, the vessel grim and daring;
    But O heart! heart! heart!
        O the bleeding drops of red,
           Where on the deck my Captain lies,
              Fallen cold and dead.

O Captain! my Captain! rise up and hear the bells;
Rise up—for you the flag is flung—for you the bugle trills,
For you bouquets and ribboned wreaths—for you the shores
    acrowding,
For you they call, the swaying mass, their eager faces turning;
    Here Captain! dear father!
        This arm beneath your head!
           It is some dream that on the deck
              You've fallen cold and dead.

My Captain does not answer, his lips are pale and still,
My father does not feel my arm, he has no pulse nor will,
The ship is anchored safe and sound, its voyage closed and
    done,
From fearful trip the victor ship comes in with object won;
    Exult O shores, and ring O bells!
        But I, with mournful tread,
           Walk the deck my Captain lies,
              Fallen cold and dead.

LOUISE CHANDLER MOULTON

Hic Jacet

SO Love is dead that has been quick so long!
Close, then, his eyes, and bear him to his rest,
With eglantine and myrtle on his breast,
And leave him there, their pleasant scents among;
And chant a sweet and melancholy song
About the charms whereof he was possessed,
And how of all things he was loveliest,
And to compare with aught were him to wrong.
Leave him beneath the still and solemn stars,
That gather and look down from their far place
With their long calm our brief woes to deride,
Until the Sun the Morning's gate unbars
And mocks, in turn, our sorrows with his face;—
And yet, had Love been Love, he had not died.

RICHARD REALF

Indirection

FAIR are the flowers and the children, but their subtle sug-
gestion is fairer;
Rare is the roseburst of dawn, but the secret that clasps it is
rarer;
Sweet the exultance of song, but the strain that precedes it is
sweeter;
And never was poem yet writ, but the meaning outmastered
the metre.

Never a daisy that grows, but a mystery guideth the growing;
Never a river that flows, but a majesty sceptres the flowing;
Never a Shakespeare that soared, but a stronger than he did
    enfold him,
Nor ever a prophet foretells, but a mightier seer hath foretold
    him.

Back of the canvas that throbs the painter is hinted and hidden;
Into the statue that breathes the soul of the sculptor is bidden;
Under the joy that is felt lie the infinite issues of feeling;
Crowning the glory revealed is the glory that crowns the
    revealing.

Great are the symbols of being, but that which is symboled is
    greater;
Vast the create and beheld, but vaster the inward creator;
Back of the sound broods the silence, back of the gift stands
    the giving;
Back of the hand that receives thrill the sensitive nerves of
    receiving.

Space is as nothing to spirit, the deed is outdone by the doing;
The heart of the wooer is warm, but warmer the heart of the
    wooing;
And up from the pits where these shiver, and up from the
    heights where those shine,
Twin voices and shadows swim starward, and the essence of
    life is divine.

EMILY DICKINSON

I

I Found the Phrase

I FOUND the phrase to every thought
  I ever had, but one;
And that defies me,—as a hand
  Did try to chalk the sun

To races nurtured in the dark:—
  How would your own begin?
Can blaze be done in cochineal,
  Or noon in mazarin?

II

Parting

MY life closed twice before its close;
  It yet remains to see
If Immortality unveil
  A third event to me,
So huge, so hopeless to conceive,
  As these that twice befell:
Parting is all we know of heaven,
  And all we need of hell.

III

Called Back

JUST lost when I was saved!
Just felt the world go by!
Just girt me for the onset with eternity,
When breath blew back,
And on the other side
I heard recede the disappointed tide;

Therefore, as one returned, I feel,
Odd secrets of the line to tell!
Some sailor, skirting foreign shores,
Some pale reporter from the awful doors
Before the seal!

Next time, to stay!
Next time, the things to see
By ear unheard,
Unscrutinized by eye.

Next time, to tarry,
While the ages steal,—
Slow tramp the centuries,
And the cycles wheel.

IV

Choice

OF all the souls that stand create
I have elected one.
When sense from spirit files away,
And subterfuge is done;

When that which is and that which was
Apart, intrinsic, stand,

And this brief tragedy of flesh
Is shifted like a sand;

When figures show their royal front
And mists are carved away,—
Behold the atom I preferred
To all the lists of clay!

V

To Hear an Oriole

TO hear an oriole sing
　　May be a common thing,
Or only a divine.

It is not of the bird
Who sings the same, unheard,
As unto crowd.

The fashion of the ear
Attireth that it hear
In dun or fair.

So whether it be rune,
Or whether it be none,
Is of within;

The "tune is in the tree,"
The sceptic showeth me;
"No, sir! In thee!"

VI

There's a Certain Slant of Light

THERE'S a certain slant of light,
　　On winter afternoons,
That oppresses, like the weight
Of cathedral tunes.

Heavenly hurt it gives us;
We can find no scar,
But internal difference
Where the meanings are.

None may teach it anything
'Tis the seal, despair,—
An imperial affliction
Sent us of the air.

When it comes, the landscape listens,
Shadows hold their breath;
When it goes, 'tis like the distance
On the look of death.

VII

Apparently with No Surprise

APPARENTLY with no surprise
To any happy flower,
The frost beheads it at its play
In accidental power.
The blond assassin passes on,
The sun proceeds unmoved
To measure off another day
For an approving God.

VIII

The Last Night

THE last night that she lived,
It was a common night,
Except the dying; this to us
Made nature different.

We noticed smallest things,—
Things overlooked before,
By this great light upon our minds
Italicized, as 'twere.

That others could exist
While she must finish quite,
A jealousy for her arose
So nearly infinite.

We waited while she passed;
It was a narrow time,
Too jostled were our souls to speak,
At length the notice came.

She mentioned, and forgot;
Then lightly as a reed
Bent to the water, shivered scarce,
Consented, and was dead.

And we, we placed the hair,
And drew the head erect;
And then an awful leisure was,
Our faith to regulate.

IX

The Bustle in a House

THE bustle in a house
The morning after death
Is solemnest of industries
Enacted upon earth,—

The sweeping up the heart,
And putting love away
We shall not want to use again
Until eternity.

X

I Know That He Exists

I KNOW that he exists
Somewhere, in silence.
He has hid his rare life
From our gross eyes.

'Tis an instant's play,
'Tis a fond ambush,
Just to make bliss
Earn her own surprise!

But should the play
Prove piercing earnest,
Should the glee glaze
In death's stiff stare,

Would not the fun
Look too expensive?
Would not the jest
Have crawled too far?

XI

We Never Know How High

WE never know how high we are
Till we are called to rise;
And then, if we are true to plan,
Our statures touch the skies.

The heroism we recite
Would be a daily thing,
Did not ourselves the cubits warp
For fear to be a king.

XII

The Soul Selects

THE soul selects her own society,
    Then shuts the door;
On her divine majority
Obtrude no more.

Unmoved, she notes the chariot's pausing
At her low gate;
Unmoved, an emperor is kneeling
Upon her mat.
I've known her from an ample nation
Choose one;
Then close the valves of her attention
Like stone.

XIII

A Thought Went Up My Mind

A THOUGHT went up my mind to-day
    That I have had before,
But did not finish,—some way back,
I could not fix the year,

Nor where it went, nor why it came
The second time to me,
Nor definitely what it was,
Have I the art to say.

But somewhere in my soul, I know
I've met the thing before;
It just reminded me—'twas all—
And came my way no more.

XIV

Dying

I HEARD a fly buzz when I died;
  The stillness round my form
Was like the stillness in the air
  Between the heaves of storm.

The eyes beside had wrung them dry,
  And breaths were gathering sure
For that last onset, when the king
  Be witnessed in his power.

I willed my keepsakes, signed away
  What portion of me I
Could make assignable—and then
  There interposed a fly,

With blue, uncertain, stumbling buzz,
  Between the light and me;
And then the windows failed, and then
  I could not see to see.

XV

A Clock Stopped

A CLOCK stopped—not the mantel's;
  Geneva's farthest skill
Can't put the puppet bowing
  That just now dangled still.

An awe came on the trinket!
  The figures hunched with pain,
Then quivered out of decimals
  Into degreeless noon.

It will not stir for doctors,
  This pendulum of snow;
The shopman importunes it,
  While cool, concernless No

Nods from the gilded pointers,
  Nods from the seconds slim,
Decades of arrogance between
  The dial life and him.

XVI

Not Any Sunny Tone

NOT any sunny tone
    From any fervent zone
Finds entrance there.
Better a grave of Balm
Toward human nature's home,
And Robins near,
Than a stupendous Tomb
Proclaiming to the gloom
How dead we are.

XVII

I Felt a Funeral

I FELT a funeral in my brain,
    And mourners, to and fro,
Kept treading, treading, till it seemed
  That sense was breaking through.

And when they all were seated,
  A service like a drum
Kept beating, beating, till I thought
  My mind was going numb.

And then I heard them lift a box,
    And creak across my soul
With those same boots of lead, again.
    Then space began to toll.

As all the heavens were a bell,
    And Being but an ear,
And I and silence some strange race,
    Wrecked, solitary, here.

XVIII

To My Quick Ear

TO my quick ear the leaves conferred;
    The bushes they were bells;
I could not find a privacy
From Nature's sentinels.

In cave if I presumed to hide,
    The walls began to tell;
Creation seemed a mighty crack
To make me visible.

XIX

In the Garden

A BIRD came down the walk:
    He did not know I saw;
He bit an angle-worm in halves
And ate the fellow raw.

And then he drank a dew
From a convenient grass,
And then hopped sidewise to the wall
To let a beetle pass.

He glanced with rapid eyes
That hurried all abroad—
They looked like frightened beads, I thought;
He stirred his velvet head

Like one in danger; cautious,
I offered him a crumb,
And he unrolled his feathers
And rowed him softer home

Than oars divide the ocean,
Too silver for a seam,
Or butterflies, off banks of noon,
Leap, plashless, as they swim.

XX

Safe in Their Alabaster Chambers

SAFE in their alabaster chambers,
Untouched by morning and untouched by noon
Sleep the meek members of the resurrection,
Rafter of satin, and roof of stone.

Light laughs the breeze in her castle of sunshine;
Babbles the bee in a stolid ear;
Pipe the sweet birds in ignorant cadence—
Ah, what sagacity perished here!

Grand go the years in the crescent above them;
Worlds scoop their arcs, and firmaments row,
Diadems drop and Doges surrender,
Soundless as dots on a disk of snow.

XXI

The Wind

OF all the sounds despatched abroad,
There's not a charge to me
Like that old measure in the boughs,
That phraseless melody

The wind does, working like a hand
Whose fingers brush the sky,
Then quiver down, with tufts of tune
Permitted gods and me.

When winds go round and round in band
And thrum upon the door,
And birds take places overhead,
To bear them orchestra,

I crave him grace, of summer boughs,
If such an outcast be,
He never heard that fleshless chant
Rise solemn in the tree,

As if some caravan of sound
On deserts, in the sky,
Had broken rank,
Then knit, and passed
In seamless company.

XXII

The Chariot

BECAUSE I could not stop for Death,
He kindly stopped for me;
The carriage held but just ourselves
And Immortality.

We slowly drove, he knew no haste,
And I had put away
My labour, and my leisure too,
For his civility.

We passed the school where children played
Their lessons scarcely done;
We passed the fields of gazing grain,
We passed the setting sun.

We paused before a house that seemed
A swelling on the ground;
The roof was scarcely visible,
The cornice but a mound.

Since then 'tis centuries; but each
Feels shorter than the day
I first surmised the horses' heads
Were toward eternity.

XXIII

I Died for Beauty

I DIED for beauty, but was scarce
Adjusted in the tomb,
When one who died for truth was lain
In an adjoining room.

He questioned softly why I failed?
"For beauty," I replied.
"And I for truth—the two are one;
We brethren are," he said.

And so, as kinsmen met a-night,
We talked between the rooms,
Until the moss had reached our lips,
And covered up our names.

XXIV

Mysteries

THE murmur of a bee
A witchcraft yieldeth me.
If any ask me why,
'Twere easier to die
Than tell.

The red upon the hill
Taketh away my will;
If anybody sneer,
Take care, for God is here,
That's all.

The breaking of the day
Addeth to my degree;
If any ask me how,
Artist, who drew me so,
Must tell!

HELEN HUNT JACKSON

Emigravit

WITH sails full set, the ship her anchor weighs.
Strange names shine out beneath her figure head
What glad farewells with eager eyes are said!
What cheer for him who goes, and him who stays!
Fair skies, rich lands, new homes, and untried days
Some go to seek: the rest but wait instead,
Watching the way wherein their comrades led,
Until the next stanch ship her flag doth raise.

Who knows what myriad colonies there are
Of fairest fields, and rich, undreamed-of gains
Thick planted in the distant shining plains
Which we call sky because they lie so far?
Oh, write of me, not "Died in bitter pains,"
But "Emigrated to another star!"

A Dream

I DREAMED that I was dead and crossed heavens,—
　　Heavens after heavens with burning feet and swift,—
And cried: "O God, where art Thou? I left one
　　On earth, whose burden I would pray Thee lift."

I was so dead I wondered at no thing,—
　　Not even that the angels slowly turned
Their faces, speechless, as I hurried by
　　(Beneath my feet the golden pavements burned);

Nor, at the first, that I could not find God,
　　Because the heavens stretched endlessly like space.
At last a terror seized my very soul;
　　I seemed alone in all the crowded place.

Then, sudden, one compassionate cried out,
　　Though like the rest his face from me he turned,
As I were one no angel might regard
　　(Beneath my feet the golden pavements burned):

"No more in heaven than earth will he find God
　　Who does not know his loving mercy swift
But waits the moment consummate and ripe,
　　Each burden from each human soul to lift."

Though I was dead, I died again for shame;
　　Lonely, to flee from heaven again I turned;
The ranks of angels looked away from me
　　(Beneath my feet the golden pavements burned).

Danger

WITH what a childish and short-sighted sense
    Fear seeks for safety; reckons up the days
Of danger and escape, the hours and ways
Of death; it breathless flies the pestilence;
It walls itself in towers of defence;
By land, by sea, against the storm it lays
Down barriers; then, comforted, it says:
"This spot, this hour is safe." Oh, vain pretence!
Man born of man knows nothing when he goes;
The winds blow where they list, and will disclose
To no man which brings safety, which brings risk.
The mighty are brought low by many a thing
Too small to name. Beneath the daisy's disk
Lies hid the pebble for the fatal sling.

EDWARD ROWLAND SILL

Five Lives

FIVE mites of monads dwelt in a round drop
    That twinkled on a leaf by a pool in the sun.
To the naked eye they lived invisible;
Specks, for a world of whom the empty shell
Of a mustard-seed had been a hollow sky.

One was a meditative monad, called a sage;
And, shrinking all his mind within, he thought:
"Tradition, handed down for hours and hours,
Tells that our globe, this quivering crystal world,
Is slowly dying. What if, seconds hence,
When I am very old, yon shimmering dome

Come drawing down and down, till all things end?"
Then with a weazen smirk he proudly felt
No other mote of God had ever gained
Such giant grasp of universal truth.

One was a transcendental monad; thin
And long and slim in the mind; and thus he mused:
"Oh, vast, unfathomable monad-souls!
Made in the image"—a hoarse frog croaks from the pool—
"Hark! 't was some god, voicing his glorious thought
In thunder music! Yea, we hear their voice,
And we may guess their minds from ours, their work.
Some taste they have like ours, some tendency
To wriggle about, and munch a trace of scum."
He floated up on a pin-point bubble of gas
That burst, pricked by the air, and he was gone.

One was a barren-minded monad, called
A positivist; and he knew positively:
"There is no world beyond this certain drop.
Prove me another! let the dreamers dream
Of their faint dreams, and noises from without,
And higher and lower; life is life enough."
Then swaggering half a hair's breadth, hungrily
He seized upon an atom of bug, and fed.

One was a tattered monad, called a poet;
And with shrill voice ecstatic thus he sang:
"Oh, the little female monad's lips!
Oh, the little female monad's eyes:
Ah, the little, little, female, female monad!"

The last was a strong-minded monadess,
Who dashed amid the infusoria,
Danced high and low, and wildly spun and dove
Till the dizzy others held their breath to see.

But while they led their wondrous little lives
Aeonian moments had gone wheeling by,
The burning drop had shrunk with fearful speed;

A glistening film—'t was gone; the leaf was dry.
The little ghost of an inaudible squeak
Was lost to the frog that goggled from his stone;
Who, at the huge, slow tread of a thoughtful ox
Coming to drink, stirred sideways fatly, plunged,
Launched backward twice, and all the pool was still.

JOHN TOWNSEND TROWBRIDGE

Midwinter

THE speckled sky is dim with snow,
    The light flakes falter and fall slow;
Athwart the hill-top, rapt and pale,
Silently drops a silvery veil;
And all the valley is shut in
By flickering curtains gray and thin.

But cheerily the chickadee
Singeth to me on fence and tree;
The snow sails round him as he sings,
White as the down of angels' wings.

I watch the slow flakes as they fall
On bank and brier and broken wall;
Over the orchard, waste and brown,
All noiselessly they settle down,
Tipping the apple-boughs, and each
Light quivering twig of plum and peach.

On turf and curb and bower-roof
The snow-storm spreads its ivory woof;
It paves with pearl the garden-walk;
And lovingly round tattered stalk
And shivering stem its magic weaves
A mantle fair as lily-leaves.

The hooded beehive, small and low,
Stands like a maiden in the snow;
And the old door-slab is half-hid
Under an alabaster lid.

All day it snows: the sheeted post
Gleams in the dimness like a ghost;
All day the blasted oak has stood
A muffled wizard of the wood;

Garland and airy cap adorn
The sumach and the wayside thorn,
And clustering spangles lodge and shine
In the dark tresses of the pine.

The ragged bramble, dwarfed and old,
Shrinks like a beggar in the cold;
In surplice white the cedar stands,
And blesses him with priestly hands.

Still cheerily the chickadee
Singeth to me on fence and tree:
But in my inmost ear is heard
The music of a holier bird;
And heavenly thoughts as soft and white
As snow-flakes, on my soul alight,
Clothing with love my lonely heart,
Healing with peace each bruisëd part,
Till all my being seems to be
Transfigured by their purity.

GEORGE HENRY BOKER

Dirge for a Soldier

CLOSE his eyes; his work is done!
    What to him is friend or foeman,
Rise of moon, or set of sun,
    Hand of man, or kiss of woman?
        Lay him low, lay him low,
        In the clover or the snow!
        What cares he? he cannot know:
            Lay him low!

As man may, he fought his fight,
    Proved his truth by his endeavor;
Let him sleep in solemn night,
    Sleep forever and forever.
        Lay him low, lay him low,
        In the clover or the snow!
        What cares he? he cannot know:
            Lay him low!

Fold him in his country's stars,
    Roll the drum and fire the volley!
What to him are all our wars,
    What but death bemocking folly?
        Lay him low, lay him low,
        In the clover or the snow!
        What cares he? he cannot know:
            Lay him low!

Leave him to God's watching eye,
    Trust him to the hand that made him
Mortal love weeps idly by:
    God alone has power to aid him.

Lay him low, lay him low,
In the clover or the snow!
What cares he? he cannot know:
Lay him low!

MAURICE THOMPSON

Wild Honey

WHERE hints of racy sap and gum
Out of the old dark forest come;

Where birds their beaks like hammers wield,
And pith is pierced and bark is peeled;

Where the green walnut's outer rind
Gives precious bitterness to the wind;

There lurks the sweet creative power,
As lurks the honey in the flower.

In winter's bud that bursts in spring,
In nut of autumn's ripening,

In acrid bulb beneath the mold,
Sleeps the elixir, strong and old,

That Rosicrucians sought in vain,—
Life that renews itself again!

What bottled perfume is so good
As fragrance of split tulip-wood?

What fabled drink of God or muse
Was rich as purple mulberry juice?

And what school-polished gem of thought
Is like the rune from Nature caught?

He is a poet strong and true
Who loves wild thyme and honey-dew;

And like a brown bee works and sings
With morning freshness on his wings,

And a gold burden on his thighs,—
The pollen-dust of centuries!

———•———

JOHN VANCE CHENEY

———•———

The Happiest Heart

WHO drives the horses of the sun
    Shall lord it but a day;
Better the lowly deed were done,
And kept the humble way.

The rust will find the sword of fame,
The dust will hide the crown;
Ay, none shall nail so high his name
Time will not tear it down.

The happiest heart that ever beat
Was in some quiet breast
That found the common daylight sweet,
And left to Heaven the rest.

STEPHEN COLLINS FOSTER

My Old Kentucky Home

THE sun shines bright in the old Kentucky home;
    'Tis summer, the darkies are gay;
The corn-top's ripe, and the meadow's in the bloom,
    While the birds make music all the day.
The young folks roll on the little cabin floor,
    All merry, all happy and bright;
By-'n'-by hard times comes a-knocking at the door:—
    Then my old Kentucky home, good-night!

        Weep no more, my lady,
        O, weep no more to-day!
    We will sing one song for the old Kentucky home,
        For the old Kentucky home, far away.

They hunt no more for the possum and the coon,
    On the meadow, the hill, and the shore;
They sing no more by the glimmer of the moon,
    On the bench by the old cabin door.
The day goes by like a shadow o'er the heart,
    With sorrow, where all was delight;
The time has come when the darkies have to part:—
    Then my old Kentucky home, good-night!

The head must bow, and the back will have to bend
    Wherever the darky may go;
A few more days, and the trouble all will end,
    In the field where the sugar-canes grow.
A few more days for to tote the weary load,—
    No matter, 'twill never be light;
A few more days till we totter on the road:—
    Then my old Kentucky home, good-night!

Weep no more, my lady,
O, weep no more to-day!
We will sing one song for the old Kentucky home,
For the old Kentucky home, far away.

THOMAS BAILEY ALDRICH

Memory

MY mind lets go a thousand things,
Like dates of wars and deaths of kings,
And yet recalls the very hour—
'Twas noon by yonder village tower,
And on the last blue noon in May
The wind came briskly up this way,
Crisping the brook beside the road;
Then, pausing here, set down its load
Of pine-scents, and shook listlessly
Two petals from that wild-rose tree.

Enamored Architect of Airy Rhyme

ENAMORED architect of airy rhyme,
Build as thou wilt; heed not what each man says:
Good souls, but innocent of dreamers' ways,
Will come, and marvel why thou wastest time;
Others, beholding how thy turrets climb
'Twixt theirs and heaven, will hate thee all thy days;
But most beware of those who come to praise.
O Wondersmith, O worker in sublime
And heaven-sent dreams, let art be all in all;
Build as thou wilt, unspoiled by praise or blame,
Build as thou wilt, and as thy light is given:
Then, if at last the airy structure fall,
Dissolve, and vanish—take thyself no shame.
They fail, and they alone, who have not striven.

JOHN BURROUGHS

Waiting

SERENE, I fold my hands and wait,
Nor care for wind, or tide, or sea;
I rave no more 'gainst time or fate,
For, lo! my own shall come to me.

I stay my haste, I make delays,
For what avails this eager pace?
I stand amid the eternal ways,
And what is mine shall know my face.

Asleep, awake, by night or day,
The friends I seek are seeking me;
No wind can drive my bark astray,
Nor change the tide of destiny.

What matter if I stand alone?
I wait with joy the coming years;
My heart shall reap where it has sown,
And garner up its fruit of tears.

The waters know their own and draw
The brook that springs in yonder height;
So flows the good with equal law
Unto the soul of pure delight.

The stars come nightly to the sky;
The tidal wave unto the sea;
Nor time, nor space, nor deep, nor high,
Can keep my own away from me.

JOAQUIN MILLER

At the Grave of Walker

HE lies low in the levelled sand,
Unsheltered from the tropic sun,
And now of all he knew not one
Will speak him fair in that far land.
Perhaps 'twas this that made me seek,
Disguised, his grave one winter-tide;
A weakness for the weaker side,
A siding with the helpless weak.

A palm not far held out a hand,
Hard by a long green bamboo swung,
And bent like some great bow unstrung,
And quivered like a willow wand;
Perched on its fruits that crooked hand,
Beneath a broad banana's leaf,
A bird in rainbow splendor sang
A low, sad song, of tempered grief.

No sod, no sign, no cross nor stone,
But at his side a cactus green
Upheld its lances long and keen;
It stood in sacred sands alone,
Flat-palmed and fierce with lifted spears;
One bloom of crimson crowned its head,
A drop of blood, so bright, so red,
Yet redolent as roses' tears.

In my left hand I held a shell,
All rosy lipped and pearly red;
I laid it by his lowly bed,
For he did love so passing well

The grand songs of the solemn sea.
O shell! sing well, wild, with a will,
When storms blow loud and birds be still,
The wildest sea-song known to thee!

I said some things with folded hands,
Soft whispered in the dim sea-sound,
And eyes held humbly to the ground,
And frail knees sunken in the sands.
He had done more than this for me,
And yet I could not well do more:
I turned me down the olive shore,
And set a sad face to the sea.

SIDNEY LANIER

The Marshes of Glynn

GLOOMS of the live-oaks, beautiful-braided and woven
With intricate shades of the vines that myriad-cloven
  Clamber the forks of the multiform boughs,—
      Emerald twilights,—
      Virginal shy lights,
Wrought of the leaves to allure to the whisper of vows,
When lovers pace timidly down through the green colonnades
Of the dim sweet woods, of the dear dark woods,
  Of the heavenly woods and glades,
That run to the radiant marginal sand-beach within
      The wide sea-marshes of Glynn;—

Beautiful glooms, soft dusks in the noon-day fire,—
Wildwood privacies, closets of lone desire,
Chamber from chamber parted with wavering arras of leaves,—
Cells for the passionate pleasure of prayer to the soul that
    grieves,

Pure with a sense of the passing of saints through the wood,
Cool for the dutiful weighing of ill with good;—
O braided dusks of the oak and woven shades of the vine,
While the riotous noon-day sun of the June-day long did shine
Ye held me fast in your heart and I held you fast in mine;
But now when the noon is no more, and riot is rest,
And the sun is a-wait at the ponderous gate of the West,
And the slant yellow beam down the wood-aisle doth seem
Like a lane into heaven that leads from a dream,—
Ay, now, when my soul all day hath drunken the soul of the
         oak,
And my heart is at ease from men, and the wearisome sound
         of the stroke
      Of the scythe of time and the trowel of trade is low,
         And belief overmasters doubt, and I know that I know,
            And my spirit is grown to a lordly great compass within,
That the length and the breadth and the sweep of the marshes
         of Glynn
Will work me no fear like the fear they have wrought me of
         yore
When length was fatigue, and when breadth was but bitterness
         sore,
And when terror and shrinking and dreary unnamable pain
Drew over me out of the merciless miles of the plain,—

Oh, now, unafraid, I am fain to face
      The vast sweet visage of space.
To the edge of the wood I am drawn, I am drawn,
Where the gray beach glimmering runs, as a belt of the dawn,
      For a mete and a mark
         To the forest-dark:—
            So:
Affable live-oak, leaning low,—
Thus—with your favor—soft, with a reverent hand
(Not lightly touching your person, Lord of the land!),
Bending your beauty aside, with a step I stand
On the firm-packed sand,
            Free
By a world of marsh that borders a world of sea.

Sinuous southward and sinuous northward the shimmering
band
Of the sand-beach fastens the fringe of the marsh to the
folds of the land.
Inward and outward to northward and southward the beach-
lines linger and curl
As a silver-wrought garment that clings to and follows the
firm sweet limbs of a girl.
Vanishing, swerving, evermore curving again into sight,
Softly the sand-beach wavers away to a dim grap looping of
light.
And what if behind me to westward the wall of the woods
stands high?
The world lies east: how ample, the marsh and the sea and the
sky!
A league and a league of marsh-grass, waist-high, broad in the
blade,
Green, and all of a height, and unflecked with a light or a
shade,
Stretch leisurely off, in a pleasant plain,
To the terminal blue of the main.

Oh, what is abroad in the marsh and the terminal sea?
Somehow my soul seems suddenly free
From the weighing of fate and the sad discussion of sin,
By the length and the breadth and the sweep of the marshes of
Glynn.

Ye marshes, how candid and simple and nothing-withholding
and free
Ye publish yourselves to the sky and offer yourselves to the sea!
Tolerant plains, that suffer the sea and the rains and the sun,
Ye spread and span like the catholic man who hath mightily
won
God out of knowledge and good out of infinite pain
And sight out of blindness and purity out of a stain.

As the marsh-hen secretly builds on the watery sod,
Behold I will build me a nest on the greatness of God:
I will fly in the greatness of God as the marsh-hen flies

In the freedom that fills all the space 'twixt the marsh and the
    skies:
By so many roots as the marsh-grass sends in the sod
I will heartily lay me a-hold on the greatness of God:
Oh, like to the greatness of God is the greatness within
The range of the marshes, the liberal marshes of Glynn.

And the sea lends large, as the marsh: lo, out of his plenty the
    sea
Pours fast: full soon the time of the flood-tide must be:
Look how the grace of the sea doth go
About and about through the intricate channels that flow
    Here and there,
        Everywhere,
Till his waters have flooded the uttermost creeks and the low-
    lying lanes,
And the marsh is meshed with a million veins,
That like as with rosy and silvery essences flow
   In the rose-and-silver evening glow.
      Farewell, my lord Sun!
The creeks overflow: a thousand rivulets run
'Twixt the roots of the sod; the blades of the marsh-grass stir;
Passeth a hurrying sound of wings that westward whir;
Passeth, and all is still; and the currents cease to run;
And the sea and the marsh are one.

How still the plains of the waters be!
The tide is in his ecstasy.
The tide is at his highest height:
    And it is night.

And now from the Vast of the Lord will the waters of sleep
Roll in on the souls of men,
But who will reveal to our waking ken
The forms that swim and the shapes that creep
    Under the waters of sleep?

Opposition

OF fret, of dark, of thorn, of chill,
    Complain no more; for these, O heart,
Direct the random of the will
    As rhymes direct the rage of art.

The lute's fixt fret, that runs athwart
    The strain and purpose of the string,
For governance and nice consort
    Doth bar his wilful wavering.

The dark hath many dear avails;
    The dark distils divinest dews;
The dark is rich with nightingales,
    With dreams, and with the heavenly Muse.

Bleeding with thorns of petty strife,
    I'll ease (as lovers do) my smart
With sonnets to my lady Life
    Writ red in issues from the heart.

What grace may lie within the chill
    Of favor frozen fast in scorn!
When Good's a-freeze, we call it Ill!
    This rosy Time is glacier-born.

Of fret, of dark, of thorn, of chill,
    Complain thou not, O heart; for these
Bank-in the current of the will
    To uses, arts, and charities.

HENRY AUGUSTIN BEERS

Ecce in Deserto

THE wilderness a secret keeps
    Upon whose guess I go:
Eye hath not seen, ear hath not heard;
    And yet I know, I know,

Some day the viewless latch will lift,
    The door of air swing wide
To one lost chamber of the wood
    Where those shy mysteries hide,—

One yet unfound, receding depth,
    From which the wood-thrush sings,
Still luring in to darker shades,
    In—in to colder springs.

There is no wind abroad to-day.
    But hark!—the pine-tops' roar,
That sleep and in their dreams repeat
    The music of the shore.

What wisdom in their needles stirs?
    What song is that they sing?
Those airs that search the forest's heart,
    What rumor do they bring?

A hushed excitement fills the gloom,
    And, in the stillness, clear
The vireo's tell-tale warning rings:
    "'Tis near—'tis near—'tis near!"

As, in the fairy-tale, more loud
   The ghostly music plays
When, toward the enchanted bower, the prince
   Draws closer through the maze.

Nay—nay. I track a fleeter game,
   A wilder than ye know,
To lairs beyond the inmost haunt
   Of thrush or vireo.

This way it passed: the scent lies fresh;
   The ferns still lightly shake.
Ever I follow hard upon,
   But never overtake.

To other woods the trail leads on,
   To other worlds and new,
Where they who keep the secret here
   Will keep the promise too.

JOHN BANISTER TABB

Clover

LITTLE masters, hat in hand
   Let me in your presence stand,
Till your silence solve for me
This your threefold mystery.

Tell me—for I long to know—
How, in darkness there below,
Was your fairy fabric spun,
Spread and fashioned, three in one.

Did your gossips gold and blue,
Sky and Sunshine, choose for you,
Ere your triple forms were seen,
Suited liveries of green?

Can ye,—if ye dwelt indeed
Captives of a prison seed,—
Like the Genie, once again
Get you back into the grain?

Little masters, may I stand
In your presence, hat in hand,
Waiting till you solve for me
This your threefold mystery?

EDWIN MARKHAM

The Man with the Hoe

GOD MADE MAN IN HIS OWN IMAGE
IN THE IMAGE OF GOD HE MADE HIM.—GENESIS.

BOWED by the weight of centuries he leans
Upon his hoe and gazes on the ground,
The emptiness of ages in his face,
And on his back the burden of the world.
Who made him dead to rapture and despair,
A thing that grieves not and that never hopes,
Stolid and stunned, a brother to the ox?
Who loosened and let down this brutal jaw?
Whose was the hand that slanted back this brow?
Whose breath blew out the light within this brain?

Is this the Thing the Lord God made and gave
To have dominion over sea and land;
To trace the stars and search the heavens for power;

To feel the passion of Eternity?
Is this the dream He dreamed who shaped the suns
And markt their ways upon the ancient deep?
Down all the caverns of Hell to their last gulf
There is no shape more terrible than this—
More tongued with censure of the world's blind greed—
More filled with signs and portents for the soul—
More packt with danger to the universe.

What gulfs between him and the seraphim!
Slave of the wheel of labor, what to him
Are Plato and the swing of Pleiades?
What the long reaches of the peaks of song,
The rift of dawn, the reddening of the rose?
Through this dread shape the suffering ages look;
Time's tragedy is in that aching stoop;
Through this dread shape humanity betrayed,
Plundered, profaned and disinherited,
Cries protest to the Powers that made the world,
A protest that is also prophecy.

O masters, lords and rulers in all lands,
Is this the handiwork you give to God,
This monstrous thing distorted and soul-quencht?
How will you ever straighten up this shape;
Touch it again with immortality;
Give back the upward looking and the light;
Rebuild in it the music and the dream;
Make right the immemorial infamies,
Perfidious wrongs, immedicable woes?

O masters, lords and rulers in all lands,
How will the future reckon with this Man?
How answer his brute question in that hour
When whirlwinds of rebellion shake all shores?
How will it be with kingdoms and with kings—
With those who shaped him to the thing he is—
When this dumb Terror shall rise to judge the world,
After the silence of the centuries?

WILLIAM VAUGHN MOODY

A Grey Day

GREY drizzling mists the moorlands drape,
Rain whitens the dead sea,
From headland dim to sullen cape
Grey sails creep wearily.
I know not how that merchantman
Has found the heart; but 'tis her plan
Seaward her endless course to shape.

Unreal as insects that appall
A drunkard's peevish brain,
O'er the grey deep the dories crawl,
Four-legged, with rowers twain:
Midgets and minims of the earth,
Across old ocean's vasty girth
Toiling—heroic, comical!

I wonder how that merchant's crew
Have ever found the will!
I wonder what the fishers do
To keep them toiling still!
I wonder how the heart of man
Has patience to live out its span,
Or wait until its dreams come true.

Pandora Song

I STOOD within the heart of God;
It seemed a place that I had known:
(I was blood-sister to the clod,
Blood-brother to the stone.)

I found my love and labor there,
My house, my raiment, meat and wine,
My ancient rage, my old despair,—
Yea, all things that were mine.

I saw the spring and summer pass,
The trees grow bare, and winter come;
All was the same as once it was
Upon my hills at home.

Then suddenly in my own heart
I felt God walk and gaze about;
He spoke; his words seemed held apart
With gladness and with doubt.

"Here is my meat and wine," He said,
"My love, my toil, my ancient care;
Here is my cloak, my book, my bed,
And here my old despair.

"Here are my seasons: winter, spring,
Summer the same, and autumn spills
The fruits I look for; everything
As on my heavenly hills."

An Ode in Time of Hesitation

I

BEFORE the solemn bronze Saint Gaudens made
To thrill the heedless passer's heart with awe,
And set here in the city's talk and trade
To the good memory of Robert Shaw,
This bright March morn I stand,
And hear the distant spring come up the land;
Knowing that what I hear is not unheard
Of this boy soldier and his Negro band,
For all their gaze is fixed so stern ahead,
For all the fatal rhythm of their tread.

The land they died to save from death and shame
Trembles and waits, hearing the spring's great name
And by her pangs these resolute ghosts are stirred.

II

Through street and mall the tides of people go
Heedless; the trees upon the Common show
No hint of green; but to my listening heart
The still earth doth impart
Assurance of her jubilant emprise,
And it is clear to my long-searching eyes
That love at last has might upon the skies.
The ice is runneled on the little pond;
A telltale patter drips from off the trees;
The air is touched with Southland spiceries,
As if but yesterday it tossed the frond
Of pendent mosses where the live-oaks grow
Beyond Virginia and the Carolines,
Or had its will among the fruits and vines
Of aromatic isles asleep beyond
Florida and the Gulf of Mexico.

III

Soon shall the Cape Ann children shout in glee,
Spying the arbutus, spring's dear recluse;
Hill lads at dawn shall hearken the wild goose
Go hanking northward over Tennessee;
West from Oswego to Sault Sainte-Marie,
And on to where the Pictured Rocks are hung,
And yonder where, gigantic, wilful, young,
Chicago sitteth at the northwest gates,
With restless violent hands and casual tongue
Moulding her mighty fates,
The Lakes shall robe them in ethereal sheen;
And like a larger sea, the vital green
Of springing wheat shall vastly be outflung
Over Dakota and the prairie states.
By desert people immemorial
On Arizonian mesas shall be done
Dim rites unto the thunder and the sun;

Nor shall the primal gods lack sacrifice
More splendid, when the white Sierras call
Unto the Rockies straightway to arise
And dance before the unveiled ark of the year.
Sounding their windy cedars as for shawms,
Unrolling rivers clear
For flutter of broad phylacteries;
While Shasta signals to Alaskan seas
That watch old sluggish glaciers downward creep
To fling their icebergs thundering from the steep,
And Mariposa through the purple calms
Gazes at far Hawaii crowned with palms
Where East and West are met,—
A rich seal on the ocean's bosom set
To say that East and West are twain,
With different loss and gain:
The Lord hath sundered them; let them be sundered yet.

IV

Alas! what sounds are these that come
Sullenly over the Pacific seas,—
Sounds of ignoble battle, striking dumb
The season's half-awakened ecstasies?
Must I be humble, then,
Now when my heart hath need of pride?
Wild love falls on me from these sculptured men;
By loving much the land for which they died
I would be justified.
My spirit was away on pinions wide
To soothe in praise of her its passionate mood
And ease it of its ache of gratitude.
Too sorely heavy is the debt they lay
On me and the companions of my day.
I would remember now
My country's goodliness, make sweet her name.
Alas! what shade art thou
Of sorrow or of blame
Liftest the lyric leafage from her brow,
And pointest a slow finger at her shame?

V

Lies! lies! It cannot be! The wars we wage
Are noble, and our battles still are won
By justice for us, ere we lift the gage.
We have not sold our loftiest heritage.
The proud republic hath not stooped to cheat
And scramble in the market-place of war;
Her forehead weareth yet its solemn star.
Here is her witness: this, her perfect son,
This delicate and proud New England soul
Who leads despisèd men, with just-unshackled feet,
Up the large ways where death and glory meet,
To show all peoples that our shame is done,
That once more we are clean and spirit-whole.

VI

Crouched in the sea-fog on the moaning sand
All night he lay, speaking some simple word
From hour to hour to the slow minds that heard,
Holding each poor life gently in his hand
And breathing on the base rejected clay
Till each dark face shone mystical and grand
Against the breaking day;
And lo, the shard the potter cast away
Was grown a fiery chalice crystal-fine,
Fulfilled of the divine
Great wine of battle wrath by God's ring-finger stirred.
Then upward, where the shadowy bastion loomed
Huge on the mountain in the wet sea light,
Whence now, and now, infernal flowerage bloomed,
Bloomed, burst, and scattered down its deadly seed,—
They swept, and died like freemen on the height,
Like freemen, and like men of noble breed;
And when the battle fell away at night
By hasty and contemptuous hands were thrust
Obscurely in a common grave with him
The fair-haired keeper of their love and trust.
Now limb doth mingle with dissolvèd limb
In nature's busy old democracy

To flush the mountain laurel when she blows
Sweet by the Southern sea,
And heart with crumbled heart climbs in the rose:—
The untaught hearts with the high heart that knew
This mountain fortress for no earthly hold
Of temporal•quarrel, but the bastion old
Of spiritual wrong,
Built by an unjust nation sheer and strong,
Expugnable but by a nation's rue
And bowing down before that equal shrine
By all men held divine,
Whereof his band and he were the most holy sign.

VII

O bitter, bitter shade!
Wilt thou not put the scorn
And instant tragic question from thine eye?
Do thy dark brows yet crave
That swift and angry stave—
Unmeet for this desirous morn—
That I have striven, striven to evade?
Gazing on him, must I not deem they err
Whose careless lips in street and shop aver
As common tidings, deeds to make his cheek
Flush from the bronze, and his dead throat to speak?
Surely some elder singer would arise,
Whose harp hath leave to threaten and to mourn
Above this people when they go astray.
Is Whitman, the strong spirit, overworn?
Has Whittier put his yearning wrath away?
I will not and I dare not yet believe!
Though furtively the sunlight seems to grieve,
And the spring-laden breeze
Out of the gladdening west is sinister
With sounds of nameless battle overseas;
Though when we turn and question in suspense
If these things be indeed after these ways,
And what things are to follow after these,
Our fluent men of place and consequence
Fumble and fill their mouths with hollow phrase,

Or for the end-all of deep arguments
Intone their dull commercial liturgies—
I dare not yet believe! My ears are shut!
I will not hear the thin satiric praise
And muffled laughter of our enemies,
Bidding us never sheathe our valiant sword
Till we have changed our birthright for a gourd
Of wild pulse stolen from a barbarian's hut;
Showing how wise it is to cast away
The symbols of our spiritual sway,
That so our hands with better ease
May wield the driver's whip and grasp the jailer's keys.

VIII

Was it for this our fathers kept the law?
This crown shall crown their struggle and their ruth?
Are we the eagle nation Milton saw
Mewing its mighty youth,
Soon to possess the mountain winds of truth,
And be a swift familiar of the sun
Where aye before God's face his trumpets run?
Or have we but the talons and the maw,
And for the abject likeness of our heart
Shall some less lordly bird be set apart?
Some gross-billed wader where the swamps are fat?
Some gorger in the sun? Some prowler with the bat?

IX

Ah, no!
We have not fallen so.
We are our fathers' sons: let those who lead us know!
'T was only yesterday sick Cuba's cry
Came up the tropic wind, "Now help us, for we die!"
Then Alabama heard,
And rising, pale, to Maine and Idaho
Shouted a burning word.
Proud state with proud impassioned state conferred,
And at the lifting of a hand sprang forth,
East, west, and south, and north,
Beautiful armies. Oh, by the sweet blood and young

Shed on the awful hill slope at San Juan,
By the unforgotten names of eager boys
Who might have tasted girl's love and been stung
With the old mystic joys
And starry griefs, now the spring nights come on,
But that the heart of youth is generous,—
We charge you, ye who lead us,
Breathe on their chivalry no hint of stain!
Turn not their new-world victories to gain!
One least leaf plucked for chaffer from the bays
Of their dear praise,
One jot of their pure conquest put to hire,
The implacable republic will require;
With clamor, in the glare and gaze of noon,
Or subtly, coming as a thief at night,
But surely, very surely, slow or soon
That insult deep we deeply will requite.
Tempt nôt our weakness, our cupidity!
For save we let the island men go free,
Those baffled and dislaureled ghosts
Will curse us from the lamentable coasts
Where walk the frustrate dead.
The cup of trembling shall be drainèd quite,
Eaten the sour bread of astonishment,
With ashes of the hearth shall be made white
Our hair, and wailing shall be in the tent;
Then on your guiltier head
Shall our intolerable self-disdain
Wreak suddenly its anger and its pain;
For manifest in that disastrous light
We shall discern the right
And do it, tardily.—O ye who lead,
Take heed!
Blindness we may forgive, but baseness we will smite.

STEPHEN CRANE

War Is Kind

DO not weep, maiden, for war is kind.
Because your lover threw wild hands toward the sky
And the affrighted steed ran on alone,
Do not weep.
War is kind.

Hoarse, booming drums of the regiment,
Little souls who thirst for fight,
These men were born to drill and die.
The unexplained glory flies above them,
Great is the battle-god, great, and his kingdom —
A field where a thousand corpses lie.

Do not weep, babe, for war is kind.
Because your father tumbled in the yellow trenches,
Raged at his breast, gulped and died,
Do not weep.
War is kind.

Swift blazing flag of the regiment,
Eagle with crest of red and gold,
These men were born to drill and die.
Point for them the virtue of slaughter,
Make plain to them the excellence of killing
And a field where a thousand corpses lie.

Mother whose heart hung humble as a button
On the bright splendid shroud of your son,
Do not weep.
War is kind.

GEORGE CABOT LODGE

Day and Dark

NOW the golden fields of sunset rose on rose to me-ward
fall,
Down the dark reverberate beaches clear and far the sea-birds
call,
Blue across the fire-stained waters, eastward thrusts the chuck-
ling tide,
Fresh as when the immortal impulse took the lifeless world
for bride.

Now the shore's thin verge of shallows keep the tense and
tender light,
Now the stars hang few and faultless, diademed on the brows
of night,
Now the moon's unstinted silver falls like dew along the sea
While from far a friendly casement softly fills with light for
me.

So it ends! I reaped the harvest, lived the long and lavish day,
Saw the earliest sunlight shiver thro' the breakers' endless play,
Felt the noonday's warm abundance, shared the hours of large
repose,
While the stately sun descended thro' the twilight's sumptuous
close.

Now the night-fall—Ah! I guess the immortal secret, glimpse
the goal,
Know the hours have scanted nothing, know each fragment
hints the whole,
While the Soul in power and freedom dares and wills to claim
its own,
Star over star, a larger, lovelier unknown heaven beyond the
known!

GEORGE SANTAYANA

On the Death of a Metaphysician

UNHAPPY dreamer, who outwinged in flight
The pleasant region of the things I love,
And soared beyond the sunshine, and above
The golden cornfields and the dear and bright
Warmth of the hearth,—blasphemer of delight,
Was your proud bosom not at peace with Jove,
That you sought, thankless for his guarded grove,
The empty horror of abysmal night?
Ah, the thin air is cold above the moon!
I stood and saw you fall, befooled in death,
As, in your numbëd spirit's fatal swoon,
You cried you were a god, or were to be;
I heard with feeble moan your boastful breath
Bubble from depths of the Icarian sea.

"As in the Midst of Battle There Is Room"

AS in the midst of battle there is room
For thoughts of love, and in foul sin for mirth,
As gossips whisper of a trinket's worth
Spied by the death-bed's flickering candle-gloom;
As in the crevices of Cæsar's tomb
The sweet herbs flourish on a little earth:
So in this great disaster of our birth
We can be happy, and forget our doom.

For morning, with a ray of tenderest joy
Gilding the iron heaven, hides the truth,
And evening gently woos us to employ

Our grief in idle catches. Such is youth;
Till from that summer's trance we wake, to find
Despair before us, vanity behind.

Solipsism

I COULD believe that I am here alone,
　　And all the world my dream;
The passion of the scene is all my own,
　　And things that seem but seem.

Perchance an exhalation of my sorrow
　　Hath raised this vaporous show,
For whence but from my soul should all things borrow
　　So deep a tinge of woe?

I keep the secret doubt within my breast
　　To be the gods' defence,
To ease the heart by too much ruth oppressed
　　And drive the horror hence.

O sorrow that the patient brute should cower
　　And die, not having sinned!
O pity that the wild and fragile flower
　　Should shiver in the wind!

Then were I dreaming dreams I know not of,
　　For that is part of me
That feels the piercing pang of grief and love
　　And doubts eternally.

But whether all to me the vision come
　　Or break in many beams,
The pageant ever shifts, and being's sum
　　Is but the sum of dreams.

Odes

I

WHAT god will choose me from this labouring
      nation
To worship him afar, with inward gladness,
At sunset and at sunrise, in some Persian
      Garden of roses;

Or under the full moon, in rapturous silence,
Charmed by the trickling fountain, and the moaning
Of the death-hallowed cypress, and the myrtle
      Hallowed by Venus?

O for a chamber in an eastern tower,
Spacious and empty, roofed in odorous cedar,
A silken soft divan, a woven carpet
      Rich, many-coloured;

A jug that, poised on her firm head, a Negress
Fetched from the well; a window to the ocean,
Lest of the stormy world too deep seclusion
      Make me forgetful!

Thence I might watch the vessel-bearing waters
Beat the slow pulses of the life eternal,
Bringing of nature's universal travail
      Infinite echoes;

And there at even I might stand and listen
To thrum of distant lutes and dying voices
Chanting the ditty an Arabian captive
      Sang to Darius.

So would I dream awhile, and ease a little
The soul long stifled and the straitened spirit,
Tasting new pleasures in a far-off country
      Sacred to beauty.

II

My heart rebels against my generation,
That talks of freedom and is slave to riches,
And, toiling 'neath each day's ignoble burden,
    Boasts of the morrow.

No space for noonday rest or midnight watches,
No purest joy of breathing under heaven!
Wretched themselves, they heap, to make them happy,
    Many possessions.

But thou, O silent Mother, wise, immortal,
To whom our toil is laughter,—take, divine one,
This vanity away, and to thy lover
    Give what is needful:—

III

Gathering the echoes of forgotten wisdom,
And mastered by a proud, adventurous purpose,
Columbus sought the golden shores of India
    Opposite Europe.

He gave the world another world, and ruin
Brought upon blameless, river-loving nations,
Cursed Spain with barren gold, and made the Andes
    Fiefs of Saint Peter;

While in the cheerless North the thrifty Saxon
Planted his corn, and, narrowing his bosom,
Made covenant with God, and by keen virtue
    Trebled his riches.

What venture hast thou left us, bold Columbus?
What honour left thy brothers, brave Magellan?
Daily the children of the rich for pastime
    Circle the planet.

And what good comes to us of all your dangers?
A smaller earth and a smaller hope of heaven.
Ye have but cheapened gold, and, measuring ocean,
    Counted the islands.

No Ponce de Leon shall drink in fountains,
On any flowering Easter, youth eternal;
No Cortes look upon another ocean;
      No Alexander

Found in the Orient dim a boundless kingdom,
And, clothing his Greek strength with barbarous
   splendour,
Build by the sea his throne, while Sacred Egypt
      Honours his godhead.

The earth, the mother once of godlike Theseus
And mighty Heracles, at length is weary,
And now brings forth a spawn of antlike creatures,
      Blackening her valleys,

Inglorious in their birth and in their living,
Curious and querulous, afraid of battle,
Rummaging earth for coals, in camps of hovels
      Crouching from winter,

As if grim fate, amid our boastful prating,
Made us the image of our brutish fathers,
When from their caves they issued, crazed with terror,
      Howling and hungry.

For all things come about in sacred cycles,
And life brings death, and light eternal darkness,
And now the world grows old apace; its glory
      Passes for ever.

Perchance the earth will yet for many ages
Bear her dead child, her moon, around her orbit;
Strange craft may tempt the ocean streams, new forests
      Cover the mountains.

If in those latter days men still remember
Our wisdom and our travail and our sorrow,
They never can be happy, with that burden
      Heavy upon them,

Knowing the hideous past, the blood, the famine,
The ancestral hate, the eager faith's disaster,
All ending in their little lives, and vulgar
      Circle of troubles.

But if they have forgot us, and the shifting
Of sands has buried deep our thousand cities,
Fell superstition then will seize upon them;
      Protean error

Will fill their panting heart with sickly phantoms
Of sudden blinding good and monstrous evil;
There will be miracles again, and torment,
      Dungeon and fagot,—

Until the patient earth, made dry and barren,
Sheds all her herbage in a final winter,
And the gods turn their eyes to some far distant
      Bright constellation.

IV

Slowly the black earth gains upon the yellow,
And the caked hill-side is ribbed soft with furrows.
Turn now again, with voice and staff, my ploughman,
      Guiding thy oxen.

Lift the great ploughshare, clear the stones and
    brambles,
Plant it the deeper, with thy foot upon it,
Uprooting all the flowering weeds that bring not
      Food to thy children.

Patience is good for man and beast, and labour
Hardens to sorrow and the frost of winter,
Turn then, again, in the brave hope of harvest,
      Singing to heaven.

V

Of thee the Northman by his beachèd galley
Dreamt, as he watched the never-setting Ursa
And longed for summer and thy light, O sacred
      Mediterranean.

Unseen he loved thee; for the heart within him
Knew earth had gardens where he might be blessed,
Putting away long dreams and aimless, barbarous
        Hunger for battle.

The foretaste of thy languors thawed his bosom;
A great need drove him to thy caverned islands
From the gray, endless reaches of the outer
        Desert of Ocean.

He saw thy pillars, saw thy sudden mountains
Wrinkled and stark, and in their crooked gorges,
'Neath peeping pine and cypress, guessed the torrent
        Smothered in flowers.

Thine incense to the sun, thy gathered vapours,
He saw suspended on the flanks of Taurus,
Or veiling the snowed bosom of the virgin
        Sister of Atlas.

He saw the luminous top of wide Olympus,
Fit for the happy gods; he saw the pilgrim
River, with rains of Ethiopia flooding
        Populous Egypt.

And having seen, he loved thee. His racked spirit,
By thy breath tempered and the light that clothes thee,
Forgot the monstrous gods, and made of Nature
        Mistress and mother.

The more should I, O fatal sea, before thee
Of alien words make echoes to thy music;
For I was born where first the rills of Tagus
        Turn to the westward.

And wandering long, alas! have need of drinking
Deep of the patience of thy perfect sadness,
O thou that constant through the change of ages,
        Beautiful ever,

Never wast wholly young and void of sorrows,
Nor ever canst be old, while yet the morning

Kindles thy ripples, or the golden evening
    Dyes thee in purple.

Thee, willing to be tamed but still untamable,
The Roman called his own until he perished,
As now the busy English hover o'er thee,
    Stalwart and noble;

But all is naught to thee, while no harsh winter
Congeals thy fountains, and the blown Sahara
Chokes not with dreadful sand thy deep and placid
    Rock-guarded havens.

Thou carest not what men may tread thy margin;
Nor I, while from some heather-scented headland
I may behold thy beauty, the eternal
    Solace of mortals.

———·—·———

TRUMBULL STICKNEY

———·—·———

Be Still. The Hanging Gardens Were a Dream

BE still. The Hanging Gardens were a dream
  That over Persian roses flew to kiss
The curlèd lashes of Semiramis.
Troy never was, nor green Skamander stream.
Provence and Troubadour are merest lies,
The glorious hair of Venice was a beam
Made within Titian's eye. The sunsets seem,
The world is very old and nothing is.
Be still. Thou foolish thing, thou canst not wake,
Nor thy tears wedge thy soldered lids apart,
But patter in the darkness of thy heart.
Thy brain is plagued. Thou art a frighted owl
Blind with the light of life thou'ldst not forsake,
And error loves and nourishes thy soul.

Live Blindly

LIVE blindly and upon the hour. The Lord,
Who was the Future, died full long ago.
Knowledge which is the Past is folly. Go,
Poor child, and be not to thyself abhorred.
Around thine earth sun-wingèd winds do blow
And planets roll; a meteor draws his sword;
The rainbow breaks his seven-coloured chord
And the long strips of river-silver flow:
Awake! Give thyself to the lovely hours.
Drinking their lips, catch thou the dream in flight
About their fragile hairs' aërial gold.
Thou art divine, thou livest,—as of old
Apollo springing naked to the light,
And all his island shivered into flowers.

He Said: "If in His Image I Was Made"

HE said: "If in his image I was made,
I am his equal and across the land
We two should make our journey hand in hand
Like brothers dignified and unafraid."
And God that day was walking in the shade.
To whom he said: "The world is idly planned,
We cross each other, let us understand
Thou who thou art, I who I am," he said.
Darkness came down. And all that night was heard
Tremendous clamour and the broken roar
Of things in turmoil driven down before.
Then silence. Morning broke, and sang a bird.
He lay upon the earth, his bosom stirred;
But God was seen no longer any more.

On Some Shells Found Inland

THESE are my murmur-laden shells that keep
A fresh voice tho' the years lie very gray.
The wave that washed their lips and tuned their lay
Is gone, gone with the faded ocean sweep,
The royal tide, gray ebb and sunken neap
And purple midday,—gone! To this hot clay
Must sing my shells, where yet the primal day,
Its roar and rhythm and splendour will not sleep.
What hand shall join them to their proper sea
If all be gone? Shall they forever feel
Glories undone and worlds that cannot be?—
'T were mercy to stamp out this agèd wrong,
Dash them to earth and crunch them with the heel
And make a dust of their seraphic song.

In Ampezzo

ONLY once more and not again—the larches
Shake to the wind their echo, "Not again,"—
We see, below the sky that over-arches
Heavy and blue, the plain

Between Tofana lying and Cristallo
In meadowy earths above the ringing stream:
Whence interchangeably desire may follow,
Hesitant as in·dream,

At sunset, south, by lilac promontories
Under green skies to Italy, or forth
By calms of morning beyond Lavinores
Tyrolward and to north:

As now, this last of latter days, when over
The brownish field by peasants are undone
Some widths of grass, some plots of mountain clover
Under the autumn sun.

With honey-warm perfume that risen lingers
In mazes of low heat, or takes the air,
Passing delicious as a woman's fingers
Passing amid the hair;

When scythes are swishing and the mower's muscle
Spans a repeated crescent to and fro,
Or in dry stalks of corn the sickles rustle,
Tangle, detach and go,

Far thro' the wide blue day and greening meadow
Whose blots of amber beaded are with sheaves,
Wherever pallidly a cloud-shadow
Deadens the earth and leaves:

Whilst high around and near, their heads of iron
Sunken in sky whose azure overlights
Ravines and edges, stand the gray and maron
Desolate Dolomites,—

And older than decay from the small summit
Unfolds a stream of pebbly wreckage down
Under the suns of midday, like some comet
Struck into gravel stone.

Faintly across this gold and amethystine
September, images of summer fade;
And gentle dreams now freshen on the pristine
Viols, awhile unplayed,

Of many a place where lovingly we wander,
More dearly held that quickly we forsake,—
A pine by sullen coasts, an oleander
Reddening on the lake.

And there, each year with more familiar motion,
From many a bird and windy forestries,
Or along shaking fringes of the ocean
Vapours of music rise.

From many easts the morning gives her splendour;
The shadows fill with colours we forget;
Remembered tints at evening grow tender,
Tarnished with violet.

Let us away! soon sheets of winter metal
On this discoloured mountain-land will close,
While elsewhere Spring-time weaves a crimson petal,
Builds and perfumes a rose.

Away! for here the mountain sinks in gravel.
Let us forget the unhappy site with change,
And go, if only happiness be travel
After the new and strange:—

Unless 'twere better to be very single,
To follow some diviner monotone,
And in all beauties, where ourselves commingle,
Love but a love, but one,

Across this shadowy minute of our living,
What time our hearts so magically sing,
To mitigate our fever, simply giving
All in a little thing?

Just as here, past yon dumb and melancholy
Sameness of ruin, while the mountains ail,
Summer and sunset-coloured autumn slowly
Dissipate down the vale;

And all these lines along the sky that measure,
Sorapis and the rocks of Mezzodi
Crumble by foamy miles into the azure
Mediterranean sea:

Whereas to-day at sunrise, under brambles,
A league above the moss and dying pines
I picked this little—in my hand that trembles—
Parcel of columbines.

Mt. Lykaion

ALONE on Lykaion since man hath been
Stand on the height two columns, where at rest
Two eagles hewn of gold sit looking East
Forever; and the sun goes up between.
Far down around the mountain's oval green
An order keeps the falling stones abreast.
Below within the chaos last and least
A river like a curl of light is seen.
Beyond the river lies the even sea,
Beyond the sea another ghost of sky,—
O God, support the sickness of my eye
Lest the far space and long antiquity
Suck out my heart, and on this awful ground
The great wind kill my little shell with sound.

Near Helikon

BY such an all-embalming summer day
As sweetens now among the mountain pines
Down to the cornland yonder and the vines,
To where the sky and sea are mixed in gray,
How do all things together take their way
Harmonious to the harvest, bringing wines
And bread and light and whatsoe'er combines
In the large wreath to make it round and gay.
To me my troubled life doth now appear
Like scarce distinguishable summits hung
Around the blue horizon: places where
Not even a traveller purposeth to steer,—
Whereof a migrant bird in passing sung,
And the girl closed her window not to hear.

Fidelity

NOT lost or won but above all endeavour
Thy life like heaven circles around mine;
Thy eyes it seems upon my eyes did shine
  Since forever.

For aught he summon up his earliest hour
No man remembers the surprise of day,
Nor where he saw with virgin wonder play
  The first flower.

And o'er the imagination's last horizon
No brain has learing descried nothing more:
Still there are stars and in the night before
  More have arisen.

Not won or lost is unto thee my being;
Our eyes were always so together met.
If mine should close, if ever thine forget,
  Time is dying.

Mnemosyne

IT'S autumn in the country I remember.

How warm a wind blew here about the ways!
And shadows on the hillside lay to slumber
During the long sun-sweetened summer-days.

It's cold abroad the country I remember.

The swallows veering skimmed the golden grain
At midday with a wing aslant and limber;
And yellow cattle browsed upon the plain.

It's empty down the country I remember.

I had a sister lovely in my sight:
Her hair was dark, her eyes were very sombre;
We sang together in the woods at night.

It's lonely in the country I remember.

The babble of our children fills my ears,
And on our hearth I stare the perished ember
To flames that show all starry thro' my tears.

It's dark about the country I remember.

Now in the Palace Gardens

NOW in the palace gardens warm with age,
On lawn and flower-bed this afternoon
The thin November-coloured foliage
Just as last year unfastens lilting down,

And round the terrace in gray attitude
The very statues are becoming sere
With long presentiment of solitude.
Most of the life that I have lived is here,

Here by the path and autumn's earthy grass
And chestnuts standing down the breadths of sky:
Indeed I know not how it came to pass,
The life I lived here so unhappily.

Yet blessing over all! I do not care
What wormwood I have ate to cups of gall;
I care not what despairs are buried there
Under the ground, no, I care not at all.

Nay, if the heart have beaten, let it break!
I have not loved and lived but only this
Betwixt my birth and grave. Dear Spirit, take
The gratitude that pains so deep it is.

When Spring shall be again, and at your door
You stand to feel the mellower evening wind,
Remember if you will my heart is pure,
Perfectly pure and altogether kind;

How much it aches to linger in these things!
I thought the perfect end of love was peace
Over the long-forgiven sufferings.
But something else, I know not what it is,

The words that came so nearly and then not,
The vanity, the error of the whole,
The strong cross-purpose, oh, I know not what
Cries dreadfully in the distracted soul.

The evening fills the garden, hardly red;
And autumn goes away, like one alone.
Would I were with the leaves that thread by thread
Soften to soil, I would that I were one.

SHAEMAS O'SHEEL

They Went Forth to Battle, but They Always Fell

THEY went forth to battle, but they always fell;
    Their eyes were fixed above the sullen shields;
Nobly they fought and bravely, but not well,
And sank heart-wounded by a subtle spell.
    They knew not fear that to the foeman yields,
    They were not weak, as one who vainly wields
A futile weapon; yet the sad scrolls tell
How on the hard-fought field they always fell.

It was a secret music that they heard,
    A sad sweet plea for pity and for peace;
And that which pierced the heart was but a word,

Though the white breast was red-lipped where the sword
    Pressed a fierce cruel kiss, to put surcease
    On its hot thirst, but drank a hot increase.
Ah, they by some strange troubling doubt were stirred,
And died for hearing what no foeman heard.

They went forth to battle, but they always fell;
    Their might was not the might of lifted spears;
Over the battle-clamor came a spell
Of troubling music, and they fought not well.
    Their wreaths are willows and their tribute, tears;
    Their names are old sad stories in men's ears;
Yet they will scatter the red hordes of Hell,
Who went to battle forth and always fell.

———————◆———————

ADELAIDE CRAPSEY

———————◆———————

Vendor's Song

MY songs to sell, good sir!
    I pray you buy.
Here's one will win a lady's tears,
    Here's one will make her gay,
Here's one will charm your true love true
    Forever and a day;
Good sir, I pray you buy!

Oh, no, he will not buy.

My songs to sell, sweet maid!
    I pray you buy.
This one will teach you Lilith's lore,
    And this what Helen knew,
And this will keep your gold hair gold.
    And this your blue eyes blue;
Sweet maid, I pray you buy!

Oh, no, she will not buy.

If I'd as much money as I could tell,
I never would cry my songs to sell.
I never would cry my songs to sell.

The Lonely Death

IN the cold I will rise, I will bathe
In waters of ice; myself
Will shiver, and shrive myself,
Alone in the dawn, and anoint
Forehead and feet and hands;
I will shutter the windows from light,
I will place in their sockets the four
Tall candles and set them aflame
In the grey of the dawn; and myself
Will lay myself straight in my bed,
And draw the sheet under my chin.

EDWIN ARLINGTON ROBINSON

Ben Jonson Entertains a Man from Stratford

YOU are a friend then, as I make it out,
Of our man Shakespeare, who alone of us
Will put an ass's head in Fairyland
As he would add a shilling to more shillings,
All most harmonious—and out of his
Miraculous inviolable increase
Fills Ilion, Rome, or any town you like
Of olden time with timeless Englishmen;

And I must wonder what you think of him—
All you down there where your small Avon flows
By Stratford, and where you're an Alderman.
Some, for a guess, would have him riding back
To be a farrier there, or say a dyer;
Or maybe one of your adept surveyors;
Or like enough the wizard of all tanners.
Not you—no fear of that; for I discern
In you a kindling of the flame that saves—
The nimble element, the true caloric;
I see it, and was told of it, moreover,
By our discriminate friend himself, no other.
Had you been one of the sad average,
As he would have it—meaning, as I take it,
The sinew and the solvent of our Island,
You'd not be buying beer for this Terpander's
Approved and estimated friend Ben Jonson;
He'd never foist it as a part of his
Contingent entertainment of a townsman
While he goes off rehearsing, as he must,
If he shall ever be the Duke of Stratford.
And my words are no shadow on your town—
Far from it; for one town's as like another
As all are unlike London. Oh, he knows it—
And there's the Stratford in him; he denies it,
And there's the Shakespeare in him. So, God help him!
I tell him he needs Greek; but neither God
Nor Greek will help him. Nothing will help that man.
You see the fates have given him so much,
He must have all or perish—or look out
Of London, where he sees too many lords.
They're part of half what ails him: I suppose
There's nothing fouler down among the demons
Than what it is he feels when he remembers
The dust and sweat and ointment of his calling
With his lords looking on and laughing at him.
King as he is, he can't be king *de facto*,
And that's as well, because he wouldn't like it;
He'd frame a lower rating of men then
Than he has now; and after that would come

An abdication or an apoplexy.
He can't be king, not even king of Stratford—
Though half the world, if not the whole of it,
May crown him with a crown that fits no king
Save Lord Apollo's homesick emissary:
Not there on Avon, or on any stream
Where Naiads and their white arms are no more
Shall he find home again. It's all too bad.
But there's a comfort, for he'll have that House—
The best you ever saw; and he'll be there
Anon, as you're an Alderman. Good God!
He makes me lie awake o' nights and laugh.

And you have known him from his origin,
You tell me; and a most uncommon urchin
He must have been to the few seeing ones—
A trifle terrifying, I dare say,
Discovering a world with his man's eyes,
Quite as another lad might see some finches,
If he looked hard and had an eye for Nature.
But this one had his eyes and their foretelling,
And he had you to fare with, and what else?
He must have had a father and a mother—
In fact I've heard him say so—and a dog,
As a boy should, I venture; and the dog,
Most likely, was the only man who knew him.
A dog, for all I know, is what he needs
As much as anything right here to-day,
To counsel him about his disillusions,
Old aches, and parturitions of what's coming—
A dog of orders, an emeritus,
To wag his tail at him when he comes home,
And then to put his paws up on his knees
And say, "For God's sake, what's it all about?"

I don't know whether he needs a dog or not—
Or what he needs. I tell him he needs Greek;
I'll talk of rules and Aristotle with him,
And if his tongue's at home he'll say to that,
"I have your word that Aristotle knows,
And you mine that I don't know Aristotle."

He's all at odds with all the unities,
And what's yet worse it doesn't seem to matter;
He treads along through Time's old wilderness
As if the tramp of all the centuries
Had left no roads—and there are none, for him;
He doesn't see them, even with those eyes—
And that's a pity, or I say it is.
Accordingly we have him as we have him—
Going his way, the way that he goes best,
A pleasant animal with no great noise
Or nonsense anywhere to set him off—
Save only divers and inclement devils
Have made of late his heart their dwelling-place.
A flame half ready to fly out sometimes
At some annoyance may be fanned up in him,
But soon it falls, and when it falls goes out;
He knows how little room there is in there
For crude and futile animosities,
And how much for the joy of being whole,
And how much for long sorrow and old pain.
On our side there are some who may be given
To grow old wondering what he thinks of us
And some above us, who are, in his eyes,
Above himself—and that's quite right and English.
Yet here we smile, or disappoint the gods
Who made it so; the gods have always eyes
To see men scratch; and they see one down here
Who itches, manor-bitten, to the bone,
Albeit he knows himself—yes, yes, he knows—
The lord of more than England and of more
Than all the seas of England in all time
Shall ever wash. D'ye wonder that I laugh?
He sees me, and he doesn't seem to care;
And why the devil should he? I can't tell you.
I'll meet him out alone of a bright Sunday,
Trim, rather spruce, and quite the gentleman.
"What, ho, my lord!" say I. He doesn't hear me;
Wherefore I have to pause and look at him.
He's not enormous, but one looks at him.
A little on the round if you insist,

For now, God save the mark, he's growing old;
He's five and forty, and to hear him talk
These days you'd call him eighty; then you'd add
More years to that. He's old enough to be
The father of a world, and so he is.
"Ben, you're a scholar, what's the time of day?"
Says he; and there shines out of him again
An aged light that has no age or station—
The mystery that's his—a mischievous
Half-mad serenity that laughs at fame
For being won so easy, and at friends
Who laugh at him for what he wants the most,
And for his dukedom down in Warwickshire;—
By which you see we're all a little jealous. . . .
Poor Greene! I fear the colour of his name
Was even as that of his ascending soul;
And he was one where there are many others—
Some scrivening to the end against their fate,
Their puppets all in ink and all to die there;
And some with hands that once would shade an eye
That scanned Euripides and Æschylus
Will reach by this time for a pot-house mop
To slush their first and last of royalties.
Poor devils! and they all play to his hand;
For so it was in Athens and old Rome.
But that's not here or there; I've wandered off.
Greene does it, or I'm careful. Where's that boy?

Yes, he'll go back to Stratford. And we'll miss him?
Dear sir, there'll be no London here without him.
We'll all be riding, one of these fine days,
Down there to see him—and his wife won't like us;
And then we'll think of what he never said
Of women—which, if taken all in all
With what he did say, would buy many horses.
Though nowadays he's not so much for women.
"So few of them," he says, "are worth the guessing."
But there's a worm at work when he says that,
And while he says it one feels in the air
A deal of circumambient hocus-pocus.

They've had him dancing till his toes were tender,
And he can feel 'em now, come chilly rains.
There's no long cry for going into it,
However, and we don't know much about it.
But you in Stratford, like most here in London,
Have more now in the *Sonnets* than you paid for;
He's put one there with all her poison on,
To make a singing fiction of a shadow
That's in his life a fact, and always will be.
But she's no care of ours, though Time, I fear,
Will have a more reverberant ado
About her than about another one
Who seems to have decoyed him, married him,
And sent him scuttling on his way to London—
With much already learned, and more to learn,
And more to follow. Lord! how I see him now,
Pretending, maybe trying, to be like us.
Whatever he may have meant, we never had him;
He failed us, or escaped, or what you will—
And there was that about him (God knows what—
We'd flayed another had he tried it on us)
That made as many of us as had wits
More fond of all his easy distances
Than one another's noise and clap-your-shoulder.
But think you not, my friend, he'd never talk!
Talk? He was eldritch at it; and we listened—
Thereby acquiring much we knew before
About ourselves, and hitherto had held
Irrelevant, or not prime to the purpose.
And there were some, of course, and there be now,
Disordered and reduced amazedly
To resignation by the mystic seal
Of young finality the gods had laid
On everything that made him a young demon;
And one or two shot looks at him already
As he had been their executioner;
And once or twice he was, not knowing it—
Or knowing, being sorry for poor clay
And saying nothing . . . Yet, for all his engines,
You'll meet a thousand of an afternoon

Who strut and sun themselves and see around 'em
A world made out of more that has a reason
Than his, I swear, that he sees here to-day;
Though he may scarcely give a Fool an exit
But we mark how he sees in everything
A law that, given that we flout it once too often,
Brings fire and iron down on our naked heads.
To me it looks as if the power that made him,
For fear of giving all things to one creature,
Left out the first—faith, innocence, illusion,
Whatever 'tis that keeps us out o' Bedlam—
And thereby, for his too consuming vision,
Empowered him out of nature; though to see him,
You'd never guess what's going on inside him.
He'll break out some day like a keg of ale
With too much independent frenzy in it;
And all for cellaring what he knows won't keep,
And what he'd best forget—but that he can't.
You'll have it, and have more than I'm foretelling;
And there'll be such a roaring at the Globe
As never stunned the bleeding gladiators.
He'll have to change the colour of its hair
A bit, for now he calls it Cleopatra.
Black hair would never do for Cleopatra.
But you and I are not yet two old women,
And you're a man of office. What he does
Is more to you than how it is he does it—
And that's what the Lord God has never told him.
They work together, and the Devil helps 'em;
They do it of a morning, or if not,
They do it of a night; in which event
He's peevish of a morning. He seems old;
He's not the proper stomach or the sleep—
And they're two sovran agents to conserve him
Against the fiery art that has no mercy
But what's in that prodigious grand new House.
I gather something happening in his boyhood
Fulfilled him with a boy's determination
To make all Stratford 'ware of him. Well, well,
I hope at last he'll have his joy of it,

And all his pigs and sheep and bellowing beeves,
And frogs and owls and unicorns, moreover,
Be less than hell to his attendant ears.
Oh, past a doubt we'll all go down to see him.

He may be wise. With London two days off,
Down there some wind of heaven may yet revive him.
But there's no quickening breath from anywhere
Shall make of him again the young poised faun
From Warwickshire, who'd made, it seems, already
A legend of himself before I came
To blink before the last of his first lightning.
Whatever there be, there'll be no more of that;
The coming on of his old monster Time
Has made him a still man; and he has dreams
Were fair to think on once, and all found hollow.
He knows how much of what men paint themselves
Would blister in the light of what they are;
He sees how much of what was great now shares
An eminence transformed and ordinary;
He knows too much of what the world has hushed
In others, to be loud now for himself;
He knows now at what height low enemies
May reach his heart, and high friends let him fall;
But what not even such as he may know
Bedevils him the worst: his lark may sing
At heaven's gate how he will, and for as long
As joy may listen, but *he* sees no gate,
Save one whereat the spent clay waits a little
Before the churchyard has it, and the worm.
Not long ago, late in an afternoon,
I came on him unseen down Lambeth way,
And on my life I was afear'd of him:
He gloomed and mumbled like a soul from Tophet,
His hands behind him and his head bent solemn.
"What is it now," said I, "another woman?"
That made him sorry for me, and he smiled.
"No, Ben," he mused; "it's Nothing. It's all Nothing.
We come, we go; and when we're done, we're done;
Spiders and flies—we're mostly one or t'other—

We come, we go; and when we're done, we're done";
"By God, you sing that song as if you knew it!"
　Said I, by way of cheering him; "what ails ye?"
"I think I must have come down here to think,"
　Says he to that, and pulls his little beard;
"Your fly will serve as well as anybody,
　And what's his hour? He flies, and flies, and flies,
　And in his fly's mind has a brave appearance;
　And then your spider gets him in her net,
　And eats him out, and hangs him up to dry.
　That's Nature, the kind mother of us all.
　And then your slattern housemaid swings her broom,
　And where's your spider? And that's Nature, also.
　It's Nature, and it's Nothing. It's all Nothing.
　It's all a world where bugs and emperors
　Go singularly back to the same dust,
　Each in his time; and the old, ordered stars
　That sang together, Ben, will sing the same
　Old stave to-morrow."

　　　　　　　　　　When he talks like that,
There's nothing for a human man to do
But lead him to some grateful nook like this
Where we be now, and there to make him drink.
He'll drink, for love of me, and then be sick;
A sad sign always in a man of parts,
And always very ominous. The great
Should be as large in liquor as in love—
And our great friend is not so large in either:
One disaffects him, and the other fails him;
Whatso he drinks that has an antic in it,
He's wondering what's to pay in his insides;
And while his eyes are on the Cyprian
He's fribbling all the time with that damned House.
We laugh here at his thrift, but after all
It may be thrift that saves him from the devil;
God gave it, anyhow—and we'll suppose
He knew the compound of His handiwork.
To-day the clouds are with him, but anon
He'll out of 'em enough to shake the tree

Of life itself and bring down fruit unheard-of—
And, throwing in the bruised and whole together,
Prepare a wine to make us drunk with wonder;
And if he live, there'll be a sunset spell
Thrown over him as over a glassed lake
That yesterday was all a black wild water.

God send he live to give us, if no more,
What now's a-rampage in him, and exhibit,
With a decent half-allegiance to the ages
An earnest of at least a casual eye
Turned once on what he owes to Gutenberg,
And to the fealty of more centuries
Than are as yet a picture in our vision.
"There's time enough—I'll do it when I'm old,
And we're immortal men," he says to that;
And then he says to me, "Ben, what's 'immortal'?
Think you by any force of ordination
It may be nothing of a sort more noisy
Than a small oblivion of component ashes
That of a dream-addicted world was once
A moving atomy much like your friend here?"
Nothing will help that man. To make him laugh
I said then he was a mad mountebank—
And by the Lord I nearer made him cry.
I could have eat an eft then, on my knees,
Tails, claws, and all of him; for I had stung
The king of men, who had no sting for me,
And I had hurt him in his memories;
And I say now, as I shall say again,
I love the man this side idolatry.
He'll do it when he's old, he says. I wonder.
He may not be so ancient as all that.
For such as he the thing that is to do
Will do itself—but there's a reckoning;
The sessions that are now too much his own,
The roiling inward of a still outside,
The churning out of all those blood-fed lines,
The nights of many schemes and little sleep,
The full brain hammered hot with too much thinking,

The vexed heart over worn with too much aching—
This weary jangling of conjoined affairs
Made out of elements that have no end,
And all confused at once, I understand,
Is not what makes a man to live forever.
O, no, not now! He'll not be going now:
There'll be time yet for God knows what explosions
Before he goes. He'll stay awhile. Just wait:
Just wait a year or two for Cleopatra,
For she's to be a balsam and a comfort;
And that's not all a jape of mine now, either.
For granted once the old way of Apollo
Sings in a man, he may then, if he's able,
Strike unafraid whatever strings he will
Upon the last and wildest of new lyres;
Nor out of his new magic, though it hymn
The shrieks of dungeoned hell, shall he create
A madness or a gloom to shut quite out
A cleaving daylight, and a last great calm
Triumphant over shipwreck and all storms.
He might have given Aristotle creeps,
But surely would have given him his *katharsis*.
He'll not be going yet. There's too much yet
Unsung within the man. But when he goes,
I'd stake ye coin o' the realm his only care
For a phantom world he sounded and found wanting
Will be a portion here, a portion there,
Of this or that thing or some other thing
That has a patent and intrinsical
Equivalence in those egregious shillings.
And yet he knows, God help him! Tell me, now,
If ever there was anything let loose
On earth by gods or devils heretofore
Like this mad, careful, proud, indifferent Shakespeare!
Where was it, if it ever was? By heaven,
'Twas never yet in Rhodes or Pergamon—
In Thebes or Nineveh, a thing like this!
No thing like this was ever out of England;
And that he knows. I wonder if he cares.
Perhaps he does. . . . O Lord, that House in Stratford!

Eros Turannos

SHE fears him, and will always ask
   What fated her to choose him;
She meets in his engaging mask
   All reasons to refuse him;
But what she meets and what she fears
Are less than are the downward years,
Drawn slowly to the foamless weirs
   Of age, were she to lose him.

Between a blurred sagacity
   That once had power to sound him,
And Love, that will not let him be
   The Judas that she found him,
Her pride assuages her almost,
As if it were alone the cost.—
He sees that he will not be lost,
   And waits and looks around him.

A sense of ocean and old trees
   Envelops and allures him;
Tradition, touching all he sees,
   Beguiles and reassures him;
And all her doubts of what he says
Are dimmed with what she knows of days—
Till even prejudice delays
   And fades, and she secures him.

The falling leaf inaugurates
   The reign of her confusion;
The pounding wave reverberates
   The dirge of her illusion;
And home, where passion lived and died,
Becomes a place where she can hide,
While all the town and harbour side
   Vibrate with her seclusion.

We tell you, tapping on our brows,
    The story as it should be—
As if the story of a house
    Were told, or ever could be;
We'll have no kindly veil between
Her visions and those we have seen—
As if we guessed what hers have been,
    Or what they are or would be.

Meanwhile we do no harm; for they
    That with a god have striven,
Not hearing much of what we say,
    Take what the god has given;
Though like waves breaking it may be,
Or like a changed familiar tree,
Or like a stairway to the sea
    Where down the blind are driven.

For a Dead Lady

NO more with overflowing light
    Shall fill the eyes that now are faded,
Nor shall another's fringe with night
Their woman-hidden world as they did.
No more shall quiver down the days
The flowing wonder of her ways,
Whereof no language may requite
The shifting and the many-shaded.

The grace, divine, definitive,
Clings only as a faint forestalling;
The laugh that love could not forgive
Is hushed, and answers to no calling;
The forehead and the little ears
Have gone where Saturn keeps the years;
The breast where roses could not live
Has done with rising and with falling.

The beauty, shattered by the laws
That have creation in their keeping,
No longer trembles at applause,
Or over children that are sleeping;
And we who delve in beauty's lore
Know all that we have known before
Of what inexorable cause
Makes Time so vicious in his reaping.

The Man Against the Sky

BETWEEN me and the sunset, like a dome
Against the glory of a world on fire,
Now burned a sudden hill,
Bleak, round, and high, by flame-lit height made higher,
With nothing on it for the flame to kill
Save one who moved and was alone up there
To loom before the chaos and the glare
As if he were the last god going home
Unto his last desire.
Dark, marvellous, and inscrutable he moved on
Till down the fiery distance he was gone,
Like one of those eternal, remote things
That range across a man's imaginings
When a sure music fills him and he knows
What he may say thereafter to few men—
The touch of ages having wrought
An echo and a glimpse of what he thought
A phantom or a legend until then;
For whether lighted over ways that save,
Or lured from all repose,
If he go on too far to find a grave,
Mostly alone he goes.
Even he, who stood where I had found him,
On high with fire all round him,
Who moved along the molten west,
And over the round hill's crest
That seemed half ready with him to go down,

Flame-bitten and flame-cleft,
As if there were to be no last thing left
Of a nameless unimaginable town—
Even he who climbed and vanished may have taken
Down to the perils of a depth not known,
From death defended, though by men forsaken,
The bread that every man must eat alone;
He may have walked while others hardly dared
Looked on to see him stand where many fell;
And upward out of that as out of hell,
He may have sung and striven
To mount where more of him shall yet be given,
Bereft of all retreat,
To sevenfold heat—
As on a day when three in Dura shared
The furnace, and were spared
For glory by that king of Babylon
Who made himself so great that God, who heard,
Covered him with long feathers, like a bird.

Again, he may have gone down easily,
By comfortable altitudes, and found,
As always, underneath him solid ground
Whereon to be sufficient and to stand
Possessed already of the promised land,
Far stretched and fair to see:
A good sight, verily,
And one to make the eyes of her who bore him
Shine glad with hidden tears.
Why question of his ease of who before him,
In one place or another where they left
Their names as far behind them as their bones,
And yet by dint of slaughter, toil, and theft,
And shrewdly sharpened stones,
Carved hard the way for his ascendancy
Through deserts of lost years?
Why trouble him now who sees and hears
No more than what his innocence requires,
And therefore to no other height aspires
Than one at which he neither quails nor tires?
He may do more by seeing what he sees

Than others eager for iniquities;
He may, by seeing all things for the best,
Incite futurity to do the rest.
Or with an even likelihood,
He may have met with atrabilious eyes
The fires of time on equal terms and passed
Indifferently down, until at last
His only kind of grandeur would have been,
Apparently, in being seen.
He may have had for evil or for good
No argument; he may have had no care
For what without himself went anywhere
To failure or to glory, and least of all
For such a stale, flamboyant miracle;
He may have been the prophet of an art
Immovable to old idolatries;
He may have been a player without a part,
Annoyed that even the sun should have the skies
For such a flaming way to advertise;
He may have been a painter sick at heart
With Nature's toiling for a new surprise;
He may have been a cynic, who now, for all
Of anything divine that his effete
Negation may have tasted,
Saw truth in his own image, rather small,
Forbore to fever the ephemeral,
Found any barren height a good retreat
From any swarming street,
And in the sun saw power superbly wasted;
And when the primitive old-fashioned stars
Came out again to shine on joys and wars
More primitive, and all arrayed for doom,
He may have proved a world a sorry thing
In his imagining,
And life a lighted highway to the tomb.
Or, mounting with unfirm unsearching tread,
His hopes to chaos led,
He may have stumbled up there from the past,
And with an aching strangeness viewed the last
Abysmal conflagration of his dreams —

A flame where nothing seems
To burn but flame itself, by nothing fed;
And while it all went out,
Not even the faint anodyne of doubt
May then have eased a painful going down
From pictured heights of power and lost renown,
Revealed at length to his outlived endeavour
Remote and unapproachable forever;
And at his heart there may have gnawed
Sick memories of a dead faith foiled and flawed
And long dishonoured by the living death
Assigned alike by chance
To brutes and hierophants;
And anguish fallen on those he loved around him
May once have dealt the last blow to confound him,
And so have left him as death leaves a child,
Who sees it all too near;
And he who knows no young way to forget
May struggle to the tomb unreconciled.
Whatever suns may rise and set
There may be nothing kinder for him here
Than shafts and agonies;
And under these
He may cry out and stay on horribly;
Or, seeing in death too small a thing to fear,
He may go forward like a stoic Roman
Where pangs and terrors in his pathway lie —
Or, seizing the swift logic of a woman,
Curse God and die.

Or maybe there, like many another one
Who might have stood aloft and looked ahead,
Black-drawn against wild red,
He may have built unawed by fiery gules
That in him no commotion stirred,
A living reason out of molecules
Why molecules occurred,
And one for smiling when he might have sighed
Had he seen far enough,
And in the same inevitable stuff

Discovered an odd reason too for pride
In being what he must have been by laws
Infrangible and for no kind of cause.
Deterred by no confusion or surprise
He may have seen with his mechanic eyes
A world without a meaning, and had room,
Alone amid magnificence and doom,
To build himself an airy monument
That should, or fail him in his vague intent,
Outlast an accidental universe—
To call it nothing worse—
Or, by the burrowing guile
Of Time disintegrated and effaced,
Like once-remembered mighty trees go down
To ruin, of which by man may now be traced
No part sufficient even to be rotten,
And in the book of things that are forgotten
Is entered as a thing not quite worth while.
He may have been so great
That satraps would have shivered at his frown,
And all he prized alive may rule a state
No larger than a grave that holds a clown;
He may have been a master of his fate,
And of his atoms—ready as another
In his emergence to exonerate
His father and his mother;
He may have been a captain of a host,
Self-eloquent and ripe for prodigies,
Doomed here to swell by dangerous degrees,
And then give up the ghost.
Nahum's great grasshoppers were such as these,
Sun-scattered and soon lost.

Whatever the dark road he may have taken,
This man who stood on high
And faced along the sky,
Whatever drove or lured or guided him—
A vision answering a faith unshaken,
An easy trust assumed by easy trials,
A sick negation born of weak denials,

A crazed abhorrence of an old condition,
A blind attendance on a brief ambition—
Whatever stayed him or derided him,
His way was even as ours;
And we, with all our wounds and all our powers,
Must each await alone at his own height
Another darkness or another light;
And there, of our poor self dominion reft,
If inference and reason shun
Hell, Heaven, and Oblivion,
May thwarted will (perforce precarious,
But for our conservation better thus)
Have no misgivings left
Of doing yet what here we leave undone?
Or if unto the last of these we cleave,
Believing or protesting we believe
In such an idle and ephemeral
Florescence of the diabolical—
If, robbed of two fond old enormities,
Our being had no onward auguries,
What then were this great love of ours to say
For launching other lives to voyage again
A little farther into time and pain,
A little faster in a futile chase
For a kingdom and a power and a Race
That would have still in sight
A manifest end of ashes and eternal night?
Is this the music of the toys we shake
So loud—as if there might be no mistake
Somewhere in our indomitable will?
Are we no greater than the noise we make
Along our blind atomic pilgrimage
Whereon by crass chance billeted we go
Because our brains and bones and cartilage
Will have it so?
If this we say, then let us all be still
About our share in it, and live and die
More quietly thereby.

Where was he going, this man against the sky?
You know not, nor do I.
But this we know, if we know anything:
That we may laugh and fight and sing
And of our transcience here make offering
To an orient Word that will not be erased,
Or, save in incommunicable gleams
Too permanent for dreams,
Be found or known.
No tonic or ambitious irritant
Of increase or of want
Has made an otherwise insensate waste
Of ages overthrown
A ruthless, veiled, implacable foretaste
Of other ages that are still to be
Depleted and rewarded variously
Because a few, by fate's economy,
Shall seem to move the world the way it goes;
No soft evangel of equality,
Safe-cradled in a communal repose
That huddles into death and may at last
Be covered well with equatorial snows—
And all for what, the devil only knows—
Will aggregate an inkling to confirm
The credit of a sage or of a worm,
Or tell us why one man in five
Should have a care to stay alive
While in his heart he feels no violence
Laid on his humour and intelligence
When infant Science makes a pleasant face
And waves again that hollow toy, the Race;
No planetary trap where souls are wrought
For nothing but the sake of being caught
And sent again to nothing will attune
Itself to any key of any reason
Why man should hunger through another season
To find out why 'twere better late than soon
To go away and let the sun and moon
And all the silly stars illuminate
A place for creeping things,

And those that root and trumpet and have wings
And herd and ruminate,
Or dive and flash and poise in rivers and seas,
Or by their loyal tails in lofty trees
Hang screeching lewd victorious derision
Of man's immortal vision.
Shall we, because Eternity records
Too vast an answer for the time-born words
We spell, whereof so many are dead that once
In our capricious lexicons
Were so alive and final, hear no more
The Word itself, the living word
That none alive has ever heard
Or ever spelt,
And few have ever felt
Without the fears and old surrenderings
And terrors that began
When Death let fall a feather from his wings
And humbled the first man?
Because the weight of our humility,
Wherefrom we gain
A little wisdom and much pain,
Falls here too sore and there too tedious,
Are we in anguish or complacency,
Not looking far enough ahead
To see by what mad couriers we are led
Along the roads of the ridiculous,
To pity ourselves and laugh at faith
And while we curse life bear it?
And if we see the soul's dead end in death,
Are we to fear it?
What folly is here that has not yet a name
Unless we say outright that we are liars?
What have we seen beyond our sunset fires
That lights again the way by which we came?
Why pay we such a price, and one we give
So clamouringly, for each racked empty day
That leads one more last human hope away,
As quiet fiends would lead past our crazed eyes
Our children to an unseen sacrifice?

If after all that we have lived and thought,
All comes to Nought—
If there be nothing after Now,
And we be nothing anyhow,
And we know that—why live?
'Twere sure but weaklings' vain distress
To suffer dungeons where so many doors
Will open on the cold eternal shores
That look sheer down
To the dark tideless floods of Nothingness
Where all who know may drown.

ANNA HEMPSTEAD BRANCH

The Monk in the Kitchen

I

ORDER is a lovely thing;
On disarray it lays its wing,
Teaching simplicity to sing.
It has a meek and lowly grace,
Quiet as a nun's face.
Lo—I will have thee in this place!
Tranquil well of deep delight,
All things that shine through thee appear
As stones through water, sweetly clear.
Thou clarity,
That with angelic charity
Revealest beauty where thou art,
Spread thyself like a clean pool,
Then all the things that in thee are,
Shall seem more spiritual and fair,
Reflection from serener air—
Sunken shapes of many a star
In the high heavens set afar.

II

Ye stolid, homely, visible things,
Above you all brood glorious wings
Of your deep entities, set high,
Like slow moons in a hidden sky.
But you, their likenesses, are spent
Upon another element.
Truly ye are but seemings—
The shadowy cast-off gleamings
Of bright solidities. Ye seem
Soft as water, vague as dream;
Image, cast in a shifting stream.

III

What are ye?
I know not.
Brazen pan and iron pot,
Yellow brick and gray flag-stone
That my feet have trod upon—
Ye seem to me
Vessels of bright mystery.
For ye do bear a shape, and so
Though ye were made by man, I know
An inner Spirit also made,
And ye his breathings have obeyed.

IV

Shape, the strong and awful spirit,
Laid his ancient hand on you.
He waste chaos doth inherit;
He can alter and subdue.
Verily, he doth lift up
Matter, like a sacred cup,
Into deep substance he reached, and lo
Where ye were not, ye were; and so
Out of useless nothing, ye
Groaned and laughed and came to be.
And I use you, as I can,

Wonderful uses, made for man.
Iron pot and brazen pan.

V

What are ye?
I know not;
Nor what I really do
When I move and govern you.
There is no small work unto God.
He required of us greatness;
Of His last creature
A high angelic nature,
Stature superb and bright completeness,
He sets to us no humble duty.
Each act that He would have us do
Is haloed round with strangest beauty:
Terrific deeds and cosmic tasks
Of His plainest child He asks.
When I polish the brazen pan
I hear a creature laugh afar
In the gardens of a star,
And from his burning presence run
Flaming wheels of many a sun.
Whoever makes a thing more bright,
He is an angel of all light.
When I cleanse this earthen floor
My spirit leaps to see
Bright garments trailing over it,
A cleanness made by me.
Purger of all men's thoughts and ways,
With labour do I sound Thy praise,
My work is done for Thee.
Whoever makes a thing more bright,
He is an angel of all light.
Therefore let me spread abroad
The beautiful cleanness of my God.

VI

One time in the cool of dawn
Angels came and worked with me.

The air was soft with many a wing.
They laughed amid my solitude
And cast bright looks on everything.
Sweetly of me did they ask
That they might do my common task.
And all were beautiful—but One
With garments whiter than the sun
Had such a face
Of deep, remembered grace;
That when I saw I cried—"Thou art
The great Blood-Brother of my heart.
Where have I seen Thee?"—And He said,
"When we are dancing round God's throne,
How often thou art there.
Beauties from thy hands have flown
Like white doves wheeling in mid air.
Nay—thy soul remembers not?
Work on, and cleanse thy iron pot."

VII

What are we? I know not.

Ere the Golden Bowl Is Broken

HE gathered for His own delight
    The sparkling waters of my soul.
A thousand creatures, bubbling bright—
    He set me in a golden bowl.

From the deep cisterns of the earth
    He bade me up—the shining daughter—
And I am exquisite with mirth,
    A brightening and a sunlit water.

The wild, the free, the radiant one,
    A happy bubble I did glide.
I poised my sweetness to the sun
    And there I sleeked my silver side.

Sometimes I lifted up my head
    And globed the moonlight with my hands,
Or thin as flying wings I spread
    Angelic wildness through the sands.

Then, woven into webs of light,
    I breathed, I sighed, I laughed aloud,
And lifting up my pinions bright
    I shone in Heaven, a bird-white cloud.

Then did I dance above the mead,
    And through the crystal fields would run,
And from my scarlet splendours breed
    The golden thunders of the sun.

Beneath the whitening stars I flew
    And floated moon-like on the breeze,
Or my frail heart was piercèd through
    With sharp sweet flowers of the trees.

Of giant crags I bear the scars,
    And I have swept along the gale,
Such multitudes as are the stars,
    My myriad faces rapt and pale.

As savage creatures strong and free
    Make wild the jungle of the wood,
The starry powers that sport in me
    Habit my silver solitude.

From out my smallness, soft as dew,
    That utter fastness, stern and deep,
Terrible meanings look at you
    Like vision from the eyes of sleep.

I cannot leap—I cannot run—
    I only glimmer, soft and mild,
A limpid water in the sun,
    A sparkling and a sunlit child.

What stranger ways shall yet be mine
　　When I am spilled, you cannot see.
But now you laugh to watch me shine,
　　And smooth the hidden stars in me.

Lightly you stroke my silver wing—
　　The folded carrier of my soul.
A soft, a shy, a silent thing,
　　A water in a golden bowl.

AMY LOWELL

Little Ivory Figures Pulled with String

IS it the tinkling of mandolins which disturbs you?
Or the dropping of bitter-orange petals among the coffee-
　　cups?
Or the slow creeping of the moonlight between the olive-trees?
　　Drop! drop! the rain
　　Upon the thin plates of my heart.

String your blood to chord with this music,
Stir your heels upon the cobbles to the rhythm of a dance-tune.
They have slim thighs and arms of silver;
The moon washes away their garments;
They make a pattern of fleeing feet in the branch shadows,
And the green grapes knotted about them
Burst as they press against one another.
　　The rain knocks upon the plates of my heart,
　　They are crumpled with its beating.

Would you drink only from your brains, Old Man?
See, the moonlight has reached your knees,
It falls upon your head in an accolade of silver.
Rise up on the music,

Fling against the moon-drifts in a whorl of young light bodies:
Leaping grape-clusters,
Vine leaves tearing from a grey wall.
You shall run, laughing, in a braid of women,
And weave flowers with the frosty spines of thorns.
Why do you gaze into your glass,
And jar the spoons with your finger-tapping?
    The rain is rigid on the plates of my heart.
    The murmur of it is loud—loud.

Patterns

I WALK down the garden paths,
  And all the daffodils
Are blowing, and the bright blue squills.
I walk down the patterned garden paths
In my stiff, brocaded gown.
With my powdered hair and jewelled fan,
I too am a rare
Pattern. As I wander down
The garden paths,
My dress is richly figured,
And the train
Makes a pink and silver stain
On the gravel, and the thrift
Of the borders.
Just a plate of current fashion,
Tripping by in high-heeled, ribboned shoes.
Not a softness anywhere about me,
Only whalebone and brocade.
And I sink on a seat in the shade
Of a lime tree. For my passion
Wars against the stiff brocade.
The daffodils and squills
Flutter in the breeze
As they please.
And I weep;
For the lime tree is in blossom
And one small flower has dropped upon my bosom.

And the plashing of waterdrops
In the marble fountain
Comes down the garden paths.
The dripping never stops.
Underneath my stiffened gown
Is the softness of a woman bathing in a marble basin,
A basin in the midst of hedges grown
So thick, she cannot see her lover hiding,
But she guesses he is near,
And the sliding of the water
Seems the stroking of a dear
Hand upon her.
What is Summer in a fine brocaded gown!
I should like to see it lying in a heap upon the ground.
All the pink and silver crumpled up on the ground.

I would be the pink and silver as I ran along the paths,
And he would stumble after,
Bewildered by my laughter.
I should see the sun flashing from his sword-hilt and the
    buckles on his shoes.
I would choose
To lead him in a maze along the patterned paths,
A bright and laughing maze for my heavy-booted lover.
Till he caught me in the shade,
And the buttons of his waistcoat bruised my body as he
    clasped me,
Aching, melting, unafraid.
With the shadows of the leaves and the sundrops,
And the plopping of the waterdrops,
All about us in the open afternoon—
I am very like to swoon
With the weight of this brocade,
For the sun sifts through the shade.

Underneath the fallen blossom
In my bosom,
Is a letter I have hid.
It was brought to me this morning by a rider from the Duke.
"Madam, we regret to inform you that Lord Hartwell
    Died in action Thursday se'nnight."

As I read it in the white, morning sunlight,
  The letters squirmed like snakes.
"Any answer, Madam," said my footman.
"No," I told him.
"See that the messenger takes some refreshment.
  No, no answer."
And I walked into the garden,
Up and down the patterned paths,
In my stiff, correct brocade.
The blue and yellow flowers stood up proudly in the sun,
  Each one.
I stood upright too,
Held rigid to the pattern
By the stiffness of my gown.
Up and down I walked,
Up and down.

In a month he would have been my husband.
In a month, here, underneath this lime,
We would have broke the pattern;
He for me, and I for him,
He as Colonel, I as Lady,
On this shady seat.
He had a whim
That sunlight carried blessing.
And I answered, "It shall be as you have said."
Now he is dead.

In Summer and in Winter I shall walk
Up and down
The patterned garden paths
In my stiff, brocaded gown.
The squills and daffodils
Will give place to pillared roses, and to asters, and to snow.
I shall go
Up and down,
In my gown.
Gorgeously arrayed,
Boned and stayed.
And the softness of my body will be guarded from embrace
By each button, hook, and lace.

For the man who should loose me is dead,
Fighting with the Duke in Flanders,
In a pattern called a war.
Christ! What are patterns for?

EDGAR LEE MASTERS

(FROM "SPOON RIVER ANTHOLOGY")

Thomas Trevelyan

READING in Ovid the sorrowful story of Itys,
Son of the love of Tereus and Procne, slain
For the guilty passion of Tereus for Philomela,
The flesh of him served to Tereus by Procne,
And the wrath of Tereus, the murderess pursuing
Till the gods made Philomela a nightingale,
Lute of the rising moon, and Procne a swallow!
Oh livers and artists of Hellas centuries gone,
Sealing in little thuribles dreams and wisdom,
Incense beyond all price, forever fragrant,
A breath whereof makes clear the eyes of the soul!
How I inhaled its sweetness here in Spoon River!
The thurible opening when I had lived and learned
How all of us kill the children of love, and all of us,
Knowing not what we do, devour their flesh;
And all of us change to singers, although it be
But once in our lives, or change—alas!—to swallows,
To twitter amid cold winds and falling leaves!

Edmund Pollard

I WOULD I had thrust my hands of flesh
Into the disk-flowers bee-infested,
Into the mirror-like core of fire
Of the light of life, the sun of delight.

For what are anthers worth or petals
Or halo-rays? Mockeries, shadows
Of the heart of the flower, the central flame!
All is yours, young passer-by;
Enter the banquet room with the thought;
Don't sidle in as if you were doubtful
Whether you're welcome—the feast is yours!
Nor take but a little, refusing more
With a bashful "Thank you," when you're hungry.
Is your soul alive? Then let it feed!
Leave no balconies where you can climb;
Nor milk-white bosoms where you can rest;
Nor golden heads with pillows to share;
Nor wine cups while the wine is sweet;
Nor ecstasies of body or soul,
You will die, no doubt, but die while living
In depths of azure, rapt and mated,
Kissing the queen-bee, Life!

Bert Kessler

I WINGED my bird,
   Though he flew toward the setting sun;
But just as the shot rang out, he soared
Up and up through the splinters of golden light,
Till he turned right over, feathers ruffled,
With some of the down of him floating near,
And fell like a plummet into the grass.
I tramped about, parting the tangles,
Till I saw a splash of blood on a stump,
And the quail lying close to the rotten roots.
I reached my hand, but saw no brier,
But something pricked and stung and numbed it.
And then, in a second, I spied the rattler—
The shutters wide in his yellow eyes,
The head of him arched, sunk back in the rings of him,
A circle of filth, the color of ashes,
Or oak leaves bleached under layers of leaves.

I stood like a stone as he shrank and uncoiled
And started to crawl beneath the stump,
When I fell limp in the grass.

Petit, the Poet

SEEDS in a dry pod, tick, tick, tick,
Tick, tick, tick, like mites in a quarrel—
Faint iambics that the full breeze wakens—
But the pine tree makes a symphony thereof.
Triolets, villanelles, rondels, rondeaus,
Ballades by the score with the same old thought:
The snows and the roses of yesterday are vanished;
And what is love but a rose that fades?
Life all around me here in the village:
Tragedy, comedy, valor and truth,
Courage, constancy, heroism, failure—
All in the loom, and oh what patterns!
Woodlands, meadows, streams and rivers—
Blind to all of it all my life long.
Triolets, villanelles, rondels, rondeaus,
Seeds in a dry pod, tick, tick, tick,
Tick, tick, tick, what little iambics,
While Homer and Whitman roared in the pines?

ROBERT FROST

Desert Places

SNOW falling and night falling fast oh fast
In a field I looked into going past,
And the ground almost covered smooth in snow,
But a few weeds and stubble showing last.

The woods around it have it—it is theirs.
All animals are smothered in their lairs.
I am too absent-spirited to count;
The loneliness includes me unawares.

And lonely as it is that loneliness
Will be more lonely ere it will be less—
A blanker whiteness of benighted snow
With no expression, nothing to express.

They cannot scare me with their empty spaces
Between stars—on stars where no human race is.
I have it in me so much nearer home
To scare myself with my own desert places.

Bereft

WHERE had I heard this wind before
Change like this to a deeper roar?
What would it take my standing there for,
Holding open a restive door,
Looking down hill to a frothy shore?
Summer was past and day was past.
Sombre clouds in the west were massed.
Out in the porch's sagging floor,
Leaves got up in a coil and hissed,
Blindly struck at my knee and missed.
Something sinister in the tone
Told me my secret must be known:
Word I was in the house alone
Somehow must have gotten abroad.
Word I was in my life alone,
Word I had no one left but God.

For Once, Then, Something

OTHERS taunt me with having knelt at well-curbs
 Always wrong to the light, so never seeing
Deeper down in the well than where the water
Gives me back in a shining surface picture
Me myself in the summer heaven godlike
Looking out of a wreath of fern and cloud puffs.
Once, when trying with chin against a well-curb
I discerned, as I thought, beyond the picture,
Through the picture, a something white, uncertain,
Something more of the depths—and then I lost it.
Water came to rebuke the too clear water.
One drop fell from a fern, and lo, a ripple
Shook whatever it was lay there at bottom,
Blurred it, blotted it out. What was that whiteness?
Truth? A pebble of quartz? For once, then, something.

Once by the Pacific

THE shattered water made a misty din.
 Great waves looked over others coming in,
And thought of doing something to the shore
That water never did to land before.
The clouds were low and hairy in the skies,
Like locks blown forward in the gleam of eyes.
You could not tell, and yet it looked as if
The shore was lucky in being backed by cliff,
The cliff in being backed by continent;
It looked as if a night of dark intent
Was coming, and not only a night, an age.
Someone had better be prepared for rage.
There would be more than ocean-water broken
Before God's last *Put out the Light* was spoken.

The Telephone

"WHEN I was just as far as I could walk
From here to-day,
There was an hour
All still
When leaning with my head against a flower
I heard you talk.
Don't say I didn't, for I heard you say—
You spoke from that flower on the window sill—
Do you remember what it was you said?"

"First tell me what it was you thought you heard."

"Having found the flower and driven a bee away,
I leaned my head,
And holding by the stalk,
I listened and I thought I caught the word—
What was it? Did you call me by my name?
Or did you say—
Someone said 'Come'—I heard it as I bowed."

"I may have thought as much, but not aloud."

"Well, so I came."

The Road Not Taken

TWO roads diverged in a yellow wood,
And sorry I could not travel both
And be one traveler, long I stood
And looked down one as far as I could
To where it bent in the undergrowth;

Then took the other, as just as fair,
And having perhaps the better claim,
Because it was grassy and wanted wear;
Though as for that the passing there
Had worn them really about the same,

And both that morning equally lay
In leaves no step had trodden black.
Oh, I kept the first foi another day!
Yet knowing how way leads on to way,
I doubted if I should ever come back.

I shall be telling this with a sigh
Somewhere ages and ages hence:
Two roads diverged in a wood, and I—
I took the one less traveled by,
And that has made all the difference.

My November Guest

MY sorrow, when she's here with me,
    Thinks these dark days of autumn rain
Are beautiful as days can be;
She loves the bare, the withered tree;
    She walks the sodden pasture lane.

Her pleasure will not let me stay.
    She talks and I am fain to list:
She's glad the birds are gone away,
She's glad her simple worsted grey
    Is silver now with clinging mist.

The desolate, deserted trees,
    The faded earth, the heavy sky,
The beauties she so truly sees,
She thinks I have no eye for these,
    And vexes me for reason why.

Not yesterday I learned to know
    The love of bare November days
Before the coming of the snow;
But it were vain to tell her so,
    And they are better for her praise.

Home Burial

HE saw her from the bottom of the stairs
Before she saw him. She was starting down,
Looking back over her shoulder at some fear.
She took a doubtful step and then undid it
To raise herself and look again. He spoke
Advancing toward her: "What is it you see
From up there always—for I want to know."
She turned and sank upon her skirts at that,
And her face changed from terrified to dull.
He said to gain time: "What is it you see?"
Mounting until she cowered under him,
"I will find out now—you must tell me, dear."
She, in her place, refused him any help
With the least stiffening of her neck and silence.
She let him look, sure that he wouldn't see,
Blind creature; and a while he didn't see.
But at last he murmured, "Oh," and again,
    "Oh."
"What is it—what?" she said.

                                        "Just that I see."
"You don't," she challenged. "Tell me what it is."

"The wonder is I didn't see at once.
I never noticed it from here before.
I must be wonted to it—that's the reason.
The little graveyard where my people are!
So small the window frames the whole of it.
Not so much larger than a bedroom, is it?
There are three stones of slate and one of marble,
Broad-shouldered little slabs there in the sunlight
On the sidehill. We haven't to mind *those*.
But I understand: it is not the stones,
But the child's mound—"

    "Don't, don't, don't, don't," she cried.

She withdrew shrinking from beneath his arm
That rested on the banister, and slid downstairs;
And turned on him with such a daunting look,
He said twice over before he knew himself:
"Can't a man speak of his own child he's lost?"

"Not you! Oh, where's my hat? Oh, I don't need it!
I must get out of here. I must get air.
I don't know rightly whether any man can."

"Amy! Don't go to someone else this time.
Listen to me. I won't come down the stairs."
He sat and fixed his chin between his fists.
"There's something I should like to ask you, dear."

"You don't know how to ask it."

"Help me, then."

Her fingers moved the latch for all reply.

"My words are nearly always an offence.
I don't know how to speak of anything
So as to please you. But I might be taught
I should suppose. I can't say I see how.
A man must partly give up being a man
With women-folk. We could have some arrangement
By which I'd bind myself to keep hands off
Anything special you're a mind to name.
Though I don't like such things 'twixt those that love.
Two that don't love can't live together without them.
But two that do can't live together with them."
She moved the latch a little. "Don't, don't go.
Don't carry it to someone else this time.
Tell me about it if it's something human.
Let me into your grief. I'm not so much
Unlike other folks as your standing there
Apart would make me out. Give me my chance.
I do think, though, you overdo it a little.
What was it brought you up to think it the thing

To take your mother-loss of a first child
So inconsolably—in the face of love.
You'd think his memory might be satisfied—"

"There you go sneering now!"

                              "I'm not, I'm not!
You make me angry. I'll come down to you.
God, what a woman! And it's come to this,
A man can't speak of his own child that's dead."

"You can't because you don't know how.
If you had any feelings, you that dug
With your own hand—how could you?—his little grave;
I saw you from that very window there,
Making the gravel leap and leap in air,
Leap up, like that, like that, and land so lightly
And roll down the mound beside the hole.
I thought, who is that man? I don't know you.
And I crept down the stairs and up the stairs
To look again, and still your spade kept lifting.
Then you came in. I heard your rumbling voice
Out in the kitchen, and I don't know why,
But I went near to see with my own eyes.
You could sit there with the stains on your shoes
Of the fresh earth from your own baby's grave
And talk about your everyday concerns.
You had stood the spade up against the wall
Outside there in the entry, for I saw it."

"I shall laugh the worst laugh I ever laughed.
I'm cursed. God, if I don't believe I'm cursed."

"I can repeat the very words you were saying.
'Three foggy mornings and one rainy day
Will rot the best birch fence a man can build.'
Think of it, talk like that at such a time!
What had how long it takes a birch to rot
To do with that was in the darkened parlour.
You *couldn't* care! The nearest friends can go

With any one to death, comes so far short
They might as well not try to go at all.
No, from the time when one is sick to death,
One is alone, and he dies more alone.

Friends make pretence of following to the grave,
But before one is in it, their minds are turned
And making the best of their way back to life
And living people, and things they understand.
But the world's evil. I won't have my grief so
If I can change it. Oh, I won't, I won't!"

"There, you have said it all and you feel better.
You won't go now. You're crying. Close the door.
The heart's gone out of it: why keep it up.
Amy! There's someone coming down the road!"

"*You*—oh, you think the talk is all. I must go—
Somewhere out of this house. How can I make **you**—"

"If—you—do!" She was opening the door wider.
"Where do you mean to go? First tell me that.
I'll follow and bring you back by force. I *will!*—"

The Sound of the Trees

I WONDER about the trees
Why do we wish to bear
Forever the noise of these
More than another noise
So close to our dwelling place?
We suffer them by the day
Till we lose all measure of pace,
And fixity in our joys,
And acquire a listening air.
They are that that talks of going
But never gets away;
And that talks no less for knowing,
As it grows wiser and older,

That now it means to stay.
My feet tug at the floor
And my head sways to my shoulder
Sometimes when I watch trees sway,
From the window or the door.
I shall set forth for somewhere,
I shall make the reckless choice
Some day when they are in voice
And tossing so as to scare
The white clouds over them on.
I shall have less to say,
But I shall be gone.

Hyla Brook

BY June our brook's run out of song and speed.
Sought for much after that, it will be found
Either to have gone groping underground
(And taken with it all the Hyla breed
That shouted in the mist a month ago,
Like ghost of sleigh-bells in a ghost of snow)—
Or flourished and come up in jewel-weed,
Weak foliage that is blown upon and bent
Even against the way its waters went.
Its bed is left a faded paper sheet
Of dead leaves stuck together by the heat—
A brook to none but who remember long.
This as it will be seen is other far
Than with brooks taken otherwhere in song.
We love the things we love for what they are.

Mowing

THERE was never a sound beside the wood but one,
And that was my long scythe whispering to the ground.
What was it it whispered? I knew not well myself;
Perhaps it was something about the heat of the sun,

Something, perhaps, about the lack of sound—
And that was why it whispered and did not speak.
It was no dream of the gift of idle hours,
Or easy gold at the hand of fay or elf:
Anything more than the truth would have seemed **too weak**
To the earnest love that laid the swale in rows,
Not without feeble-pointed spikes of flowers
(Pale orchises), and scared a bright green snake.
The fact is the sweetest dream that labor knows.
My long scythe whispered and left the hay to make.

To Earthward

LOVE at the lips was touch
   As sweet as I could bear;
And once that seemed too much;
I lived on air

That crossed me from sweet things,
The flow of—was it musk
From hidden grapevine springs
Down hill at dusk?

I had the swirl and ache
From sprays of honeysuckle
That when they're gathered shake
Dew on the knuckle.

I craved strong sweets, but those
Seemed strong when I was young;
The petal of the rose
It was that stung.

Now no joy but lacks salt
That is not dashed with pain
And weariness and fault;
I crave the stain

Of tears, the aftermark
Of almost too much love,
The sweet of bitter bark
And burning clove.

When stiff and sore and scarred
I take away my hand
From leaning on it hard
In grass and sand,

The hurt is not enough:
I long for weight and strength
To feel the earth as rough
To all my length.

Fire and Ice

SOME say the world will end in fire,
Some say in ice.
From what I've tasted of desire
I hold with those who favor fire.
But if it had to perish twice,
I think I know enough of hate
To say that for destruction ice
Is also great
And would suffice.

Stopping by Woods on a Snowy Evening

WHOSE woods these are I think I know.
His house is in the village though;
He will not see me stopping here
To watch his woods fill up with snow.

My little horse must think it queer
To stop without a farmhouse near
Between the woods and frozen lake
The darkest evening of the year.

He gives his harness bells a shake
To ask if there is some mistake.
The only other sound's the sweep
Of easy wind and downy flake.

The woods are lovely, dark and deep,
But I have promises to keep,
And miles to go before I sleep,
And miles to go before I sleep.

WILLIAM ELLERY LEONARD

The Image of Delight

O HOW came I that loved stars, moon, and flame,
    And unimaginable wind and sea,
All inner shrines and temples of the free,
Legends and hopes and golden books of fame;
I that upon the mountain carved my name
With cliffs and clouds and eagles over me,
O how came I to stoop to loving thee—
I that had never stooped before to shame?

O 'twas not thee! Too eager of a white
Far beauty and a voice to answer mine,
Myself I built an image of delight,
Which all one purple day I deemed divine—
And when it vanished in the fiery night,
I lost not thee, nor any shape of thine.

CARL SANDBURG

Cool Tombs

WHEN Abraham Lincoln was shoveled into the tombs,
he forgot the copperheads and the assassin . . . in the
dust, in the cool tombs.

And Ulysses Grant lost all thought of con men and Wall Street,
cash and collateral turned ashes . . . in the dust, in the
cool tombs.

Pocahontas' body, lovely as a poplar, sweet as a red haw in
November or a pawpaw in May, did she wonder? does she
remember? . . . in the dust, in the cool tombs?

Take any streetful of people buying clothes and groceries, cheer-
ing a hero or throwing confetti and blowing tin horns
. . . tell me if the lovers are losers . . . tell me if any
get more than the lovers . . . in the dust . . . in the cool
tombs.

Four Preludes on Playthings of the Wind

"THE PAST IS A BUCKET OF ASHES"

I

THE woman named Tomorrow
sits with a hairpin in her teeth
and takes her time
and does her hair the way she wants it
and fastens at last the last braid and coil
and puts the hairpin where it belongs

and turns and drawls: Well, what of it?
My grandmother, Yesterday, is gone.
What of it? Let the dead be dead.

2

The doors were cedar
and the panel strips of gold
and the girls were golden girls
and the panels read and the girls chanted:
    We are the greatest city,
      and the greatest nation:
    nothing like us ever was.
The doors are twisted on broken hinges,
Sheets of rain swish through on the wind
    where the golden girls ran and the panels read:
    We are the greatest city,
    the greatest nation,
    nothing like us ever was.

3

It has happened before.
Strong men put up a city and got
    a nation together,
And paid singers to sing and women
    to warble: We are the greatest city,
    the greatest nation,
    nothing like us ever was.

And while the singers sang
and the strong men listened
and paid the singers well,
    there were rats and lizards who listened
    . . . and the only listeners left now
    . . . are . . . the rats . . . and the lizards.
    And there are black crows
    crying, "Caw, caw,"
    bringing mud and sticks
    building a nest
    over the words carved

on the doors where the panels were cedar
and the strips on the panels were gold
and the golden girls came singing:
We are the greatest city,
the greatest nation:
nothing like us ever was.

The only singers now are crows crying, "Caw, caw,"
And the sheets of rain whine in the wind and doorways.
And the only listeners now are . . . the rats . . . and the
lizards.

4

The feet of the rats
scribble on the doorsills;
the hieroglyphs of the rat footprints
chatter the pedigrees of the rats
and babble of the blood
and gabble of the breed
of the grandfathers and the great-grandfathers
of the rats.

And the wind shifts
and the dust on a doorsill shifts
and even the writing of the rat footprints
tells us nothing, nothing at all
about the greatest city, the greatest nation
where the strong men listened
and the women warbled: Nothing like us ever was.

Jazz Fantasia

DRUM on your drums, batter on your banjos, sob on the
long cool winding saxophones. Go to it, O jazzmen.

Sling your knuckles on the bottoms of the happy tin pans, let
your trombones ooze, and go husha-husha-hush with the
slippery sandpaper.

Moan like an autumn wind high in the lonesome treetops,
   moan soft like you wanted somebody terrible, cry like a
   racing car slipping away from a motorcycle-cop, bang-bang!
   you jazzmen, bang altogether drums, traps, banjos, horns,
   tin cans—make two people fight on the top of a stairway and
   scratch each other's eyes in a clinch tumbling down the
   stairs.

Can the rough stuff. . . . Now a Mississippi steamboat pushes
   up the night river with a hoo-hoo-hoo-oo . . . and the
   green lanterns calling to the high soft stars . . . a red
   moon rides on the humps of the low river hills. . . . Go
   to it, O jazzmen.

Gone

EVERYBODY loved Chick Lorimer in our town
    Far off.
    Everybody loved her.
So we all love a wild girl keeping a hold
    On a dream she wants.
Nobody knows now where Chick Lorimer went.
Nobody knows why she packed her trunk . . . a few old things
And is gone,
        Gone with her little chin
        Thrust ahead of her
        And her soft hair blowing careless
        From under a wide hat,
Dancer, singer, a laughing passionate lover.

Were there ten men or a hundred hunting Chick?
Were there five men or fifty with aching hearts?
    Everybody loved Chick Lorimer.
        Nobody knows where she's gone.

VACHEL LINDSAY

Abraham Lincoln Walks at Midnight

(IN SPRINGFIELD, ILLINOIS)

T is portentous, and a thing of state
That here at midnight, in our little town
A mourning figure walks, and will not rest,
Near the old court-house pacing up and down,

Or by his homestead, or in shadowed yards
He lingers where his children used to play,
Or through the market, on the well-worn stones
He stalks until the dawn-stars burn away.

A bronzed, lank man! His suit of ancient black,
A famous high top-hat and plain worn shawl
Make him the quaint great figure that men love,
The prairie-lawyer, master of us all.

He cannot sleep upon his hillside now.
He is among us:—as in times before!
And we who toss and lie awake for long
Breathe deep, and start, to see him pass the door.

His head is bowed. He thinks on men and kings.
Yes, when the sick world cries, how can he sleep?
Too many peasants fight, they know not why,
Too many homesteads in black terror weep.

The sins of all the war-lords burn his heart.
He sees the dreadnoughts scouring every main.
He carries on his shawl-wrapped shoulders now
The bitterness, the folly and the pain.

He cannot rest until a spirit-dawn
Shall come;—the shining hope of Europe free:
The league of sober folk, the Workers' Earth,
Bringing long peace to Cornland, Alp and Sea.

It breaks his heart that kings must murder still,
That all his hours of travail here for men
Seem yet in vain. And who will bring white peace
That he may sleep upon his hill again?

The Eagle That Is Forgotten

[JOHN P. ALTGELD. BORN DECEMBER 30, 1847;
DIED MARCH 12, 1902]

SLEEP softly . . . eagle forgotten . . . under the stone,
Time has its way with you there, and the clay has its own.
"We have buried him now," thought your foes, and in secret
rejoiced.
They made a brave show of their mourning, their hatred un-
voiced,
They had snarled at you, barked at you, foamed at you, day
after day,
Now you were ended. They praised you, . . . and laid you
away.

The others that mourned you in silence and terror and truth,
The widow bereft of her pittance, the boy without youth,
The mocked and the scorned and the wounded, the lame and
the poor
That should have remembered foreever, . . . remember no
more.

Where are those lovers of yours, on what name do they call
The lost, that in armies wept over your funeral pall?
They call on the names of a hundred high-valiant ones,
A hundred white eagles have risen, the sons of your sons,
The zeal in their wings is a zeal that your dreaming began,
The valor that wore out your soul in the service of man.

Sleep softly, . . . eagle forgotten, . . . under the stone,
Time has its way with you there, and the clay has its own.
Sleep on, O brave hearted, O wise man, that kindled the
    flame—
To live in mankind is far more than to live in a name,
To live in mankind, far, far more . . . than to live in a name.

Aladdin and the Jinn

BRING me soft song," said Aladdin.
    "This tailor-shop sings not at all.
Chant me a word of the twilight,
Of roses that mourn in the fall.
Bring me a song like hashish
That will comfort the stale and the sad,
For I would be mending my spirit,
Forgetting these days that are bad,
Forgetting companions too shallow,
Their quarrels and arguments thin,
Forgetting the shouting Muezzin:"—
"I AM YOUR SLAVE," said the Jinn.

"Bring me old wines," said Aladdin.
"I have been a starved pauper too long.
 Serve them in vessels of jade and of shell,
 Serve them with fruit and with song:—
Wines of pre-Adamite Sultans
Digged from beneath the black seas:—
New-gathered dew from the heavens
Dripped down from Heaven's sweet trees,
Cups from the angels' pale tables
That will make me both handsome and wise,
For I have beheld her, the princess,
Firelight and starlight her eyes.
Pauper I am, I would woo her.
And—let me drink wine, to begin,
Though the Koran expressly forbids it."
"I AM YOUR SLAVE," said the Jinn.

"Plan me a dome," said Aladdin,
"That is drawn like the dawn of the MOON,
  When the sphere seems to rest on the mountains,
  Half-hidden, yet full-risen soon.
  Build me a dome," said Aladdin,
"That shall cause all young lovers to sigh,
  The fullness of life and of beauty,
  Peace beyond peace to the eye—
  A palace of foam and of opal,
  Pure moonlight without and within,
  Where I may enthrone my sweet lady."
"I AM YOUR SLAVE," said the Jinn.

WALLACE STEVENS

Domination of Black

AT night, by the fire,
  The colors of the bushes
And of the fallen leaves,
Repeating themselves,
Turned in the room,
Like the leaves themselves
Turning in the wind.
Yes: but the color of the heavy hemlocks
Came striding.
And I remembered the cry of the peacocks.

The colors of their tails
Were like the leaves themselves
Turning in the wind,
In the twilight wind.
They swept over the room,
Just as they flew from the boughs of the hemlocks
Down to the ground.

I heard them cry—the peacocks.
Was it a cry against the twilight
Or against the leaves themselves
Turning in the wind,
Turning as the flames
Turned in the fire,
Turning as the tails of the peacocks
Turned in the loud fire,
Loud as the hemlocks
Full of the cry of the peacocks?
Or was it a cry against the hemlocks?

Out of the window,
I saw how the planets gathered
Like the leaves themselves
Turning in the wind.
I saw how the night came,
Came striding like the color of the heavy hemlocks,
I felt afraid.
And I remembered the cry of the peacocks.

Sea Surface Full of Clouds

I

IN that November off Tehuantepec,
The slopping of the sea grew still one night
And in the morning summer hued the deck

And made one think of rosy chocolate
And gilt umbrellas. Paradisal green
Gave suavity to the perplexed machine

Of ocean, which like limpid water lay.
Who, then, in that ambrosial latitude
Out of the light evolved the moving blooms,

Who, then, evolved the sea-blooms from the clouds
Diffusing balm in that Pacific calm?
C'était mon enfant, mon bijou, mon âme.

The sea-clouds whitened far below the calm
And moved, as blooms move, in the swimming green
And in its watery radiance, while the hue

Of heaven in an antique reflection rolled
Round those flotillas. And sometimes the sea
Poured brilliant iris on the glistening blue.

II

In that November off Tehuantepec
The slopping of the sea grew still one night.
At breakfast jelly yellow streaked the deck

And made one think of chop-house chocolate
And sham umbrellas. And a sham-like green
Capped summer-seeming on the tense machine

Of ocean, which in sinister flatness lay.
Who, then, beheld the rising of the clouds
That strode submerged in that malevolent sheen,

Who saw the mortal massives of the blooms
Of water moving on the water-floor?
C'était mon frère du ciel, ma vie, mon or.

The gongs rang loudly as the windy blooms
Hoo-hooed it in the darkened ocean-blooms.
The gongs grew still. And then blue heaven spread

Its crystalline pendentives on the sea
And the macabre of the water-glooms.
In an enormous undulation fled.

III

In that November off Tehuantepec,
The slopping of the sea grew still one night,
And a pale silver patterned on the deck

Made one think of porcelain chocolate
And pied umbrellas. An uncertain green,
Piano-polished, held the tranced machine

Of ocean, as a prelude holds and holds.
Who, seeing silver petals of white blooms
Unfolding in the water, feeling sure

Of the milk within the saltiest spurge, heard, then,
The sea unfolding in the sunken clouds?
Oh! C'était mon extase et mon amour.

So deeply sunken were they that the shrouds,
The shrouding shadows, made the petals black
Until the rolling heaven made them blue,

A blue beyond the rainy hyacinth,
And smiting the crevasses of the leaves
Deluged the ocean with a sapphire hue.

IV

In that November off Tehuantepec
The night-long slopping of the sea grew still.
A mallow morning dozed upon the deck

And made one think of musky chocolate
And frail umbrellas. A too-fluent green
Suggested malice in the dry machine

Of ocean, pondering dank stratagem.
Who then beheld the figures of the clouds,
Like blooms secluded in the thick marine?

Like blooms? Like damasks that were shaken off
From the loosed girdles in the spangling must.
C'était ma foi, la nonchalance divine.

The nakedness would rise and suddenly turn
Salt masks of beard and mouths of bellowing,
Would— But more suddenly the heaven rolled

Its bluest sea-clouds in the thinking green
And the nakedness became the broadest blooms,
Mile-mallows that a mallow sun cajoled.

V

In that November off Tehuantepec
Night stilled the slopping of the sea. The day
Came, bowing and voluble, upon the deck,

Good clown. . . . One thought of Chinese chocolate
And large umbrellas. And a motley green
Followed the drift of the obese machine

Of ocean, perfected in indolence.
What pistache one, ingenious and droll,
Beheld the sovereign clouds as jugglery

And the sea as turquoise-turbaned Sambo, neat
At tossing saucers—cloudy-conjuring sea?
C'était mon esprit batard, l'ignominie.

The sovereign clouds came clustering. The conch
Of loyal conjuration trumped. The wind
Of green blooms turning crisped the motley hue

To clearing opalescence. Then the sea
And heaven rolled as one and from the two
Came fresh transfigurings of freshest blue.

To the One of Fictive Music

SISTER and mother and diviner love,
And of the sisterhood of the living dead
Most near, most clear, and of the clearest bloom,
And of the fragrant mothers the most dear
And queen, and of diviner love the day
And flame and summer and sweet fire, no thread
Of cloudy silver sprinkles in your gown
Its venom of renown, and on your head
No crown is simpler than the simple hair.

Now, of the music summoned by the birth
That separates us from the wind and sea,
Yet leaves us in them, until earth becomes,
By being so much of the things we are,
Gross effigy and simulacrum, none
Gives motion to perfection more serene
Than yours, out of our imperfections wrought,
Most rare, or ever of more kindred air
In the laborious weaving that you wear.

For so retentive of themselves are men
That music is intensest which proclaims
The near, the clear, and vaunts the clearest bloom,
And of all vigils musing the obscure,
That apprehends the most which sees and names,
As in your name, an image that is sure,
Among the arrant spices of the sun,
O bough and bush and scented vine, in whom
We give ourselves our likest issuance.

Yet not too like, yet not so like to be
Too near, too clear, saving a little to endow
Our feigning with the strange unlike, whence springs
The difference that heavenly pity brings.
For this, musician, in your girdle fixed
Bear other perfumes. On your pale head wear
A band entwining, set with fatal stones.
Unreal, give back to us what once you gave:
The imagination that we spurned and crave.

Peter Quince at the Clavier

I

JUST as my fingers on these keys
Make music, so the self-same sounds
On my spirit make a music too.

Music is feeling then, not sound;
And thus it is that what I feel,
Here in this room, desiring you,

Thinking of your blue-shadowed silk,
Is music. It is like the strain
Waked in the elders by Susanna:

Of a green evening, clear and warm,
She bathed in her still garden, while
The red-eyed elders, watching, felt

The basses of their being throb
In witching chords, and their thin blood
Pulse pizzicati of Hosanna.

II

In the green evening, clear and warm,
Susanna lay.
She searched
The touch of springs,
And found
Concealed imaginings.
She sighed
For so much melody.

Upon the bank she stood
In the cool
Of spent emotions.
She felt, among the leaves,
The dew
Of old devotions.

She walked upon the grass,
Still quavering.
The winds were like her maids,
On timid feet,
Fetching her woven scarves,
Yet wavering.

A breath upon her hand
Muted the night.
She turned—
A cymbal clashed,
And roaring horns.

III

Soon, with a noise like tambourines,
Came her attendant Byzantines.

They wondered why Susanna cried
Against the elders by her side:

And as they whispered, the refrain
Was like a willow swept by rain.

Anon their lamps' uplifted flame
Revealed Susanna and her shame.

And then the simpering Byzantines,
Fled, with a noise like tambourines.

IV

Beauty is momentary in the mind—
The fitful tracing of a portal;
But in the flesh it is immortal.

The body dies; the body's beauty lives.
So evenings die, in their green going,
A wave, interminably flowing.

So gardens die, their meek breath scenting
The cowl of Winter, done repenting.
So maidens die, to the auroral
Celebration of a maiden's choral.

Susanna's music touched the bawdy strings
Of those white elders; but, escaping,
Left only Death's ironic scraping.
Now in its immortality, it plays
On the clear viol of her memory,
And makes a constant sacrament of praise.

Sunday Morning

I

COMPLACENCIES of the peignoir, and late
Coffee and oranges in a sunny chair,
And the green freedom of a cockatoo
Upon a rug, mingle to dissipate
The holy hush of ancient sacrifice.
She dreams a little, and she feels the dark
Encroachment of that old catastrophe,
As a calm darkens among water-lights.
The pungent oranges and bright green wings
Seem things in some procession of the dead,
Winding across wide water, without sound.
The day is like wide water, without sound,
Stilled for the passing of her dreaming feet
Over the seas, to silent Palestine,
Dominion of the blood and sepulchre.

II

She hears, upon that water without sound,
A voice that cries: "The tomb in Palestine
Is not the porch of spirits lingering;
It is the grave of Jesus, where He lay."
We live in an old chaos of the sun,
Or old dependency of day and night,
Or island solitude, unsponsored, free,
Of that wide water, inescapable.
Deer walk upon our mountains, and the quail
Whistle about us their spontaneous cries;
Sweet berries ripen in the wilderness;
And in the isolation of the sky,
At evening, casual flocks of pigeons make
Ambiguous undulations as they sink,
Downward to darkness, on extended wings.

III

She says: "I am content when wakened birds,
Before they fly, test the reality

Of misty fields, by their sweet questionings;
But when the birds are gone, and their warm fields
Return no more, where, then, is paradise?"
There is not any haunt of prophecy,
Nor any old chimera of the grave,
Neither the golden underground, nor isle
Melodious, where spirits gat them home,
Nor visionary South, nor cloudy palm
Remote on heaven's hill, that has endured
As April's green endures; or will endure
Like her remembrance of awakened birds,
Or her desire for June and evening, tipped
By the consummation of the swallow's wings.

IV

She says, "But in contentment I still feel
The need of some imperishable bliss."
Death is the mother of beauty; hence from her,
Alone, shall come fulfilment to our dreams
And our desires. Although she strews the leaves
Of sure obliteration on our paths—
The path sick sorrow took, the many paths
Where triumph rang its brassy phrase, or love
Whispered a little out of tenderness—
She makes the willow shiver in the sun
For maidens who were wont to sit and gaze
Upon the grass, relinquished to their feet.
She causes boys to bring sweet-smelling pears
And plums in ponderous piles. The maidens taste
And stray impassioned in the littering leaves.

V

Supple and turbulent, a ring of men
Shall chant in orgy on a summer morn
Their boisterous devotion to the sun—
Not as a god, but as a god might be,
Naked among them, like a savage source.
Their chant shall be a chant of paradise,
Out of their blood, returning to the sky;
And in their chant shall enter, voice by voice,

The windy lake wherein their lord delights,
The trees, like seraphim, and echoing hills,
That choir among themselves long afterward.
They shall know well the heavenly fellowship
Of men that perish and of summer morn—
And whence they came and whither they shall go,
The dew upon their feet shall manifest.

Le Monocle de Mon Oncle

I

"MOTHER of heaven, regina of the clouds,
O sceptre of the sun, crown of the moon,
There is not nothing, no, no, never nothing,
Like the clashed edges of two words that kill."
And so I mocked her in magnificent measure.
Or was it that I mocked myself alone?
I wish that I might be a thinking stone.
The sea of spuming thoughts foists up again
The radiant bubble that she was. And then
A deep up-pouring from some saltier well
Within me, bursts its watery syllable.

II

A red bird flies across the golden floor.
It is a red bird that seeks out his choir
Among the choirs of wind and wet and wing.
A torrent will fall from him when he finds.
Shall I uncrumple this much-crumpled thing?
I am a man of fortune greeting heirs;
For it has come that thus I greet the Spring.
These choirs of welcome choir for me farewell.
No Spring can follow past meridian.
Yet you persist with anecdotal bliss
To make believe a starry *connaissance.*

III

Is it for nothing, then, that old Chinese
Sat titivating by their mountain pools

Or in the Yangtse studied out their beards?
I shall not play the flat historic scale.
You know how Utamaro's beauties sought
The end of love in their all-speaking braids.
You know the mountainous coiffures of Bath.
Alas! Have all the barbers lived in vain
That not one curl in Nature has survived?
Why, without pity on these studious ghosts,
Do you come dripping in your hair from sleep?

IV

This luscious and impeccable fruit of life
Falls, it appears, of its own weight to earth.
When you were Eve, its acrid juice was sweet,
Untasted, in its heavenly, orchard air—
An apple serves as well as any skull
To be the book in which to read a round,
And is as excellent, in that it is composed
Of what, like skulls, comes rotting back to ground.
But it excels in this that as the fruit
Of love, it is a book too mad to read
Before one merely reads to pass the time.

V

In the high West there burns a furious star.
It is for fiery boys that star was set
And for sweet-smelling virgins close to them.
The measure of the intensity of love
Is measure, also, of the verve of earth.
For me, the firefly's quick, electric stroke
Ticks tediously the time of one more year.
And you? Remember how the crickets came
Out of their mother grass, like little kin . . .
In the pale nights, when your first imagery
Found inklings of your bond to all that dust.

VI

If men at forty will be painting lakes
The ephemeral blues must merge for them in one,
The basic slate, the universal hue.

There is a substance in us that prevails.
But in our amours amorists discern
Such fluctuations that their scrivening
Is breathless to attend each quirky turn.
When amorists grow bald, then amours shrink
Into the compass and curriculum
Of introspective exiles, lecturing.
It is a theme for Hyacinth alone.

VII

The mules that angels ride come slowly down
The blazing passes, from beyond the sun.
Descensions of their tinkling bells arrive.
These muleteers are dainty of their way.
Meantime centurions guffaw and beat
Their shrilling tankards on the table-boards.
This parable, in sense, amounts to this:
The honey of heaven may or may not come,
But that of earth both comes and goes at once.
Suppose these couriers brought amid their train
A damsel heightened by eternal bloom. . . .

VIII

Like a dull scholar, I behold, in love,
An ancient aspect touching a new mind.
It comes, it blooms, it bears its fruit and dies.
This trivial trope reveals a way of truth.
Our bloom is gone. We are the fruit thereof.
Two golden gourds distended on our vines,
We hang like warty squashes, streaked and rayed,
Into the Autumn weather, splashed with frost,
Distorted by hale fatness, turned grotesque.
The laughing sky will see the two of us
Washed into rinds by rotting winter rains.

IX

In verses wild with motion, full of din,
Loudened by cries, by clashes, quick and sure
As the deadly thought of men accomplishing
Their curious fates in war, come, celebrate

The faith of forty, ward of Cupido.
Most venerable heart, the lustiest conceit
Is not too lusty for your broadening.
I quiz all sounds, all thoughts, all everything
For the music and manner of the paladins
To make oblation fit. Where shall I find
Bravura adequate to this great hymn?

X

The fops of fancy in their poems leave
Memorabilia of the mystic sprouts,
Spontaneously watering their gritty soils.
I am a yeoman, as such fellows go.
I know no magic trees, no balmy boughs,
No silver-ruddy, gold-vermilion fruits.
But, after all, I know a tree that bears
A semblance to the thing I have in mind.
It stands gigantic, with a certain tip
To which all birds come sometime in their time.
But when they go that tip still tips the tree.

XI

If sex were all, then every trembling hand
Could make us speak, like dolls, the wished-for words.
But note the unconscionable treachery of fate,
That makes us weep, laugh, grunt and groan, and shout
Doleful heroics, pinching gestures forth
From madness or delight, without regard
To that first foremost law. Anguishing hour!
Last night, we sat beside a pool of pink,
Clippered with lilacs, scudding the bright chromes,
Keen to the point of starlight, while a frog
Boomed from his very belly, odious chords.

XII

A blue pigeon it is, that circles the blue sky,
On side-long wing, around and round and round.
A white pigeon it is, that flutters to the ground,
Grown tired of flight. Like a dark rabbi, I
Observed, when young, the nature of mankind,

In lordly study. Every day, I found
Man proved a gobbet in my mincing world.
Like a rose rabbi, later, I pursued,
And still pursue, the origin and course
Of love, but until now I never knew
That fluttering things have so distinct a shade

Tattoo

THE light is like a spider.
    It crawls over the water.
It crawls over the edges of the snow.
It crawls under your eyelids
And spreads its webs there—
Its two webs.

The webs of your eyes
Are fastened
To the flesh and bones of you
As to rafters or grass.

There are filaments of your eyes
On the surface of the water
And in the edges of the snow.

The Bird with the Coppery, Keen Claws

ABOVE the forest of the parakeets,
    A parakeet of parakeets prevails,
A pip of life amid a mort of tails.

(The rudiments of tropics are around,
Aloe of ivory, pear of rusty rind.)
His lids are white because his eyes are blind.

He is not paradise of parakeets,
Of his gold ether, golden alguazil.
Except because he broods there and is still

Panache upon panache, his tails deploy
Upward and outward, in green-vented forms,
His tip a drop of water full of storms.

But though the turbulent tinges undulate
As his pure intellect applies its laws,
He moves not on his coppery, keen claws.

He munches a dry shell while he exerts
His will, yet never ceases, perfect cock,
To flare, in the sun-pallor of his rock.

Of Heaven Considered as a Tomb

WHAT word have you, interpreters, of men
    Who in the tomb of heaven walk by night,
The darkened ghosts of our old comedy?
Do they believe they range the gusty cold,
With lanterns borne aloft to light the way,
Freemen of death, about and still about
To find whatever it is they seek? Or does
That burial, pillared up each day as porte
And spiritous passage into nothingness,
Foretell each night the one abysmal night,
When the host shall no more wander, nor the light
Of the steadfast lanterns creep across the dark?
Make hue among the dark comedians,
Halloo them in the topmost distances
For answer from their icy Elysée.

Of the Manner of Addressing Clouds

GLOOMY grammarians in golden gowns,
    Meekly you keep the mortal rendezvous,
Eliciting the still sustaining pomps
Of speech which are like music so profound
They seem an exaltation without sound.

Funest philosophers and ponderers,
Their evocations are the speèch of clouds.
So speech of your processionals returns
In the casual evocations of your tread
Across the stale, mysterious seasons. These
Are the music of meet resignation; these
The responsive, still sustaining pomps for you
To magnify, if in that drifting waste
You are to be accompanied by more
Than mute bare splendors of the sun and moon.

WITTER BYNNER

Spouse

NOW this Ophelia was a wiser woman,—
She wanted all his life and all his worth;
And yet she said, Since he is only human,
I can lie down upon my lonely earth.
I can allow him Tuesdays, if he chooses,
To stay away from me and let me nurse
My sentimental madnesses and bruises.
I have six days of him. It might be worse.
The others come, the others go, she said,
But I can madden only upon him.
So let me moan along the river-bed,
That he is absent from the river-brim
And weave these flowers in my hair for sorrow,
For this is Tuesday,—Wednesday is tomorrow.

Ghost

HE rises from his guests, abruptly leaves,
Because of memory that long moons ago
Others now dead had dined with him, and grieves
Because these newer persons he must know
Might not have loved his ghosts, his unknown dead.
There are new smiles, new answers to his quips;
But there are intervals when, having said
His dinner-table say, he hears dead lips . . .
The dead have ways of mingling in the uses
Of life they leave behind, the dead can rise
When dinner's done. But one of them refuses
To go away and gazes with dead eyes
Piercing him deeper than a rain can reach,
Leaving him only motion, only speech.

Correspondent

WORDS, words and words! What else, when men
are dead,
Their small lives ended and their sayings said,
Is left of them? Their children go to dust,
As also all their children's children must,
And their belongings are of paltry worth
Against the insatiable consuming earth . . .
I knew a man and almost had forgot
The wisdom of the letters that he wrote;
But words, if words are wise, go on and on
To make a longer note of unison
With man and man than living persons make
With one another for whatever sake.
Therefore I wept tonight when quick words rose
Out of a dead man's grave, whom no one knows.

Ganymede

WHEN love begins with Ganymede, he gathers
        All blossoms that a cloudy rain can bring
And, heedless of the warning of his fathers,
Folds in his arms the elements of spring.
This is a world that vernal things should count in,
There should be only happiness to know,—   :
A breath of wild-flowers carried from the mountain
And changed, along the waves, to falling snow.
Shade may be cool and comfortable for lovers;
But what great shadow darkening in the sky
Circles and distances, then nears and hovers
As though a vulturous bird of death were by? . . .
Ganymede feels the talon in his spine
Lift him Olympian to lustier wine.

Captain's Table

CASSANDRA, treading the Titanic deck,
        Her eye still proud, although the boat may sink,
What shall she do against the coming wreck
But wrap her pride within a cloak of mink?
She hears an ominous whisper in the sky
But hides with gaiety her guessing heart.
She is as willing as a ghost to die
But—willing still to play a social part—
Pretends to think that dinners are the Lord,
Though the last supper happen every day.
Others than she are travelling aboard,
But not inured, like her, to tragic play.
And so she sits at everybody's right
A female Oedipus with half his sight.

Charioteer

HERE is a woman whom a man can greet
Equal to equal, which is something said;
For seldom will a man forego conceit
And grant a woman room, till she is dead.
But here's a woman different: a young mind
In a body aging with no age at all.
She's like a living portrait whom you find
Some rainy night in your ancestral hall,
The spark within her eye aware and human . . .
Having Athena's mind, Achilles' heel,
She's mythological, this modern woman.
Torn from the chariot, a loosened wheel
Which kept the chariot upon its course,
She runs ahead, beyond the fallen horse.

ELINOR WYLIE

This Corruptible

THE Body, long oppressed
And pierced, then prayed for rest
(Being but apprenticed to the other Powers);
And kneeling in that place
Implored the thrust of grace
Which makes the dust lie level with the flowers.

Then did that fellowship
Of three, the Body strip;
Beheld his wounds, and none among them mortal;
The Mind severe and cool;
The Heart still half a fool;
The fine-spun Soul, a beam of sun can startle.

These three, a thousand years
Had made adventurers
Amid all villainies the earth can offer,
Applied them to resolve
From the universal gulph
What pangs the poor material flesh may suffer.

"This is a pretty pass;
To hear the growing grass
Complain; the clay cry out to be translated;
Will not this grosser stuff
Receive reward enough
If stabled after labouring, and baited?"

Thus spoke the Mind in scorn:
The Heart, which had outworn
The Body, and was weary of its fashion,
Preferring to be dressed
In skin of bird or beast,
Replied more softly, in a feigned compassion.

"Anatomy most strange
Crying to chop and change;
Inferior copy of a higher image;
While I, the noble guest,
Sick of your second-best
Sigh for embroidered archangelic plumage:

"For shame, thou fustian cloak!"
And then the Spirit spoke;
Within the void it swung securely tethered
By strings composed of cloud;
It spoke both low and loud
Above a storm no lesser star had weathered

"O lodging for the night!
O house of my delight!
O lovely hovel builded for my pleasure!
Dear tenement of clay
Endure another day
As coffin sweetly fitted to my measure.

"Take Heart, and call to Mind
  Although we are unkind;
  Although we steal your shelter, strength, and clothing;
'Tis you who shall escape
  In some enchanting shape
  Or be dissolved to elemental nothing.

"You, the unlucky slave,
  Are the lily on the grave;
  The wave that runs above the bones a-whitening;
You are the new-mown grass;
  And the wheaten bread of the Mass;
  And the fabric of the rain, and the lightning.

"If one of us elect
  To leave the poor suspect
  Imperfect bosom of the earth our parent;
And from the world avert
  The Spirit or the Heart
  Upon a further and essential errand;

"His chain he cannot slough
  Nor cast his substance off;
  He bears himself upon his flying shoulder;
The Heart, infirm and dull;
  The Mind, in any skull;
  Are captive still, and wearier and colder.

" 'Tis you who are the ghost,
  Disintegrated, lost;
  The burden shed; the dead who need not bear it;
O grain of God in power,
  Endure another hour!
  It is but for an hour," said the Spirit.

The Eagle and the Mole

AVOID the reeking herd,
  Shun the polluted flock,
Live like that stoic bird,
  The eagle of the rock.

The huddled warmth of crowds
Begets and fosters hate;
He keeps, above the clouds,
His cliff inviolate.

When flocks are folded warm,
And herds to shelter run,
He sails above the storm,
He stares into the sun.

If in the eagle's track
Your sinews cannot leap,
Avoid the lathered pack,
Turn from the steaming sheep.

If you would keep your soul
From spotted sight or sound,
Live like the velvet mole;
Go burrow under ground.

And there hold intercourse
With roots of trees and stones,
With rivers at their source,
And disembodied bones.

Escape

WHEN foxes eat the last gold grape,
And the last white antelope is killed,
I shall stop fighting and escape
Into a little house I'll build.

But first I'll shrink to fairy size,
With a whisper no one understands,
Making blind moons of all your eyes,
And muddy roads of all your hands.

And you may grope for me in vain
In hollows under the mangrove root,
Or where, in apple-scented rain,
The silver wasp-nests hang like fruit.

Confession of Faith

I LACK the braver mind
   That dares to find
The lover friend, and kind.

I fear him to the bone;
I lie alone
By the beloved one,

And, breathless for suspense,
Erect defense
Against love's violence

Whose silences portend
A bloody end
For lover never friend.

But, in default of faith,
In futile breath,
I dream no ill of Death.

Address to My Soul

MY soul, be not disturbed
   By planetary war;
Remain securely orbed
In this contracted star.

Fear not, pathetic flame;
Your sustenance is doubt:
Glassed in translucent dream
They cannot snuff you out.

Wear water, or a mask
Of unapparent cloud;
Be brave and never ask
A more defunctive shroud.

The universal points
Are shrunk into a flower;
Between its delicate joints
Chaos keeps no power.

The pure integral form,
Austere and silver-dark,
Is balanced on the storm
In its predestined arc.

Small as a sphere of rain
It slides along the groove
Whose path is furrowed plain
Among the suns that move.

The shapes of April buds
Outlive the phantom year:
Upon the void at odds
The dewdrop falls severe.

Five-petalled flame, be cold:
Be firm, dissolving star;
Accept the stricter mould
That makes you singular.

True Vine

THERE is a serpent in perfection tarnished
The thin shell pierced, the purity grown fainter,
The virgin silver shield no longer burnished,
The pearly fruit with ruin at its centre.

The thing that sits expectant in our bosoms
Contriving heaven out of very little
Demands such delicate immaculate blossoms
As no malicious verity makes brittle.

This wild fastidious hope is quick to languish;
Its smooth diaphanous escape is swifter

Than the pack of truth; no mortal can distinguish
Its trace upon the durable hereafter.

Not so the obdurate and savage lovely
Whose roots are set profoundly upon trouble;
This flower grows so fiercely and so bravely
It does not even know that it is noble.

This is the vine to love, whose balsams flourish
Upon a living soil corrupt and faulty,
Whose leaves have drunk the skies, and stooped to nourish
The earth again with honey sweet and salty.

EZRA POUND

Envoi (1919)

G O, dumb-born book,
   Tell her that sang me once that song of Lawes:
Hadst thou but song
As thou hast subjects known,
Then were there cause in thee that should condone
Even my faults that heavy upon me lie,
And build her glories their longevity.

Tell her that sheds
Such treasure in the air,
Recking naught else but that her graces give
Life to the moment,
I would bid them live
As roses might, in magic amber laid,
Red overwrought with orange and all made
One substance and one colour
Braving time.

Tell her that goes
With song upon her lips
But sings not out the song, nor knows
The maker of it, some other mouth,
May be as fair as hers,
Might, in new ages, gain her worshippers,
When our two dusts with Waller's shall be laid,
Siftings on siftings in oblivion,
Till change hath broken down
All things save Beauty alone.

The Tree

I STOOD still and was a tree amid the wood,
Knowing the truth of things unseen before:
Of Daphne and the laurel bough
And that god-feasting couple old
That grew elm-oak amid the wold.
'Twas not until the gods had been
Kindly entreated, and been brought within
Unto the hearth of their heart's home
That they might do this wonder thing;
Nathless I have been a tree amid the wood
And many a new thing understood
That was rank folly to my head before.

The Tomb at Aƙr Çaar

"I AM thy soul, Nikoptis. I have watched
These five millennia, and thy dead eyes
Moved not, nor ever answer my desire,
And thy light limbs, wherethrough I leapt aflame,
Burn not with me nor any saffron thing.
See, the light grass sprang up to pillow thee,
And kissed thee with a myriad grassy tongues;
But not thou me.
I have read out the gold upon the wall,

And wearied out my thought upon the signs.
And there is no new thing in all this place.

I have been kind. See, I have left the jars sealed,
Lest thou shouldst wake and whimper for thy wine.
And all thy robes I have kept smooth on thee.

O thou unmindful! How should I forget!
—Even the river many days ago,
The river? thou wast over young.
And three souls came upon Thee—
And I came.
And I flowed in upon thee, beat them off;
I have been intimate with thee, known thy ways.
Have I not touched thy palms and finger-tips,
Flowed in, and through thee and about thy heels?
How 'came I in'? Was I not thee and Thee?

And no sun comes to rest me in this place,
And I am torn against the jagged dark,
And no light beats upon me, and you say
No word, day after day.

Oh! I could get me out, despite the marks
And all their crafty work upon the door,
Out through the glass-green fields. . . .

Yet it is quiet here:

I do not go."

Portrait d'une Femme

YOUR mind and you are our Sargasso Sea,
London has swept about you this score years
And bright ships left you this or that in fee:
Ideas, old gossip, oddments of all things,
Strange spars of knowledge and dimmed wares of price.
Great minds have sought you—lacking someone else.

You have been second always. Tragical?
No. You preferred it to the usual thing:
One dull man, dulling and uxorious,
One average mind—with one thought less, each year.
Oh, you are patient, I have seen you sit
Hours, where something might have floated up.
And now you pay one. Yes, you richly pay.
You are a person of some interest, one comes to you
And takes strange gain away:
Trophies fished up; some curious suggestion;
Fact that leads nowhere; and a tale or two,
Pregnant with mandrakes, or with something else
That might prove useful and yet never proves,
That never fits a corner or shows use,
Or finds its hour upon the loom of days:
The tarnished, gaudy, wonderful old work;
Idols and ambergris and rare inlays,
These are your riches, your great store; and yet
For all this sea-hoard of deciduous things,
Strange woods half sodden, and new brighter stuff:
In the slow float of differing light and deep,
No! there is nothing! In the whole and all,
Nothing that's quite your own.
                    Yet this is you.

Apparuit

GOLDEN rose the house, in the portal I saw
thee, a marvel, carven in subtle stuff, a
portent. Life died down in the lamp and flickered,
    caught at the wonder.

Crimson, frosty with dew, the roses bend where
thou afar, moving in the glamorous sun,
drinkst in life of earth, of the air, the tissue
    golden about thee.

Green the ways, the breath of the fields is thine there,
open lies the land, yet the steely going
darkly hast thou dared and the dreaded æther
    parted before thee.

Swift at courage thou in the shell of gold, cast-
ing a-loose the cloak of the body, camest
straight, then shone thine oriel and the stunned light
    faded about thee.

Half the graven shoulder, the throat aflash with
strands of light inwoven about it, loveli-
est of all things, frail alabaster, ah me!
    swift in departing.

Clothed in goldish weft, delicately perfect,
gone as wind! The cloth of the magical hands:
Thou a slight thing, thou in access of cunning
    dar'dst to assume this?

A Virginal

NO, no! Go from me. I have left her lately.
    I will not spoil my sheath with lesser brightness.
For my surrounding air hath a new lightness;
Slight are her arms, yet they have bound me straitly
And left me cloaked as with a gauze of æther;
As with sweet leaves; as with subtle clearness.
Oh, I have picked up magic in her nearness
To sheathe me half in half the things that sheathe her.
No, no! Go from me. I have still the flavour,
Soft as spring wind that's come from birchen bowers.
Green come the shoots, aye April in the branches,
As winter's wound with her sleight hand she staunches,
Hath of the trees a likeness of the savour:
As white their bark, so white this lady's hours.

The Return

SEE, they return; ah, see the tentative
Movements, and the slow feet,
The trouble in the pace and the uncertain
Wavering!

See, they return, one, and by one,
With fear, as half-awakened;
As if the snow should hesitate
And murmur in the wind,
            and half turned back;
These were the "Wing'd-with-Awe,"
            Inviolable.

Gods of the wingèd shoe!
With them the silver hounds,
            sniffing the trace of air!

Haie! Haie!
      These were the swift to harry;
These the keen-scented;
These were the souls of blood.

Slow on the leash,
            pallid the leash-men!

The River-Merchant's Wife:
A Letter

WHILE my hair was still cut straight across my forehead
I played about the front gate, pulling flowers.
You came by on bamboo stilts, playing horse,
You walked about my seat, playing with blue plums.
And we went on living in the village of Chokan:
Two small people, without dislike or suspicion.

At fourteen I married My Lord you.
I never laughed, being bashful.
Lowering my head, I looked at the wall.
Called to, a thousand times, I never looked back.

At fifteen I stopped scowling,
I desired my dust to be mingled with yours
Forever and forever and forever.
Why should I climb the look out?

At sixteen you departed,
You went into far Ku-to-yen, by the river of swirling eddies,
And you have been gone five months.
The monkeys make sorrowful noise overhead.

You dragged your feet when you went out.
By the gate now, the moss is grown, the different mosses,
Too deep to clear them away!
The leaves fall early this autumn, in wind.
The paired butterflies are already yellow with August
Over the grass in the West garden;
They hurt me. I grow older.
If you are coming down through the narrows of the river Kiang,
Please let me know beforehand,
And I will come out to meet you
                    As far as Cho-fu-Sa.

                                                Rihaku

The Flame

T IS not a game that plays at mates and mating,
     Provençe knew;
'Tis not a game of barter, lands and houses,
Provençe knew.
We who are wise beyond your dream of wisdom,
Drink our immortal moments; we "pass through."
We have gone forth beyond your bonds and borders,
Provençe knew;
And all the tales of Oisin say but this:

That man doth pass the net of days and hours.
Where time is shrivelled down to time's seed corn
We of the Ever-living, in that light
Meet through our veils and whisper, and of love.

O smoke and shadow of a darkling world,
These, and the rest, and all the rest we knew.

'Tis not a game that plays at mates and mating,
'Tis not a game of barter, lands and houses,
'Tis not "of days and nights" and troubling years,
Of cheeks grown sunken and glad hair gone gray
There *is* the subtler music, the clear light
Where time burns back about the eternal ember.
We are not shut from all the thousand heavens:
Lo, there are many gods whom we have seen,
Folk of unearthly fashion, places splendid,
Bulwarks of beryl and of chrysoprase.

Sapphire Benacus, in thy mists and thee
Nature herself's turned metaphysical,
Who can look on that blue and not believe?

Thou hooded opal, thou eternal pearl,
O thou dark secret with a shimmering floor,
Through all thy various mood I know thee mine;
If I have merged my soul, or utterly
Am solved and bound in, through aught here on earth,
There canst thou find me, O thou anxious thou,
Who call'st about my gates for some lost me;
I say my soul flowed back, became translucent.
Search not my lips, O Love, let go my hands,
This thing that moves as man is no more mortal.
If thou hast seen my shade sans character,
If thou hast seen that mirror of all moments,
That glass to all things that o'ershadow it,
Call not that mirror me, for I have slipped
Your grasp, I have eluded.

Dance Figure

FOR THE MARRIAGE IN CANA OF GALILEE

DARK eyed,
 O woman of my dreams,
Ivory sandaled,
There is none like thee among the dancers,
None with swift feet.

I have not found thee in the tents,
In the broken darkness.
I have not found thee at the well-head
Among the women with pitchers.

Thine arms are as a young sapling under the bark;
Thy face as a river with lights.

White as an almond are thy shoulders;
As new almonds stripped from the husk.
They guard thee not with eunuchs;
Not with bars of copper.

Gilt turquoise and silver are in the place of thy rest.
A brown robe, with threads of gold woven in patterns
        hast thou gathered about thee,
O Nathat-Ikanaie, "Tree-at-the-river."

As a rillet among the sedge are thy hands upon me;
Thy fingers a frosted stream.

Thy maidens are white like pebbles;
Their music about thee!

There is none like thee among the dancers;
None with swift feet.

Lament of the Frontier Guard

BY the North Gate, the wind blows full of sand,
Lonely from the beginning of time until now!
Trees fall, the grass goes yellow with autumn.
I climb the towers and towers
      to watch out the barbarous land:
Desolate castle, the sky, the wide desert.
There is no wall left to this village.
Bones white with a thousand frosts,
High heaps, covered with trees and grass;
Who brought this to pass?
Who has brought the flaming imperial anger?
Who has brought the army with drums and with
      kettle-drums?
Barbarous kings.
A gracious spring, turned to blood-ravenous autumn,
A turmoil of wars-men, spread over the middle kingdom,
Three hundred and sixty thousand,
And sorrow, sorrow like rain.
Sorrow to go, and sorrow, sorrow returning.
Desolate, desolate fields,
And no children of warfare upon them,
      No longer the men for offence and defence.
Ah, how shall you know the dreary sorrow at the
      North Gate,
With Rihaku's name forgotten,
And we guardsmen fed to the tigers.

Rihaku

Taking Leave of a Friend

BLUE mountains to the north of the walls,
White river winding about them;
Here we must make separation
And go out through a thousand miles of dead grass.

Mind like a floating wide cloud,
Sunset like the parting of old acquaintances
Who bow over their clasped hands at a distance.
Our horses neigh to each other
    as we are departing.

           Rihaku

———— •••• ————

ALFRED KREYMBORG

———— •••• ————

Nun Snow

A Pantomime of Beads

Earth Voice

  IS she
  Thoughtless of life,
A lover of imminent death,
Nun Snow
Touching her strings of white beads?
Is it her unseen hands
Which urge the beads to tremble?
Does Nun Snow,
Aware of the death she must die alone,
Away from the nuns
Of the green beads,
Of the ochre and brown,
Of the purple and black—
Does she improvise
Along those soundless strings
In the worldly hope
That the answering, friendly tune,
The faithful, folk-like miracle,
Will shine in a moment or two?

Moon Voice

> Or peradventure,
> Are the beads merely wayward,
> On an evening so soft,
> And One Wind
> Is so gentle a mesmerist
> As he draws them and her with his hand?

Earth Voice

> Was it Full Moon,
> Who contrives tales of this order,
> And himself loves the heroine,
> Nun Snow—

Wind Voice

> Do you see his beads courting hers? —
> Lascivious monk! —

Earth Voice

> Was it Full Moon,
> Slyly innocent of guile,
> Propounder of sorrowless whimseys,
> Who breathed that suspicion?
> Is it One Wind,
> The wily, scholarly pedant—
> Is it he who retorts—

Wind Voice

> Like olden allegros
> In olden sonatas,
> All tales have two themes,
> *She is beautiful,*
> *He is beautiful,*
> With the traditional movement,
> *Their beads court each other,*
> Revealing a cadence as fatally true
> As the sum which follows a one-plus-one—
> So, why inquire further?
> Nay, inquire further,

Deduce it your fashion!
Nun Snow,
As you say,
Touches her strings of white beads,
Full Moon,
Let you add,
His lute of yellow strings;
And, our Night
Is square, nay,
Our Night
Is round, nay
Our Night
Is a blue balcony—
And therewith close your inquisition!

Earth Voice

Who urged the beads to tremble?
They're still now!
Fallen, or cast over me!
Nun, Moon, and Wind are gone!
Are they betraying her?—

Moon Voice

Ask our Night—

Earth Voice

Did the miracle appear?—

Moon Voice

Ask our Night,
Merely a child on a balcony,
Letting down her hair and
Black beads, a glissando—
Ask her what she means,
Dropping the curtain so soon!

JOHN GOULD FLETCHER

Irradiations

I

THE spattering of the rain upon pale terraces
   Of afternoon is like the passing of a dream
Amid the roses shuddering 'gainst the wet green stalks
Of the streaming trees—the passing of the wind
Upon the pale lower terraces of my dream
Is like the crinkling of the wet grey robes
Of the hours that come to turn over the urn
Of the day and spill its rainy dream.
Vague movement over the puddled terraces:
Heavy gold pennons—a pomp of solemn gardens
Half hidden under the liquid veil of spring:
Far trumpets like a vague rout of faded roses
Burst 'gainst the wet green silence of distant forests:
A clash of cymbals—then the swift swaying footsteps
Of the wind that undulates along the languid terraces.
Pools of rain—the vacant terraces
Wet, chill and glistening
Towards the sunset beyond the broken doors of to-day.

II

The iridescent vibrations of midsummer light
Dancing, dancing, suddenly flickering and quivering
Like little feet or the movement of quick hands clapping,
Or the rustle of furbelows or the clash of polished gems.
The palpitant mosaic of the midday light
Colliding, sliding, leaping and lingering:
O, I could lie on my back all day,
And mark the mad ballet of the midsummer sky.

III

Over the roof-tops race the shadows of clouds;
Like horses the shadows of clouds charge down the street.

Whirlpools of purple and gold,
Winds from the mountains of cinnabar,
Lacquered mandarin moments, palanquins swaying and bal
    ancing
Amid the vermilion pavilions, against the jade balustrades.
Glint of the glittering wings of dragon-flies in the light:
Silver filaments, golden flakes settling downwards,
Rippling, quivering flutters, repulse and surrender,
The sun broidered upon the rain,
The rain rustling with the sun.

Over the roof-tops race the shadows of clouds;
Like horses the shadows of clouds charge down the street.

IV

The balancing of gaudy broad pavilions
Of summer against the insolent breeze:
The bellying of the sides of striped tents,
Swelling taut, shuddering in quick collapse,
Silent under the silence of the sky.

Earth is streaked and spotted
With great splashes and dapples of sunlight:
The sun throws an immense circle of hot light upon the world,
Rolling slowly in ponderous rhythm
Darkly, musically forward.
All is silent under the steep cone of afternoon:
The sky is imperturbably profound.
The ultimate divine union seems about to be accomplished,
All is troubled at the attainment
Of the inexhaustible infinite.

The rolling and the tossing of the sides of immense pavilions
Under the whirling wind that screams up the cloudless sky.

V

Flickering of incessant rain
On flashing pavements:
Sudden scurry of umbrellas:
Bending, recurved blossoms of the storm.

The winds came clanging and clattering
From long white highroads whipping in ribbons up summits:
They strew upon the city gusty wafts of apple-blossom,
And the rustling of innumerable translucent leaves.
Uneven tinkling, the lazy rain
Dripping from the eaves.

VI

The fountain blows its breathless spray
From me to you and back to me.

Whipped, tossed, curdled,
Crashing, quivering:
I hurl kisses like blows upon your lips.
The dance of a bee drunken with sunlight:
Irradiant ecstasies, white and gold,
Sigh and relapse.

The fountain tosses pallid spray
Far in the sorrowful, silent sky.

Green Symphony

I

THE glittering leaves of the rhododendrons
Balance and vibrate in the cool air;
While in the sky above them
White clouds chase each other.

Like scampering rabbits,
Flashes of sunlight sweep the lawn;

They fling in passing
Patterns of shadow,
Golden and green.

With long cascades of laughter,
The mating birds dart and swoop to the turf:
'Mid their mad trillings
Glints the gay sun behind the trees.

Down there are deep blue lakes:
Orange blossom droops in the water.
In the tower of the winds,
All the bells are set adrift:
Jingling
For the dawn.

Thin fluttering streamers
Of breeze lash through the swaying boughs,
Palely expectant
The earth receives the slanting rain.

I am a glittering raindrop
Hugged close by the cool rhododendron.
I am a daisy starring
The exquisite curves of the close-cropped turf.

The glittering leaves of the rhododendron
Are shaken like blue-green blades of grass,
Flickering, cracking, falling:
Splintering in a million fragments.
The wind runs laughing up the slope
Stripping off handfuls of wet green leaves,
To fling in peoples' faces.
Wallowing on the daisy-powdered turf,
Clutching at the sunlight,
Cavorting in the shadow.

Like baroque pearls,
Like cloudy emeralds,
The clouds and the trees clash together;

Whirling and swirling,
In the tumult
Of the spring,
And the wind.

II

The trees splash the sky with their fingers,
A restless green rout of stars.

With whirling movement
They swing their boughs
About their stems:
Planes on planes of light and shadow
Pass among them,
Opening fan-like to fall.

The trees are like a sea;
Tossing,
Trembling,
Roaring,
Wallowing,
Darting their long green flickering fronds up at the sky,
Spotted with white blossom-spray.

The trees are roofs:
Hollow caverns of cool blue shadow,
Solemn arches
In the afternoons.
The whole vast horizon
In terrace beyond terrace,
Pinnacle above pinnacle,
Lifts to the sky
Serrated ranks of green on green.

They caress the roofs with their fingers,
They sprawl about the river to look into it;
Up the hill they come
Gesticulating challenge:
They cower together
In dark valleys;
They yearn out over the fields.

Enamelled domes
Tumble upon the grass,
Crashing in ruin
Quiet at last.

The trees lash the sky with their leaves,
Uneasily shaking their dark green manes.

III

Far let the voices of the mad wild birds be calling me,
I will abide in this forest of pines.

When the wind blows
Battling through the forest,
I hear it distantly,
The crash of a perpetual sea.

When the rain falls,
I watch silver spears slanting downwards
From pale river-pools of sky,
Enclosed in dark fronds.

When the sun shines,
I weave together distant branches till they enclose
    mighty circles,
I sway to the movement of hooded summits,
I swim leisurely in deep blue seas of air.

I hug the smooth bark of stately red pillars
And with cones carefully scattered
I mark the progression of dark dial-shadows
Flung diagonally downwards through the afternoon.

This turf is not like turf:
It is a smooth dry carpet of velvet,
Embroidered with brown patterns of needles and cones
These trees are not like trees:
They are innumerable feathery pagoda-umbrellas,
Stiffly ungracious to the wind,
Teetering on red-lacquered stems.

In the evening I listen to the winds' lisping,
While the conflagrations of the sunset flicker and clash
    behind me,
Flamboyant crenellations of glory amid the charred
    ebony boles.

In the night the fiery nightingales
Shall clash and trill through the silence:
Like the voices of mermaids crying
From the sea.

Long ago has the moon whelmed this uncompleted
    temple.
Stars swim like gold fish far above the black arches.

Far let the timid feet of dawn fly to catch me:
I will abide in this forest of pines:
For I have unveiled naked beauty,
And the things that she whispered to me in the
    darkness,
Are buried deep in my heart.

Now let the black tops of the pine-trees break like a
    spent wave,
Against the grey sky:
These are tombs and memorials and temples and altars
    sun-kindled for me.

White Symphony

I

FORLORN and white,
    Whorls of purity about a golden chalice,
Immense the peonies
Flare and shatter their petals over my face.

They slowly turn paler,
They seem to be melting like blue-grey flakes of ice,

Thin greyish shivers
Fluctuating 'mid the dark green lance-thrust of the
    leaves.

Like snowballs tossed,
Like soft white butterflies,
The peonies poise in the twilight.
And their narcotic insinuating perfume
Draws me into them
Shivering with the coolness,
Aching with the void.
They kiss the blue chalice of my dreams
Like a gesture seen for an instant and then lost forever.

.   .

Outwards the petals
Thrust to embrace me,
Pale daggers of coldness
Run through my aching breast.

Outwards, still outwards,
Till on the brink of twilight
They swirl downwards silently,
Flurry of snow in the void.

Outwards, still outwards,
Till the blue walls are hidden,
And in the blinding white radiance
Of a whirlpool of clouds, I awake.

.   ,

Like spraying rockets
My peonies shower
Their glories on the night.
Wavering perfumes,
Drift about the garden;
Shadows of the moonlight,
Drift and ripple over the dew-gemmed leaves.

Soar, crash, and sparkle,
Shoa of stars drifting
Like silver fishes,
Through the black sluggish boughs.
Towards the impossible,
Towards the inaccessible,
Towards the ultimate,
Towards the silence,
Towards the eternal,
These blossoms go.

The peonies spring like rockets in the twilight,
And out of them all I rise.

II

Downwards through the blue abyss it slides,
The white snow-water of my dreams,
Downwards crashing from slippery rock
Into the boiling chasm:
In which no eye dare look, for it is the chasm of death.
Upwards from the blue abyss it rises,
The chill water-mist of my dreams;
Upwards to greyish weeping pines,
And to skies of autumn ever about my heart,
It is blue at the beginning,
And blue-white against the grey-greenness;
It wavers in the upper air,
Catching unconscious sparkles, a rainbow-glint of
    sunlight,
And fading in the sad depths of the sky.

Outwards rush the strong pale clouds,
Outwards and ever outwards;
The blue-grey clouds indistinguishable one from
    another:
Nervous, sinewy, tossing their arms and brandishing,
Till on the blue serrations of the horizon
They drench with their black rain a great peak of
    changeless snow.

As evening came on, I climbed the tower,
To gaze upon the city far beneath:
I was not weary of day; but in the evening
A white mist assembled and gathered over the earth
And blotted it from sight.
But to escape:
To chase with the golden clouds galloping over the
    horizon:
Arrows of the northwest wind
Singing amid them,
Ruffling up my hair!

As evening came on the distance altered,
Pale wavering reflections rose from out the city,
Like sighs of the beckoning of half-invisible hands.
Monotonously and sluggishly they crept upwards
A river that had spent itself in some chasm,
And dwindled and foamed at last at my weary feet.

Autumn! Golden fountains,
And the winds neighing
Amid the monotonous hills:
Desolation of the old gods,
Rain that lifts and rain that moves away;
In the green-black torrent
Scarlet leaves.

It was now perfectly evening:
And the tower loomed like a gaunt peak in mid-air
Above the city: its base was utterly lost.
It was slowly coming on to rain,
And the immense columns of white mist
Wavered and broke before the faint-hurled spears.

I will descend the mountains like a shepherd,
And in the folds of tumultuous misty cities,
I will put all my thoughts, all my old thoughts, safely
    to sleep.
For it is already autumn,
O whiteness of the pale southwestern sky!
O wavering dream that was not mine to keep!

In midnight, in mournful moonlight,
By paths I could not trace,
I walked in the white garden,
Each flower had a white face.

Their perfume intoxicated me: thus I began my dream.

I was alone; I had no one to guide me,
But the moon was like the sun:
It stooped and kissed each waxen petal,
One after one.
Green and white was that garden: diamond rain hung
    in the branches,
You will not believe it!

In the morning, at the dayspring,
I wakened, shivering; lo,
The white garden that blossomed at my feet
Was a garden hidden in snow.

It was my sorrow to see that all this was a dream.

III

Blue, clogged with purple,
Mists uncoil themselves:
Sparkling to the horizon,
I see the snow alone.

In the deep blue chasm,
Boats sleep under gold thatch;
Icicle-like trees fret
Faintly rose-touched sky.

Under their heaped snow-eaves,
Leaden houses shiver.
Through thin blue crevasses,
Trickles an icy stream.

The pines groan white-laden,
The waves shiver, struck by the wind;

Beyond from treeless horizons,
Broken snow-peaks crawl to the sea.

    .

  .   .

Wearily the snow glares,
Through the grey silence, day after day,
Mocking the colourless cloudless sky
With the reflection of death.

There is no smoke through the pine tops,
No strong red boatmen in pale green reeds
No herons to flicker an instant,
No lanterns to glow with gay ray.

No sails beat up to the harbour,
With creaking cordage and sailors' song.
Somnolent, bare-poled, indifferent,
They sleep, and the city sleeps.

Mid-winter about them casts
Its dreary fortifications:
Each day is a gaunt grey rock,
And death is the last of them all.

    .

  .   .

Over the sluggish snow,
Drifts now a pallid weak shower of bloom:
Boredom of fresh creation,
Death-weariness of old returns.

White, white blossom,
Fall of the shattered cups day on day:
Is there anything here that is not ancient,
That has not bloomed a thousand years ago?

Under the glare of the white-hot day,
Under the restless wind-rakes of the winter,
White blossom or white snow scattered,
And beneath them, dark, the graves.

Dark graves never changing,
White dream, drifting, never changing above them:
O that the white scroll of heaven might be rolled up,
And the naked red lightning thrust at the smouldering
    earth!

———•——•———

H. D.

———•——•———

At Baia

I SHOULD have thought
In a dream you would have brought
Some lovely perilous thing,
Orchids piled in a great sheath,
As who would say (in a dream)
I send you this,
Who left the blue veins
Of your throat unkissed.
Why was it that your hands
(That never took mine)
Your hands that I could see
Drift over the orchid heads
So carefully,
Your hands, so fragile, sure to lift
So gently, the fragile flower stuff—
Ah, ah, how was it

You never sent (in a dream)
The very form, the very scent,
Not heavy, not sensuous.
But perilous—perilous—
Of orchids, piled in a great sheath,
And folded underneath on a bright scroll
Some word:

Flower sent to flower;
For white hands, the lesser white,
Less lovely of flower leaf,

Or

Lover to lover, no kiss,
No touch, but forever and ever this.

"Not Honey"

NOT honey,
  Not the plunder of the bee
From meadow or sand-flower
Or mountain bush;
From winter-flower or shoot
Born of the later heat:
Not honey, not the sweet
Stain on the lips and teeth:
Not honey, not the deep
Plunge of soft belly
And the clinging of the gold-edged
Pollen-dusted feet.

Not so—
Though rapture blind my eyes,
And hunger crisp
Dark and inert my mouth,
Not honey, not the south,
Not the tall stalk
Of red twin-lilies,
Nor light branch of fruit tree
Caught in flexible light branch.

Not honey, not the south;
Ah, flower of purple iris,
Flower of white,
Or of the iris, withering the grass—
For fleck of the sun's fire,

Gathers such heat and power,
That shadow-print is light,
Cast through the petals
Of the yellow iris flower.

Not iris—old desire—old passion—
Old forgetfulness—old pain—
Not this, nor any flower,
But if you turn again,
Seek strength of arm and throat,
Touch as the god:
Neglect the lyre-note;
Knowing that you shall feel,
About the frame,
No trembling of the string
But heat more passionate
Of bone and the white shell
And fiery tempered steel.

Song

YOU are as gold
As the half-ripe grain
That merges to gold again,
As white as the white rain
That beats through
The half-opened flowers
Of the great flower tufts
Thick on the black limbs
Of an Illyrian apple bough.

Can honey distil such fragrance
As your bright hair—
For your face is as fair as rain,
Yet as rain that lies clear
On white honey-comb,
Lends radiance to the white wax,
So your hair on your brow
Casts light for a shadow.

The Garden

I

YOU are clear,
O rose, cut in rock.

I could scrape the colour
From the petals,
Like spilt dye from a rock.

If I could break you
I could break a tree.

If I could stir
I could break a tree,
I could break you.

II

O wind, rend open the heat,
Cut apart the heat,
Slit it to tatters.

Fruit cannot drop
Through this thick air;
Fruit cannot fall into heat
That presses up and blunts
The points of pears,
And rounds grapes.

Cut the heat:
Plough through it,
Turning it on either side
Of your path.

Orchard

I SAW the first pear
as it fell—
the honey-seeking, golden banded,
the yellow swarm,
was not more fleet than I,
(spare us from loveliness!)
and I fell prostrate,
crying:
you have flayed us with your blossoms,
spare us the beauty
of fruit-trees!

The honey-seeking
paused not;
the air thundered their song,
and I alone was prostrate.

O rough-hewn
god of the orchard,
I bring you an offering—
do you, alone unbeautiful,
son of the god,
spare us from loveliness:
these fallen hazel-nuts,
stripped late of their green sheaths,
grapes, red-purple,
their berries
dripping with wine;
pomegranates already broken,
and shrunken figs,
and quinces untouched,
I bring you as offering.

LOUIS UNTERMEYER

Long Feud

WHERE, without bloodshed, can there be
     A more relentless enmity
Than the long feud fought silently

Between man and the growing grass?
Man's the aggressor, for he has
Weapons to humble and harass

The impudent spears that charge upon
His sacred privacy of lawn,
He mows them down, and they are gone

Only to lie in wait, although
He builds above and digs below
Where never a root would dare to go.

His are the triumphs till the day
There's no more grass to cut away,
And, tired of labor, tired of play,

Having exhausted every whim,
He stretches out each conquering limb.
And then the small grass covers him.

JOHN HALL WHEELOCK

Earth

GRASSHOPPER, your fairy song
And my poem alike belong
To the dark and silent earth
From which all poetry has birth;
All we say and all we sing
Is but as the murmuring
Of that drowsy heart of hers
When from her deep dream she stirs:
If we sorrow, or rejoice,
You and I are but her voice.

Deftly does the dust express
In mind her hidden loveliness,
And from her cool silence stream
The cricket's cry and Dante's dream;
For the earth that breeds the trees
Breeds cities too, and symphonies.

Equally her beauty flows
Into a savior, or a rose—
Looks down in dream, and from above
Smiles at herself in Jesus' love.
Christ's love and Homer's art
Are but the workings of her heart;
Through Leonardo's hand she seeks
Herself, and through Beethoven speaks
In holy thunderings around
The awful message of the ground.

The serene and humble mold
Does in herself all selves enfold—

Kingdoms, destinies, and creeds,
Great dreams, and dauntless deeds,
Science that metes the firmament,
The high, inflexible intent
Of one for many sacrificed—
Plato's brain, the heart of Christ;
All love, all legend, and all lore
Are in the dust forevermore.

Even as the growing grass,
Up from the soil religions pass,
And the field that bears the rye
Bears parables and prophecy.
Out of the earth the poem grows
Like the lily, or the rose;
And all man is, or yet may be,
Is but herself in agony
Toiling up the steep ascent
Toward the complete accomplishment
When all dust shall be, the whole
Universe, one conscious soul.

Yea, the quiet and cool sod
Bears in her breast the dream of God.
If you would know what earth is, scan
The intricate, proud heart of man,
Which is the earth articulate,
And learn how holy and how great,
How limitless and how profound
Is the nature of the ground—
How without terror or demur
We may entrust ourselves to her
When we are wearied out and lay
Our faces in the common clay.

For she is pity, she is love,
All wisdom, she, all thoughts that move
About her everlasting breast
Till she gathers them to rest:
All tenderness of all the ages,
Seraphic secrets of the sages,

Vision and hope of all the seers,
All prayer, all anguish, and all tears
Are but the dust that from her dream
Awakes, and knows herself supreme—
Are but earth, when she reveals
All that her secret heart conceals
Down in the dark and silent loam,
Which is ourselves, asleep, at home.

Yea, and this, my poem, too,
Is part of her as dust and dew,
Wherein herself she doth declare
Through my lips, and say her prayer.

CALE YOUNG RICE

Chanson of the Bells of Oseney

THIRTEENTH CENTURY

THE bells of Osenèy
    (Hautclère, Doucement, Austyn)
Chant sweetly every day,
And sadly, for our sin.
The bells of Osenèy
(John, Gabriel, Marie)
Chant lowly,
        Chant slowly,
Chant wistfully and holy
Of Christ, our Paladin.

Hautclère chants to the East
(His tongue is silvery high),
And Austyn like a priest
Sends west a weighty cry.
But Doucement set between
(Like an appeasive nun)

Chants cheerly,
        Chants clearly,
As if Christ heard her nearly,
A plea to every sky.

A plea that John takes up
(He is the evangelist)
Till Gabriel's angel cup
Pours sound to sun or mist.
And last of all Marie
(The virgin-voice of God)
Peals purely,
        Demurely,
And with a tone so surely
Divine, that all must hear.

The bells of Osenèy
(Doucement, Austyn, Hautclère)
Pour ever day by day
Their peals on the rapt air;
And with their mellow mates
(John, Gabriel, Marie)
Tell slowly,
        Tell lowly,
Of Christ the High and Holy,
Who makes the whole world fair.

MARIANNE MOORE

The Fish

WADE
        through black jade
Of the crow-blue mussel shells, one
        keeps
        adjusting the ash heaps;
opening and shutting itself like

an
injured fan.
  The barnacles which encrust the
   side
    of the wave, cannot hide
  there for the submerged shafts of the

sun,
split like spun
  glass, move themselves with spotlight
   swiftness
    into the crevices—
  in and out, illuminating

the
turquoise sea
  of bodies. The water drives a
   wedge
    of iron through the iron edge
  of the cliff, whereupon the stars,

pink
rice grains, ink
  bespattered jelly-fish, crabs like
   green
    lilies and submarine
  toadstools, slide each on the other.

All
external
  marks of abuse are present on
   this
    defiant edifice—
  all the physical features of

ac-
cident—lack
  of cornice, dynamite grooves, burns
   and
    hatchet strokes, these things stand
  out on it: the chasm side is

dead.
Repeated
    evidence has proved that it can
      live
        on what cannot revive
   its youth. The sea grows old in it.

My Apish Cousins

WINKED too much and were afraid of snakes. The
   zebras, supreme in
their abnormality; the elephants with their fog-colored skin
  and strictly practical appendages
    were there, the small cats; and the parakeet—
      trivial and humdrum on examination, destroying
   bark and portions of the food it could not eat.

I recall their magnificence, now not more magnificent
than it is dim. It is difficult to recall the ornament,
  speech, and precise manner of what one might
    call the minor acquaintances twenty
      years back; but I shall not forget him—that
        Gilgamesh among
   the hairy carnivora—that cat with the

wedge-shaped, slate-gray marks on its forelegs and the resolute
    tail,
astringently remarking: "They have imposed on us with their
    pale
  half-fledged protestations, trembling about
    in inarticulate frenzy, saying
      it is not for us to understand art; finding it
    all so difficult, examining the thing

as if it were inconceivably arcanic, as symmet-
rically frigid as if it had been carved out of chrysoprase
  or marble—strict with tension, malignant
    in its power over us and deeper
      than the sea when it proffers flattery in exchange for
      hemp,
  rye, flax, horses, platinum, timber, and fur."

Pedantic Literalist

PRINCE RUPERT'S drop, paper muslin ghost,
White torch—"with power to say unkind
Things with kindness, and the most
Irritating things in the midst of love and
Tears," you invite destruction.

You are like the meditative man
With the perfunctory heart; its
Carved cordiality ran
To and fro at first like an inlaid and royal
Immutable production;

Then afterward "neglected to be
Painful, deluding him with
Loitering formality,"
"Doing its duty as if it did it not,"
Presenting an obstruction

To the motive that it served. What stood
Erect in you has withered. A
Little "palm tree of turned wood"
Informs your once spontaneous core in its
Immutable production.

Poetry

I TOO, dislike it: there are things that are important be-
yond all this fiddle.
Reading it, however, with a perfect contempt for it, one dis-
covers that there is in
it after all, a place for the genuine.
Hands that can grasp, eyes
that can dilate, hair that can rise
if it must, these things are important not because a

high sounding interpretation can be put upon them but be
             cause they are
      useful; when they become so derivative as to become unin-
             telligible,
   the same thing may be said for all of us, that we
         do not admire what
       we cannot understand: the bat,
             holding on upside down or in quest of something to
eat, elephants pushing, a wild horse taking a roll, a tireless
             wolf under
   a tree, the immovable critic twitching his skin like a horse
             that feels a flea, the base-
      ball fan, the statistician—
         nor is it valid
            to discriminate against "business documents and

school-books"; all these phenomena are important. One must
             make a distinction
      however: when dragged into prominence by half poets, the
             result is not poetry,
   nor till the poets among us can be
         "literalists of
         the imagination"—above
             insolence and triviality and can present

for inspection, imaginary gardens with real toads in them,
             shall we have
      it. In the meantime, if you demand on one hand,
         the raw material of poetry in
         all its rawness and
         that which is on the other hand
             genuine, then you are interested in poetry.

A Talisman

UNDER a splintered mast,
   Torn from the ship and cast
Near her hull,

A stumbling shepherd found
Embedded in the ground,
   A seagull

Of lapis lazuli,
A scarab of the sea,
   With wings spread—

Curling its coral feet,
Parting its beak to greet
   Men long dead.

Roses Only

YOU do not seem to realize that beauty is a liability rather
    than an asset—that in view of the fact that spirit creates
      form we are justified in supposing
        that you must have brains. For you, a symbol of the unit,
        stiff and sharp,
    conscious of surpassing by dint of native superiority and
      liking for everything
self-dependent, anything an

ambitious civilization might produce: for you, unaided, to at
      tempt through sheer
    reserve, to confuse presumptions resulting from observation,
      is idle. You cannot make us
        think you a delightful happen-so. But rose, if you are
        brilliant, it
    is not because your petals are the without-which-nothing of
      pre-eminence. Would you not, minus
thorns, be a what-is-this, a mere

peculiarity? They are not proof against a worm, the elements,
    or mildew;
    but what about the predatory hand? What is brilliance
      without co-ordination? Guarding the
      infinitesimal pieces of your mind, compelling audience to

the remark that it is better to be forgotten than to be re-
          membered too violently,
your thorns are the best part of you.

ROBINSON JEFFERS

Continent's End

AT the equinox when the earth was veiled in a late rain,
          wreathed with wet poppies, waiting spring,
The ocean swelled for a far storm and beat its boundary, the
     ground-swell shook the beds of granite.

I gazing at the boundaries of granite and spray, the established
     sea-marks, felt behind me
Mountain and plain, the immense breadth of the continent,
     before me the mass and doubled stretch of water.

I said: You yoke the Aleutian seal-rocks with the lava and coral
     sowings that flower the south,
Over your flood the life that sought the sunrise faces ours that
     has followed the evening star.

The long migrations meet across you and it is nothing to you,
     you have forgotten us, mother.
You were much younger when we crawled out of the womb
     and lay in the sun's eye on the tideline.

It was long and long ago; we have grown proud since then
     and you have grown bitter; life retains
Your mobile soft unquiet strength; and envies hardness, the
     insolent quietness of stone.

The tides are in our veins, we still mirror the stars, life is your
     child, but there is in me

Older and harder than life and more impartial, the eye that
    watched before there was an ocean.

That watched you fill your beds out of the condensation of thin
    vapor and watched you change them,
That saw you soft and violent wear your boundaries down, eat
    rock, shift places with the continents.

Mother, though my song's measure is like your surf-beat's an-
    cient rhythm I never learned it of you.
Before there was any water there were tides of fire, both our
    tones flow from the older fountain.

Apology for Bad Dreams

I

IN the purple light, heavy with redwood, the slopes drop
    seaward,
Headlong convexities of forest, drawn in together to the steep
    ravine. Below, on the sea-cliff,
A lonely clearing; a little field of corn by the streamside; a roof
    under spared trees. Then the ocean
Like a great stone someone has cut to a sharp edge and polished
    to shining. Beyond it, the fountain
And furnace of incredible light flowing up from the sunk sun.
    In the little clearing a woman
Was punishing a horse; she had tied the halter to a sapling at
    the edge of the wood; but when the great whip
Clung to the flanks the creature kicked so hard she feared he
    would snap the halter; she called from the house
The young man her son; who fetched a chain tie-rope, they
    working together
Noosed the small rusty links round the horse's tongue
And tied him by the swollen tongue to the tree.
Seen from this height they are shrunk to insect size,
Out of all human relation. You cannot distinguish
The blood dripping from where the chain is fastened,
The beast shuddering; but the thrust neck and the legs

Far apart. You can see the whip fall on the flanks. . . .
The gesture of the arm. You cannot see the face of the woman.
The enormous light beats up out of the west across the cloud-
  bars of the trade-wind. The ocean
Darkens, the high clouds brighten, the hills darken together.
Unbridled and unbelievable beauty
Covers the evening world . . . not covers, grows apparent out
  of it, as Venus down there grows out
From the lit sky. What said the prophet? "I create good: and
  I create evil: I am the Lord."

II

This coast crying out for tragedy like all beautiful places,
(The quiet ones ask for quieter suffering; but here the granite
  cliff the gaunt cypresses' crown
Demands what victim? The dykes of red lava and black what
  Titan? The hills like pointed flames
Beyond Soberanes, the terrible peaks of the bare hills under the
  sun, what immolation?)
This coast crying out for tragedy like all beautiful places: and
  like the passionate spirit of humanity
Pain for its bread: God's, many victims', the painful deaths,
  the horrible transfigurations: I said in my heart,
"Better invent than suffer: imagine victims
Lest your own flesh be chosen the agonist, or you
Martyr some creature to the beauty of the place." And I said,
"Burn sacrifices once a year to magic
Horror away from the house, this little house here
You have built over the ocean with your own hands
Beside the standing boulders: for what are we,
The beast that walks upright, with speaking lips
And little hair, to think we should always be fed,
Sheltered, intact, and self-controlled? We sooner more liable
Than the other animals. Pain and terror, the insanities of
  desire; not accidents, but essential,
And crowd up from the core." I imagined victims for those
  wolves, I made the phantoms to follow.
They have hunted the phantoms and missed the house. It is
  not good to forget over what gulls the spirit

Of the beauty of humanity, the petal of a lost flower **blown sea-**
ward by the night-wind, floats to its quietness.

III

Boulders blunted like an old bear's teeth break up from the
headland; below them
All the soil is thick with shells, the tide-rock feasts of a dead
people.
Here the granite flanks are scarred with ancient fire, the ghosts
of the tribe
Crouch in the nights beside the ghost of a fire, they try to re-
member the sunlight,
Light has died out of their skies. These have paid something
for the future
Luck of the country, while we living keep old griefs in mem-
ory: though God's
Envy is not a likely fountain of ruin, to forget evil calls down
Sudden reminders from the cloud: remembered deaths be our
redeemers;
Imagined victims our salvation: white as the half moon at mid-
night
Someone flamelike passed me, saying, "I am Tamar Cauldwell,
I have my desire,"
Then the voice of the sea returned, when she had gone by, the
stars to their towers.
. . . Beautiful country, burn again, Point Pinos down to the
Sur Rivers
Burn as before with bitter wonders, land and ocean and the
Carmel water.

IV

He brays humanity in a mortar to bring the savor
From the bruised root: a man having bad dreams, who invents
victims, is only the ape of that God.
He washes it out with tears and many waters, calcines it with
fire in the red crucible,
Deforms it, makes it horrible to itself: the spirit flies out and
stands naked, he sees the spirit.
He takes it in the naked ecstasy; it breaks in his hand, the atom
is broken, the power that massed it

Cries to the power that moves the stars, "I have come home to
   myself, behold me.
I bruised myself in the flint mortar and burnt me
In the red shell, I tortured myself, I flew forth,
Stood naked of myself and broke me in fragments,
And here am I moving the stars that are me."
I have seen these ways of God: I know of no reason
For fire and change and torture and the old returnings.
He being sufficient might be still. I think they admit no reason;
   they are the ways of my love.
Unmeasured power, incredible passion, enormous craft: no
   thought apparent but burns darkly
Smothered with its own smoke in the human brain-vault: no
   thought outside: a certain measure in phenomena:
The fountains of the boiling stars, the flowers on the foreland,
   the ever-returning roses of dawn.

Love the Wild Swan

I HATE my verses, every line, every word.
Oh pale and brittle pencils ever to try
One grass-blade's curve, or the throat of one bird
That clings to twig, ruffled against white sky.
Oh cracked and twilight mirrors ever to catch
One color, one glinting flash, of the splendor of things.
Unlucky hunter, Oh bullets of wax,
The lion beauty, the wild-swan wings, the storm of the wings."
—This wild swan of a world is no hunter's game.
Better bullets than yours would miss the white breast,
Better mirrors than yours would crack in the flame.
Does it matter whether you hate your . . . self? At least
Love your eyes that can see, your mind that can
Hear the music, the thunder of the wings. Love the wild swan.

MARSDEN HARTLEY

Confidence

WE'LL have the sun now,"
    the quaking sea gulls said—
"We've run the gamut of the thundering sea,
one by one—one by one,
and though the wave is full of bread
a wing is often tendon-weary
of a thing so varied-vast;
we do our geodetic surveillance,
for herring are a shining thing,
a shape of sleek imagining,
a pretty circumstance.
The shiver of an ash leaf and of pine
makes other music for a day's determining,
even sea gulls love the shape of roses
ere day closes."

Warblers

AN hundred warblers in the nearest aching gap,
    it seems as though it loved its aching
filled with hyper-ikonistic misery.
I did not expect such staggering wealth
to come to me by dawn-delivered stealth,
though morning is the time—and spring
the way love knows of its best being.

All through the leaves a burning
rush of gilded, swift, whirling wing.
All warblers of the world have come

to me, and are in me living—
I only cool retreat and humble shade
giving,
my leaves with excess of sun
trampled.

I said an hundred warblers came
to me,
and now that I am clear, what it
was, was very near—
it was but two, or three,
But—how they fastened me.

In Robin Hood Cove

THE tide comes in, and out goes tide;
it skirts the cliffs, and in their shadow sees
the remnants of the days that fall
between a seagull's and a robin's call.
There is the bridge, and under flows
the rests of evening with its primulous
shows—
it is a river made of listless sea
after it has explained its fierce integrity;
no thunder makes, or on rock heaves—
it learns the place for plain humility,
and keeps reflection of some mindless
leaves.

These evening greens
that gather wistfully among
the ripening coronals of summer
when rain has done its streaming
and the sea has washed back
its waters into these little cities
made of whispered wish
and gentle, seabird thought, homely consecration;
airs—vibrant with the felt glimmer of a day

gone down to glory of a sunken yesterday;
night stepping in, soft-shod and separate
in her smooth design;
these evening greens
that gather wistfully, making melody
of nothings in their tuneful
prime.

T. S. ELIOT

The Love Song of J. Alfred Prufrock

S'io credesse che mia risposta fosse
A persona che mai tornasse al mondo,
Questa fiamma staria senza piu scosse.
Ma perciocche giammai di questo fondo
Non torno vivo alcun s'i'odo il vero,
Senza tema d'infamia ti rispondo.

LET us go then, you and I,
When the evening is spread out against the sky
Like a patient etherized upon a table;
Let us go, through certain half-deserted streets,
The muttering retreats
Of restless nights in one-night cheap hotels
And sawdust restaurants with oyster-shells:
Streets that follow like a tedious argument
Of insidious intent
To lead you to an overwhelming question. . . .
Oh, do not ask, "What is it?"
Let us go and make our visit.
In the room the women come and go
Talking of Michelangelo.

The yellow fog that rubs its back upon the window-panes,
The yellow smoke that rubs its muzzle on the window-
      panes,
Licked its tongue into the corners of the evening,
Lingered upon the pools that stand in drains,
Let fall upon its back the soot that falls from chimneys
Slipped by the terrace, made a sudden leap,
And seeing that it was a soft October night,
Curled once about the house, and fell asleep.

And indeed there will be time
For the yellow smoke that slides along the street,
Rubbing its back upon the window-panes;
There will be time, there will be time
To prepare a face to meet the faces that you meet;
There will be time to murder and create,
And time for all the works and days of hands
That lift and drop a question on your plate;
Time for you and time for me,
And time yet for a hundred indecisions,
And for a hundred visions and revisions,
Before the taking of a toast and tea.
In the room the women come and go
Talking of Michelangelo.

And indeed there will be time
To wonder, "Do I dare?" and, "Do I dare?"
Time to turn back and descend the stair,
With a bald spot in the middle of my hair—
(They will say: "How his hair is growing thin!")
My morning coat, my collar mounting firmly to the chin,
My necktie rich and modest, but asserted by a simple
      pin—
(They will say: "But how his arms and legs are thin!")
Do I dare
Disturb the universe?
In a minute there is time
For decisions and revisions which a minute will reverse.

For I have known them all already, known them all:
Have known the evenings, mornings, afternoons,

I have measured out my life with coffee spoons;
I know the voices dying with a dying fall
Beneath the music from a farther room.
    So how should I presume?

And I have known the eyes already, known them all—
The eyes that fix you in a formulated phrase,
And when I am formulated, sprawling on a pin,
When I am pinned and wriggling on the wall,
Then how should I begin
To spit out all the butt-ends of my days and ways?
    And how should I presume?

And I have known the arms already, known them all—
Arms that are braceleted and white and bare
(But in the lamplight, downed with light brown hair!)
Is it perfume from a dress
That makes me so digress?
Arms that lie along a table, or wrap about a shawl.
    And should I then presume?
    And how should I begin?

      .   .   .   .

Shall I say, I have gone at dusk through narrow streets
And watched the smoke that rises from the pipes
Of lonely men in shirt-sleeves, leaning out of
      windows? . . .
I should have been a pair of ragged claws
Scuttling across the floors of silent seas.

      .   .   .   .

And the afternoon, the evening, sleeps so peacefully!
Smoothed by long fingers,
Asleep . . . tired . . . or it malingers,
Stretched on the floor, here beside you and me.
Should I, after tea and cakes and ices,
Have the strength to force the moment to its crisis?
But though I have wept and fasted, wept and prayed,
Though I have seen my head (grown slightly bald)
      brought in upon a platter,
I am no prophet—and here's no great matter;
I have seen the moment of my greatness flicker,

And I have seen the eternal Footman hold my coat,
    and snicker,
And in short, I was afraid.

And would it have been worth it, after all,
After the cups, the marmalade, the tea,
Among the porcelain, among some talk of you and me,
Would it have been worth while,
To have bitten off the matter with a smile,
To have squeezed the universe into a ball
To roll it toward some overwhelming question,
To say: "I am Lazarus, come from the dead,
Come back to tell you all, I shall tell you all"—
If one, settling a pillow by her head,
    Should say: "That was not what I meant at all;
    That is not it, at all."

And would it have been worth it, after all,
Would it have been worth while,
After the sunsets and the dooryards and the sprinkled
    streets,
After the novels, after the teacups, after the skirts that
    trail along the floor—
And this, and so much more?—
It is impossible to say just what I mean!
But as if a magic lantern threw the nerves in patterns on
    a screen:
Would it have been worth while
If one, settling a pillow or throwing off a shawl,
And turning toward the window, should say:
    "That is not it at all,
    That is not what I meant at all."

      .   .   .

No! I am not Prince Hamlet, nor was meant to be;
Am an attendant lord, one that will do
To swell a progress, start a scene or two,
Advise the prince; no doubt, an easy tool,
Deferential, glad to be of use,
Politic, cautious, and meticulous;
Full of high sentence, but a bit obtuse;

At times, indeed, almost ridiculous—
Almost, at times, the Fool.

I grow old . . . I grow old . . .
I shall wear the bottoms of my trousers rolled.

Shall I part my hair behind? Do I dare to eat a peach?
I shall wear white flannel trousers, and walk upon the
    beach.
I have heard the mermaids singing, each to each.

I do not think that they will sing to me.
I have seen them riding seaward on the waves
Combing the white hair of the waves blown back
When the wind blows the water white and black.
We have lingered in the chambers of the sea
By sea-girls wreathed with seaweed red and brown
Till human voices wake us, and we drown.

Sweeney Among the Nightingales

ὤμοι πέπληγμαι καιρίαν πληγὴν ἔσω.

*Why should I speak of the nightingale? The nightingale
sings of adulterous wrong.*

APENECK SWEENEY spreads his knees
   Letting his arms hang down to laugh,
The zebra stripes along his jaw
Swelling to maculate giraffe.

The circles of the stormy moon
Slide westward to the River Plate,
Death and the Raven drift above
And Sweeney guards the hornèd gate.

Gloomy Orion and the Dog
Are veiled; and hushed the shrunken seas;
The person in the Spanish cape
Tries to sit on Sweeney's knees

Slips and pulls the table cloth
Overturns a coffee cup,
Reorganized upon the floor
She yawns and draws a stocking up;

The silent man in mocha brown
Sprawls at the window-sill and gapes;
The waiter brings in oranges,
Bananas, figs and hot-house grapes;

The silent vertebrate exhales,
Contracts and concentrates, withdraws;
Rachel *née* Rabinovitch
Tears at the grapes with murderous paws;

She and the lady in the cape
Are suspect, thought to be in league;
Therefore the man with heavy eyes
Declines the gambit, shows fatigue,

Leaves the room and reappears
Outside the window, leaning in,
Branches of wistaria
Circumscribe a golden grin;

The host with someone indistinct
Converses at the door apart,
The nightingales are singing near
The Convent of the Sacred Heart,

And sang within the bloody wood
When Agamemnon cried aloud,
And let their liquid siftings fall
To stain the stiff dishonoured shroud.

Whispers of Immortality

WEBSTER was much possessed by death
And saw the skull beneath the skin;
And breastless creatures underground
Leaned backward with a lipless grin.

Daffodil bulbs instead of balls
Stared from the sockets of the eyes!
He knew that thought clings round dead limbs
Tightening its lusts and luxuries.

Donne, I suppose, was such another
Who found no substitute for sense
To seize and clutch and penetrate,
Expert beyond experience.

He knew the anguish of the marrow
The ague of the skeleton;
No contact possible to flesh
Allayed the fever of the bone.

.   .   .   .   .

Grishkin is nice; her Russian eye
Is underlined for emphasis;
Uncorseted, her friendly bust
Gives promise of pneumatic bliss.

The couched Brazilian jaguar
Compels the scampering marmoset
With subtle effluence of a cat;
Grishkin has a maisonette:

The sleek and sinuous jaguar
Does not in his arboreal gloom
Distil so rank a feline smell
As Grishkin in a drawing-room.

And even abstracter entities
Circumambulate her charm;
But our lot crawls between dry ribs
To keep its metaphysics warm.

Gerontion

Thou hast nor youth nor age
But as it were an after dinner sleep
Dreaming of both.

HERE I am, an old man in a dry month,
Being read to by a boy, waiting for rain.
I was neither at the hot gates
Nor fought in the warm rain
Nor knee deep in the salt marsh, heaving a cutlass,
Bitten by flies, fought.
My house is a decayed house,
And the Jew squats on the window sill, the owner,
Spawned in some estaminet of Antwerp,
Blistered in Brussels, patched and peeled in London.
The goat coughs at night in the field overhead;
Rocks, moss, stonecrop, iron, merds.
The woman keeps the kitchen, makes tea,
Sneezes at evening, poking the peevish gutter.

                    I an old man,
A dull head among windy spaces.

Signs are taken for wonders. "We would see a sign!"
The word within a word, unable to speak a word,
Swaddled with darkness. In the juvescence of the year
Came Christ the tiger.

In depraved May, dogwood and chestnut, flowering
    judas,
To be eaten, to be divided, to be drunk
Among whispers; by Mr. Silvero
With caressing hands, at Limoges
Who walked all night in the next room;
By Hakagawa, bowing among the Titians;
By Madame de Tornquist, in the dark room

Shifting the candles; Fraulein von Kulp
Who turned in the hall, one hand on the door. Vacant
    shuttles
Weave the wind. I have no ghosts,
An old man in a draughty house
Under a windy knob.

After such knowledge, what forgiveness? Think now
History has many cunning passages, contrived corridors
And issues, deceives with whispering ambitions,
Guides us by vanities. Think now
She gives when our attention is distracted
And what she gives, gives with such supple confusions
That the giving famishes the craving. Gives too late
What's not believed in, or if still believed,
In memory only, reconsidered passion. Gives too soon
Into weak hands, what's thought can be dispensed with
Till the refusal propagates a fear. Think
Neither fear nor courage saves us. Unnatural vices
Are fathered by our heroism. Virtues
Are forced upon us by our impudent crimes.
These tears are shaken from the wrath-bearing tree.

The tiger springs in the new year. Us he devours.
    Think at last
We have not reached conclusion, when I
Stiffen in a rented house. Think at last
I have not made this show purposelessly
And it is not by any concitation
Of the backward devils.
I would meet you upon this honestly.
I that was near your heart was removed therefrom
To lose beauty in terror, terror in inquisition.
I have lost my passion: why should I need to keep it
Since what is kept must be adulterated?
I have lost my sight, smell, hearing, taste and touch:
How should I use it for your closer contact?

These with a thousand small deliberations
Protract the profit, of their chilled delirium,

Excite the membrane, when the sense has cooled,
With pungent sauces, multiply variety
In a wilderness of mirrors. What will the spider do,
Suspend its operations, will the weevil
Delay? De Bailhache, Fresca, Mrs. Cammell, whirled
Beyond the circuit of the shuddering Bear
In fractured atoms. Gull against the wind, in the
    windy straits
Of Belle Isle, or running on the Horn,
White feathers in the snow, the Gulf claims,
And an old man driven by the Trades
To a sleepy corner.

                      Tenants of the house,
Thoughts of a dry brain in a dry season.

The Hollow Men

A penny for the Old Guy.

              MISTAH KURTZ—HE DEAD

I

WE are the hollow men
   We are the stuffed men
Leaning together
Headpiece filled with straw. Alas!
Our dried voices, when
We whisper together
Are quiet and meaningless
As wind in dry grass
Or rats' feet over broken glass
In our dry cellar

Shape without form, shade without colour,
Paralysed force, gesture without motion;

Those who have crossed
With direct eyes, to death's other Kingdom
Remember us—if at all—not as lost

Violent souls, but only
As the hollow men
The stuffed men.

II

Eyes I dare not meet in dreams
In death's dream kingdom
These do not appear:
There, the eyes are
Sunlight on a broken column
There, is a tree swinging
And voices are
In the wind's singing
More distant and more solemn
Than a fading star.

Let me be no nearer
In death's dream kingdom
Let me also wear
Such deliberate disguises
Rat's coat, crowskin, crossed staves
In a field
Behaving as the wind behaves
No nearer—
Not that final meeting
In the twilight kingdom

III

This is the dead land
This is cactus land
Here the stone images
Are raised, here they receive
The supplication of a dead man's hand
Under the twinkle of a fading star.

Is it like this
In death's other kingdom
Waking alone
At the hour when we are
Trembling with tenderness

Lips that would kiss
Form prayers to broken stone.

IV

The eyes are not here
There are no eyes here
In this valley of dying stars
In this hollow valley
This broken jaw of our lost kingdoms

In this last of meeting places
We grope together
And avoid speech
Gathered on this beach of the tumid river
Sightless, unless
The eyes reappear
As the perpetual star
Multifoliate rose
Of death's twilight kingdom
The hope only
Of empty men.

V

Here we go round the prickly pear
Prickly pear, prickly pear
Here we go round the prickly pear
At five o'clock in the morning.

Between the idea
And the reality
Between the motion
And the act
Falls the Shadow
            For Thine is the Kingdom.

Between the conception
And the creation
Between the emotion
And the response
Falls the Shadow
            Life is very long.

Between the desire
And the spasm
Between the potency
And the existence
Between the essence
And the descent
Falls the Shadow
      For Thine is the Kingdom.

For Thine is
Life is
For Thine is the

This is the way the world ends
This is the way the world ends
This is the way the world ends
Not with a bang but a whimper.

La Figlia Che Piange

O quam te memorem virgo . . .

STAND on the highest pavement of the stair—
Lean on a garden urn—
Weave, weave the sunlight in your hair—
Clasp your flowers to you with a pained surprise—
Fling them to the ground and turn
With a fugitive resentment in your eyes:
But weave, weave the sunlight in your hair.

So I would have had him leave,
So I would have had her stand and grieve,
So he would have left
As the soul leaves the body torn and bruised,
As the mind deserts the body it has used.

I should find
Some way incomparably light and deft,
Some way we both should understand,
Simple and faithless as a smile and shake of the hand.

She turned away, but with the autumn weather
Compelled my imagination many days,
Many days and many hours:
Her hair over her arms and her arms full of flowers,
And I wonder how they should have been together!
I should have lost a gesture and a pose.
Sometimes these cognitions still amaze
The troubled midnight and the noon's repose.

Portrait of a Lady

I

AMONG the smoke and fog of a December afternoon
You have the scene arrange itself—as it will seem to do—
With "I have saved this afternoon for you";
And four wax candles in the darkened room,
Four rings of light upon the ceiling overhead,
And atmosphere of Juliet's tomb
Prepared for all the things to be said, or left unsaid.
We have been, let us say, to hear the latest Pole
Transmit the Preludes, through his hair and finger-tips.
"So intimate, this Chopin, that I think his soul
Should be resurrected only among friends
Some two or three, who will not touch the bloom
That is rubbed and questioned in the concert room."
—And so the conversation slips
Among velleities and carefully caught regrets
Through attenuated tones of violins
Mingled with remote cornets
And begins.
"You do not know how much they mean to me, my friends,
And how, how rare and strange it is, to find
In a life composed so much, so much of odds and ends
(For indeed I do not love it . . . you knew? You are not blind!
How keen you are!)
To find a friend who has these qualities,
Who has, and gives
Those qualities upon which friendship lives.
How much it means that I say this to you—

Without these friendships—life, what *cauchemar!*[15]
Among the windings of the violins
And the ariettes
Of cracked cornets
Inside my brain a dull tom-tom begins
Absurdly hammering a prelude of its own,
Capricious monotone
That is at least one definite "false note."
—Let us take the air, in a tobacco trance,
Admire the monuments,
Discuss the late events,
Correct our watches by the public clocks,
Then sit for half an hour and drink our bocks.

II

Now that lilacs are in bloom
She has a bowl of lilacs in her room
And twists one in her fingers while she talks.
'Ah, my friend, you do not know, you do not know
What life is, you should hold it in your hands";
  (Slowly twisting the lilac stalks)
"You let it flow from you, you let it flow,
And youth is cruel, and has no remorse
And smiles at situations which it cannot see."

I smile, of course,
And go on drinking tea.
"Yet with these April sunsets, that somehow recall
My buried life, and Paris in the Spring,
I feel immeasurably at peace, and find the world
To be wonderful and youthful, after all."

The voice returns like the insistent out-of-tune
Of a broken violin on an August afternoon:
"I am always sure that you understand
My feelings, always sure that you feel,
Sure that across the gulf you reach your hand.
You are invulnerable, you have no Achilles' heel.
You will go on, and when you have prevailed
You can say: at this point many a one has failed.

"But what have I, but what have I, my friend,
   To give you, what can you receive from me?
   Only the friendship and the sympathy
   Of one about to reach her journey's end.
   I shall sit here, serving tea to friends. . . ."

I take my hat: how can I make a cowardly amends
For what she has said to me?

You will see me any morning in the park
Reading the comics and the sporting page.
Particularly I remark
An English countess goes upon the stage.
A Greek was murdered at a Polish dance.
Another bank defaulter has confessed.
I keep my countenance,
I remain self-possessed
Except when a street piano, mechanical and tired,
Reiterates some worn-out common song
With the smell of hyacinths across the garden,
Recalling things that other people have desired.
Are these ideas right or wrong?

III

The October night comes down; returning as before
Except for a slight sensation of being ill at ease
I mount the stairs and turn the handle of the door
And feel as if I had mounted on my hands and knees.
"And so you are going abroad; and when do you return?
   But that's a useless question.
   You hardly know when you are coming back;
   You will find so much to learn."
My smile falls heavily among the bric-à-brac.

"Perhaps you can write to me."
My self-possession flares up for a second;
This is as I had reckoned.
"I have been wondering frequently of late
   (But our beginnings never know our ends!)
   Why we have not developed into friends."

I feel like one who smiles, and turning shall remark
Suddenly, his expression in a glass.
My self-possession gutters; we are really in the dark.

"For everybody said so, all our friends,
They all were sure our feelings would relate
So closely! I myself can hardly understand.
We must leave it now to fate.
You will write, at any rate.
Perhaps it is not too late.
I shall sit here, serving tea to friends."

And I must borrow every changing shape
To find expression . . . dance, dance
Like a dancing bear,
Cry like a parrot, chatter like an ape. . . .
Let us take the air, in a tobacco trance—
Well! and what if she should die some afternoon,
Afternoon gray and smoky, evening yellow and rose;
Should die and leave me sitting pen in hand
With the smoke coming down above the housetops;
Doubtful, for quite a while
Not knowing what to feel or if I understand
Or whether wise or foolish, tardy or too soon . . .
Would she not have the advantage, after all?
This music is successful with a "dying fall"
Now that we talk of dying—
And should I have the right to smile?

Burnt Norton

I

TIME present and time past
　Are both perhaps present in time future,
And time future contained in time past.
If all time is eternally present
All time is unredeemable.
What might have been is an abstraction

Remaining a perpetual possibility
Only in a world of speculation.
What might have been and what has been
Point to one end, which is always present.
Footfalls echo in the memory
Down the passage which we did not take
Towards the door we never opened
Into the rose-garden. My words echo
Thus, in your mind.
                              But to what purpose
Disturbing the dust on a bowl of rose-leaves
I do not know.
                              Other echoes
Inhabit the garden. Shall we follow?
Quick, said the bird, find them, find them,
Round the corner. Through the first gate,
Into our first world, shall we follow
The deception of the thrush? Into our first world.
There they were, dignified, invisible,
Moving without pressure, over the dead leaves,
In the autumn heat, through the vibrant air,
And the bird called, in response to
The unheard music hidden in the shrubbery,
And the unseen eyebeam crossed, for the roses
Had the look of flowers that are looked at.
There they were as our guests, accepted and accepting.
So we moved, and they, in a formal pattern,
Along the empty alley, into the box circle,
To look down into the drained pool.
Dry the pool, dry concrete, brown edged,
And the pool was filled with water out of sunlight,
And the lotos rose, quietly, quietly,
The surface glittered out of heart of light,
And they were behind us, reflected in the pool.
Then a cloud passed, and the pool was empty.
Go, said the bird, for the leaves were full of children,
Hidden excitedly, containing laughter.
Go, go, go, said the bird: human kind
Cannot bear very much reality.
Time past and time future

What might have been and what has been
Point to one end, which is always present.

II

Garlic and sapphires in the mud
Clot the bedded axle-tree.
The trilling wire in the blood
Sings below inveterate scars
And reconciles forgotten wars.
The dance along the artery
The circulation of the lymph
Are figured in the drift of stars
Ascend to summer in the tree
We move above the moving tree
In light upon the figured leaf
And hear upon the sodden floor
Below, the boarhound and the boar
Pursue their pattern as before
But reconciled among the stars.

At the still point of the turning world. Neither flesh nor flesh-
   less;
Neither from nor towards; at the still point, there the dance is,
But neither arrest nor movement. And do not call it fixity,
Where past and future are gathered. Neither movement from
   nor towards,
Neither ascent nor decline. Except for the point, the still point,
There would be no dance, and there is only the dance.
I can only say, *there* we have been: but I cannot say where.
And I cannot say, how long, for that is to place it in time.

The inner freedom from the practical desire,
The release from action and suffering, release from the inner
And the outer compulsion, yet surrounded
By a grace of sense, a white light still and moving,
Erhebung without motion, concentration
Without elimination, both a new world
And the old made explicit, understood
In the completion of its partial ecstasy,

The resolution of its partial horror.
Yet the enchainment of past and future
Woven in the weakness of the changing body,
Protects mankind from heaven and damnation
Which flesh cannot endure.
                              Time past and time future
Allow but a little consciousness.
To be conscious is not to be in time
But only in time can the moment in the rose-garden,
The moment in the arbour where the rain beat,
The moment in the draughty church at smokefall
Be remembered; involved with past and future.
Only through time time is conquered.

III

Here is a place of disaffection
Time before and time after
In a dim light: neither daylight
Investing form with lucid stillness
Turning shadow into transient beauty
With slow rotation suggesting permanence
Nor darkness to purify the soul
Emptying the sensual with deprivation
Cleansing affection from the temporal.
Neither plenitude nor vacancy. Only a flicker
Over the strained time-ridden faces
Distracted from distraction by distraction
Filled with fancies and empty of meaning
Tumid apathy with no concentration
Men and bits of paper, whirled by the cold wind
That blows before and after time,
Wind in and out of unwholesome lungs
Time before and time after.
Eructation of unhealthy souls
Into the faded air, the torpid
Driven on the wind that sweeps the gloomy hills of London
Hampstead and Clerkenwell, Campden and Putney,
Highgate, Primrose and Ludgate. Not here
Not here the darkness, in this twittering world.

Descend lower, descend only
Into the world of perpetual solitude,
World not world, but that which is not world,
Internal darkness, deprivation
And destitution of all property,
Desiccation of the world of sense,
Evacuation of the world of fancy,
Inoperancy of the world of spirit;
This is the one way, and the other
Is the same, not in movement
But abstention from movement; while the world moves
In appetency, on its metalled ways
Of time past and time future.

IV

Time and the bell have buried the day,
The black cloud carries the sun away.
Will the sunflower turn to us, will the clematis
Stray down, bend to us; tendril and spray
Clutch and cling?
Chill
Fingers of yew be curled
Down on us? After the kingfisher's wing
Has answered light to light, and is silent, the light is still
At the still point of the turning world.

V

Words move, music moves
Only in time; but that which is only living
Can only die. Words, after speech, reach
Into the silence. Only by the form, the pattern,
Can words or music reach
The stillness, as a Chinese jar still
Moves perpetually in its stillness.
Not the stillness of the violin, while the note lasts,
Not that only, but the co-existence,
Or say that the end precedes the beginning,
And the end and the beginning were always there
Before the beginning and after the end.
And all is always now. Words strain,

Crack and sometimes break, under the burden,
Under the tension, slip, slide, perish,
Decay with imprecision, will not stay in place,
Will not stay still. Shrieking voices
Scolding, mocking, or merely chattering,
Always assail them. The Word in the desert
Is most attacked by voices of temptation,
The crying shadow in the funeral dance,
The loud lament of the disconsolate chimera.

The detail of the pattern is movement,
As in the figure of the ten stairs.
Desire itself is movement
Not in itself desirable;
Love is itself unmoving,
Only the cause and end of movement,
Timeless, and undesiring
Except in the aspect of time
Caught in the form of limitation
Between un-being and being.
Sudden in a shaft of sunlight
Even while the dust moves
There rises the hidden laughter
Of children in the foliage
Quick now, here, now, always—
Ridiculous the waste sad time
Stretching before and after.

Ash Wednesday

I

BECAUSE I do not hope to turn again
Because I do not hope
Because I do not hope to turn
Desiring this man's gift and that man's scope
I no longer strive to strive towards such things
(Why should the aged eagle stretch its wings?)
Why should I mourn
The vanished power of the usual reign?

Because I do not hope to know again
The infirm glory of the positive hour
Because I do not think
Because I know I shall not know
The one veritable transitory power
Because I cannot drink
There, where trees flower, and springs flow, for there is nothing
    again

Because I know that time is always time
And place is always and only place
And what is actual is actual only for one time
And only for one place
I rejoice that things are as they are and
I renounce the blessèd face
And renounce the voice

Because I cannot hope to turn again
Consequently I rejoice, having to construct something
Upon which to rejoice

And pray to God to have mercy upon us
And I pray that I may forget
These matters that with myself I too much discuss
Too much explain
Because I do not hope to turn again
Let these words answer
For what is done, not to be done again,
May the judgment not be too heavy upon us

Because these wings are no longer wings to fly
But merely vans to beat the air
The air which is now thoroughly small and dry
Smaller and dryer than the will
Teach us to care and not to care
Teach us to sit still.

Pray for us sinners now and at the hour of our death
Pray for us now and at the hour of our death.

II

Lady, three white leopards sat under a juniper-tree
In the cool of the day, having fed to satiety
On my legs my heart my liver and that which had been con-
     tained
In the hollow round of my skull. And God said
Shall these bones live? shall these
Bones live? And that which had been contained
In the bones (which were already dry) said chirping:
Because of the goodness of this Lady
And because of her loveliness, and because
She honors the Virgin in meditation,
We shine with brightness. And I who am here dissembled
Proffer my deeds to oblivion, and my love
To the posterity of the desert and the fruit of the gourd.
It is this which recovers
My guts the strings of my eyes and the indigestible portions
Which the leopards reject. The Lady is withdrawn
In a white gown, to contemplation, in a white gown.
Let the whiteness of bones atone to forgetfulness.
There is no life in them. As I am forgotten
And would be forgotten, so I would forget
Thus devoted, concentrated in purpose. And God said
Prophesy to the wind, to the wind only, for only
The wind will listen. And the bones sang chirping
With the burden of the grasshopper, saying

Lady of silences
Calm and distressed
Torn and most whole
Rose of memory
Rose of forgetfulness
Exhausted and life-giving
Worried reposeful
The single Rose
Is now the Garden
Where all loves end
Terminate torment
Of love unsatisfied

The greater torment
Of love satisfied
End of the endless
Journey to no end
Conclusion of all that
Is inconclusible
Speech without word and
Word of no speech
Grace to the Mother
For the Garden
Where all love ends.

Under a juniper-tree the bones sang, scattered and shining
We are glad to be scattered, we did little good to each other,
Under a tree in the cool of the day, with the blessing of sand,
Forgetting themselves and each other, united
In the quiet of the desert. This is the land which ye
Shall divide by lot. And neither division nor unity
Matters. This is the land. We have our inheritance.

III

At the first turning of the second stair
I turned and saw below
The same shape twisted on the banister
Under the vapor in the fetid air
Struggling with the devil of the stairs who wears
The deceitful face of hope and of despair.

At the second turning of the second stair
I left them twisting, turning below;
There were no more faces and the stair was dark,
Damp, jaggèd, like an old man's mouth drivelling, beyond re-
    pair,
Or the toothed gullet of an agèd shark.

At the first turning of the third stair
Was a slotted window bellied like the fig's fruit
And beyond the hawthorn blossom and a pasture scene
The broadbacked figure drest in blue and green
Enchanted the maytime with an antique flute.

Blown hair is sweet, brown hair over the mouth blown,
Lilac and brown hair;
Distraction, music of the flute, stops and steps of the mind over
    the third stair,
Fading, fading; strength beyond hope and despair
Climbing the third stair.
Lord, I am not worthy
Lord, I am not worthy

      but speak the word only.

IV

Who walked between the violet and the violet
Who walked between
The various ranks of varied green
Going in white and blue, in Mary's color,
Talking of trivial things
In ignorance and in knowledge of eternal dolour
Who moved among the others as they walked,
Who then made strong the fountains and made fresh the
    springs

Made cool the dry rock and made firm the sand
In blue of larkspur, blue of Mary's color,
Sovegna vos

Here are the years that walk between, bearing
Away the fiddles and the flutes, restoring
One who moves in the time between sleep and waking, wearing

White light folded, sheathed about her, folded.
The new years walk, restoring
Through a bright cloud of tears, the years, restoring
With a new verse the ancient rhyme. Redeem
The time. Redeem
The unread vision in the higher dream
While jewelled unicorns draw by the gilded hearse

The silent sister veiled in white and blue
Between the yews, behind the garden god,

Whose flute is breathless, bent her head and sighed but spoke
no word

But the fountain sprang up and the bird sang down
Redeem the time, redeem the dream
The token of the word unheard, unspoken

Till the wind shake a thousand whispers from the yew

And after this our exile

V

If the lost word is lost, if the spent word is spent
If the unheard, unspoken
Word is unspoken, unheard;
Still is the unspoken word, the Word unheard,
The Word without a word, the Word within
The world and for the world;
And the light shone in darkness and
Against the Word the unstilled world still whirled
About the center of the silent Word.

O my people, what have I done unto thee.

Where shall the word be found, where will the word
Resound? Not here, there is not enough silence,
Not on the sea or on the islands, not
On the mainland, in the desert or the rain land,
For those who walk in darkness
Both in the day time and in the night time
The right time and the right place are not here
No place of grace for those who avoid the face
No time to rejoice for those who walk among noise and deny
the voice

Will the veiled sister pray for
Those who walk in darkness, who chose thee and oppose thee,
Those who are torn on the horn between season and season,
time and time, between

Hour and hour, word and word, power and power, those who
    wait
In darkness? Will the veiled sister pray
For children at the gate
Who will not go away and cannot pray:
Pray for those who chose and oppose

     O my people, what have I done unto thee.

Will the veiled sister between the slender
Yew trees pray for those who offend her
And are terrified and cannot surrender
And affirm before the world and deny between the rocks
In the last desert between the last blue rocks
The desert in the garden the garden in the desert
Of drouth, spitting from the mouth the withered apple-seed

     O my people.

VI

Although I do not hope to turn again
Although I do not hope
Although I do not hope to turn

Wavering between the profit and the loss
In this brief transit where the dreams cross
The dreamcrossed twilight between birth and dying
(Bless me father) though I do not wish to wish these things
From the wide window towards the granite shore
The white sails still fly seaward, seaward flying
Unbroken wings
And the lost heart stiffens and rejoices
In the lost lilac and the lost sea voices
And the weak spirit quickens to rebel
For the bent golden-rod and the lost sea smell
Quickens to recover
The cry of quail and the whirling plover
And the blind eye creates
The empty forms between the ivory gates
And smell renews the salt savor of the sandy earth

This is the time of tension between dying and birth
The place of solitude where three dreams cross
Between blue rocks
But when the voices shaken from the yew-tree drift away
Let the other yew be shaken and reply.

Blessed sister, holy mother, spirit of the fountain, spirit of the
    garden,
Suffer us not to mock ourselves with falsehood
Teach us to care and not to care
Teach us to sit still
Even among these rocks,
Our peace in His will
And even among these rocks
Sister, mother,
And spirit of the river, spirit of the sea,
Suffer me not to be separated

And let my cry come unto Thee.

------ ••• ------

JOHN CROWE RANSOM

------ ••• ------

Blue Girls

TWIRLING your blue skirts, travelling the sward
    Under the towers of your seminary,
Go listen to your teachers old and contrary
Without believing a word.

Tie the white fillets then about your lustrous hair
And think no more of what will come to pass
Than bluebirds that go walking on the grass
And chattering on the air.

Practise your beauty, blue girls, before it fail;
And I will cry with my loud lips and publish

Beauty which all our power shall never establish,
It is so frail.

For I could tell you a story which is true:
I know a lady with a terrible tongue,
Blear eyes fallen from blue,
All her perfections tarnished—and yet it is not long
Since she was lovelier than any of you.

Antique Harvesters

(SCENE: OF THE MISSISSIPPI THE BANK SINISTER, AND OF THE
OHIO THE BANK SINISTER.)

TAWNY are the leaves turned, but they still hold.
It is the harvest; what shall this land produce?
A meager hill of kernels, a runnel of juice.
Declension looks from our land, it is old.
Therefore let us assemble, dry, grey, spare,
And mild as yellow air.

"I hear the creak of a raven's funeral wing."
The young men would be joying in the song
Of passionate birds; their memories are not long.
What is it thus rehearsed in sable? "Nothing."
Trust not but the old endure, and shall be older
Than the scornful beholder.

We pluck the spindling ears and gather the corn.
One spot has special yield? "On this spot stood
Heroes and drenched it with their only blood."
And talk meets talk, as echoes from the horn
Of the hunter—echoes are the old men's arts,
Ample are the chambers of their hearts.

Here come the hunters, keepers of a rite.
The horn, the hounds, the lank mares coursing by
Under quaint archetypes of chivalry;
And the fox, lovely ritualist, in flight
Offering his unearthly ghost to quarry;
And the fields, themselves to harry.

Resume, harvesters. The treasure is full bronze
Which you will garner for the Lady, and the moon
Could tinge it no yellower than does this noon;
But the grey will quench it shortly—the fields, men,
    stones.
Pluck fast, dreamers; prove as you rumble slowly
Not less than men, not wholly.

Bare the arm too, dainty youths, bend the knees
Under bronze burdens. And by an autumn tone
As by a grey, as by a green, you will have known
Your famous Lady's image; for so have these.
And if one say that easily will your hands
More prosper in other lands,

Angry as wasp-music be your cry then:
"Forsake the Proud Lady, of the heart of fire,
The look of snow, to the praise of a dwindled choir,
Song of degenerate specters that were men?
The sons of the fathers shall keep her, worthy of
What these have done in love."

True, it is said of our Lady, she ageth.
But see, if you peep shrewdly, she hath not stooped;
Take no thought of her servitors that have drooped,
For we are nothing; and if one talk of death—
Why, the ribs of the earth subsist frail as a breath
If but God wearieth.

Captain Carpenter

CAPTAIN CARPENTER rose up in his prime
Put on his pistols and went riding out
But had got wellnigh nowhere at that time
Till he fell in with ladies in a rout.

It was a pretty lady and all her train
That played with him so sweetly but before
An hour she'd taken a sword with all her main
And twined him of his nose for evermore.

Captain Carpenter mounted up one day
And rode straightway into a strange rogue
That looked unchristian but be that as may
The Captain did not wait upon prologue.

But drew upon him out of his great heart
The other swung against him with a club
And cracked his two legs at the shinny part
And let him roll and stick like any tub.

Captain Carpenter rode many a time
From male and female took he sundry harms
He met the wife of Satan crying "I'm
The she-wolf bids you shall bear no more arms.'

Their strokes and counters whistled in the wind
I wish he had delivered half his blows
But where she should have made off like a hind
The bitch bit off his arms at the elbows.

And Captain Carpenter parted with his ears
To a black devil that used him in this wise
O jesus ere his threescore and ten years
Another had plucked out his sweet blue eyes.

Captain Carpenter got up on his roan
And sallied from the gate in hell's despite
I heard him asking in the grimmest tone
If any enemy yet there was to fight?

"To any adversary it is fame
If he risk to be wounded by my tongue
Or burnt in two beneath my red heart's flame
Such are the perils he is cast among.

"But if he can he has a pretty choice
From an anatomy with little to lose
Whether he cut my tongue and take my voice
Or whether it be my round red heart he choose."

It was the neatest knave that ever was seen
Stepping in perfume from his lady's bower
Who at this word put in his merry mien
And fell on Captain Carpenter like a tower.

I would not knock old fellows in the dust
But there lay Captain Carpenter on his back
His weapons were the old heart in his bust
And a blade shook between rotten teeth alack.

The rogue in scarlet and grey soon knew his mind
He wished to get his trophy and depart
With gentle apology and touch refined
He pierced him and produced the Captain's heart.

God's mercy rest on Captain Carpenter now
I thought him Sirs an honest gentleman
Citizen husband soldier and scholar enow
Let jangling kites eat of him if they can.

But God's deep curses follow after those
That shore him of his goodly nose and ears
His legs and strong arms at the two elbows
And eyes that had not watered seventy years.

The curse of hell upon the sleek upstart
Who got the Captain finally on his back
And took the red red vitals of his heart
And made the kites to whet their beaks clack clack.

Bells for John Whiteside's Daughter

THERE was such speed in her little body,
   And such lightness in her footfall,
It is no wonder that her brown study
Astonishes us all.

Her wars were bruited in our high window.
We looked among orchard trees and beyond,
Where she took arms against her shadow,
Or harried unto the pond

The lazy geese, like a snow cloud
Dripping their snow on the green grass,
Tricking and stopping, sleepy and proud,
Who cried in goose, Alas,

For the tireless heart within the little
Lady with rod that made them rise
From their noon apple-dreams, and scuttle
Goose-fashion under the skies:

But now go the bells, and we are ready;
In one house we are sternly stopped
To say we are vexed at her brown study,
Lying so primly propped.

Lady Lost

THIS morning, there flew up the lane
A timid lady-bird to our bird-bath
And eyed her image dolefully as death;
This afternoon, knocked on our windowpane
To be let in from the rain.

And when I caught her eye
She looked aside, but at the clapping thunder
And sight of the whole earth blazing up like tinder
Looked in on us again most miserably,
Indeed as if she would cry.

So I will go out into the park and say,
"Who has lost a delicate brown-eyed lady
In the West End Section? Or has anybody
Injured some fine woman in some dark way,
Last night or yesterday?

"Let the owner come and claim possession,
No questions will be asked. But stroke her gently
With loving words, and she will evidently
Resume her full soft-haired white-breasted fashion,
And her right home and her right passion."

Here Lies a Lady

HERE lies a lady of beauty and high degree.
Of chills and fever she died, of fever and chills,
The delight of her husband, her aunts, an infant of three,
And of medicos marveling sweetly on her ills.

For either she burned, and her confident eyes would
    blaze,
And her fingers fly in a manner to puzzle their heads—
What was she making? Why, nothing; she sat in a maze
Of old scraps of laces, snipped into curious shreds—

Or this would pass, and the light of her fire decline
Till she lay discouraged and cold as a thin stalk white
    and blown,
And would not open her eyes, to kisses, to wine.
The sixth of these states was her last; the cold settled
    down.

Sweet ladies, long may ye bloom, and toughly I hope
    ye may thole,
But was she not lucky? In flowers and lace and
    mourning,
In love and great honor we bade God rest her soul
After six little spaces of chill, and six of burning.

EDNA ST. VINCENT MILLAY

Elegy Before Death

THERE will be rose and rhododendron
    When you are dead and under ground;
Still will be heard from white syringas
    Heavy with bees, a sunny sound.

Still will the tamaracks be raining
    After the rain has ceased, and still
Will there be robins in the stubble,
    Brown sheep upon the warm green hill.

Spring will not ail nor autumn falter;
    Nothing will know that you are gone,
Saving alone some sullen plough-land
    None but yourself set foot upon;

Saving the may-weed and the pig-weed
    Nothing will know that you are dead,—
These, and perhaps a useless wagon
    Standing beside some tumbled shed.

Oh, there will pass with your great passing
    Little of beauty not your own,—
Only the light from common water,
    Only the grace from simple stone.

What Lips My Lips Have Kissed

WHAT lips my lips have kissed, and where, and why,
    I have forgotten, and what arms have lain
Under my head till morning; but the rain
Is full of ghosts tonight, that tap and sigh
Upon the glass and listen for reply;
And in my heart there stirs a quiet pain
For unremembered lads that not again
Will turn to me at midnight with a cry.

Thus in the winter stands the lonely tree,
Nor knows what birds have vanished one by one,
Yet knows its boughs more silent than before:
I cannot say what loves have come and gone;
I only know that summer sang in me
A little while, that in me sings no more.

ARCHIBALD MACLEISH

L'An Trentiesme de Mon Âge

AND I have come upon this place
By lost ways, by a nod, by words,
By faces, by an old man's face
At Morlaix lifted to the birds,

By hands upon the tablecloth
At Aldebori's, by the thin
Child's hands that opened to the moth
And let the flutter of the moonlight in,

By hands, by voices, by the voice
Of Mrs. Husman on the stair,
By Margaret's "If we had the choice
To choose or not"—through her thick hair,

By voices, by the creak and fall
Of footsteps on the upper floor,
By silence waiting in the hall
Between the doorbell and the door,

By words, by voices, a lost way—
And here above the chimney stack
The unknown constellations sway—
And by what way shall I go back?

The Too-Late Born

WE too, we too, descending once again
The hills of our own land, we too have heard
Far off—Ah, que ce cor a longue haleine—
The horn of Roland in the passages of Spain,

The first, the second blast, the failing third,
And with the third turned back and climbed once more
The steep road southward, and heard faint the sound
Of swords, of horses, the disastrous war,
And crossed the dark defile at last, and found
At Ronçevaux upon the darkening plain
The dead against the dead and on the silent ground
The silent slain—

Einstein

STANDING between the sun and moon
preserves
A certain secrecy. Or seems to keep
Something inviolate if only that
His father was an ape.
                Sweet music makes
All of his walls sound hollow and he heard
Sighs in the panelling and underfoot
Melancholy voices. So there is a door
Behind the seamless arras and within
A living something:—but no door that will
Admit the sunlight nor no windows where
The mirror moon can penetrate his bones
With cold deflection. He is small and tight
And solidly contracted into space
Opaque and perpendicular which blots
Earth with its shadow. And he terminates
In shoes which bearing up against the sphere
Attract his concentration,

Einstein upon
a public bench
Wednesday the
ninth contem-
plates finity

                    for he ends
If there why then no farther, as, beyond
Extensively the universe itself,
Or chronologically the two dates
Original and ultimate of time,

Nor could Jehovah and the million stars
Staring within their solitudes of light,
Nor all night's constellations be contained

Between his boundaries,
　　　　　　　　nor could the sun
Receive him nor his groping roots run down
Into the loam and steaming sink of time
Where coils the middle serpent and the ooze
Breeds maggots.
　　　　　　　But it seems assured he ends
Precisely at his shoes in proof whereof
He can revolve in orbits opposite
The orbit of the earth and so refuse
All planetary converse. And he wears
Clothes that distinguish him from what is not
His own circumference, as first a coat
Shaped to his back or modelled in reverse
Of the surrounding cosmos and below
Trousers preserving his detachment from
The revolutions of the stars.

Einstein descends the Hartmannsweilerstrasse

　　　　　　　　　　　His hands
And face go naked and alone converse
With what encloses him, as rough and smooth
And sound and silence and the intervals
Of rippling ether and the swarming motes
Clouding a privy: move to them and make
Shadows that mirror them within his skull
In perpendiculars and curves and planes
And bodiless significances blurred
As figures undersea and images
Patterned from eddies of the air.

Einstein ultimately before a mirror accepts the hypothesis of exterior reality

　　　　　　　　　　Which are
Perhaps not shadows but the thing itself
And may be understood.
　　　　　　　Decorticate
The petals of the enfolding world and leave
A world in reason which is in himself
And has his own dimensions. Here do trees
Adorn the hillsides and hillsides enrich
The hazy marches of the sky and skies
Kindle and char to ashes in the wind,
And winds blow toward him from the verge,
　　　and suns

Rise on his dawn and on his dusk go down
And moons prolong his shadow. And he moves
Here as within a garden in a close
And where he moves the bubble of the world
Takes centre and there circle round his head
Like golden flies in summer the gold stars.

Disintegrates.

        For suddenly he feels
The planet plunge beneath him, and a flare
Falls from the upper darkness to the dark
And awful shadows loom across the sky
That have no life from him and suns go out
And livid as a drowned man's face the moon
Floats to the lapsing surface of the night
And sinks discolored under.

                So he knows
Less than a world and must communicate
Beyond his knowledge.

Einstein unsuccessfully after lunch attempts to enter, essaying synthesis with what's not he, the Bernese Oberland

                  Outstretched on the earth
He plunges both his arms into the swirl
Of what surrounds him but the yielding grass
Excludes his finger tips and the soft soil
Will not endure confusion with his hands,
Nor will the air receive him nor the light
Dissolve their difference but recoiling turns
Back from his touch. By which denial he can
Crawl on the earth and sense the opposing sun
But not make answer to them.

                 Put out leaves
And let the old remembering wind think
   through
A green intelligence, or under sea
Float out long filaments of amber in
The numb and wordless revery of tides.

In autumn the black branches dripping rain
Bruise his uncovered bones and in the spring

His swollen tips are gorged with aching blood
That bursts the laurel.

But although they seize
His sense he has no name for them, no word
To give them meaning and no utterance
For what they say. Feel the new summer's sun
Crawl up the warmed relaxing hide of earth
And weep for his lost youth, his childhood
     home
And a wide water on an inland shore!
Or to the night's mute asking in the blood
Give back a girl's name and three notes together!

He cannot think the smell of after rain
Nor close his thought around the long
     smooth lag
And falter of a wind, nor bring to mind
Dusk and the whippoorwill.

*Einstein
dissolved in
violins invades
the molecular
structure of
F. P. Paepke's
Sommergarten.
Is repulsed*

But violins
Split out of trees and strung to tone can sing
Strange nameless words that image to the ear
What has no waiting image in the brain.
She plays in darkness and the droning wood
Dissolves to reverberations of a world
Beating in waves against him, till his sense
Trembles to rhythm and his naked brain
Feels without utterance in form the flesh
Of dumb and incommunicable earth,
And knows at once, and without knowl-
     edge how,
The stroke of the blunt rain, and blind receives
The sun.

When he a moment occupies
The hollow of himself and like an air
Pervades all other.

But the violin
Presses its dry insistence through the dream
That swims above it, shivering its speech
Back to a rhythm that becomes again
Music and vaguely ravels into sound.

*To Einstein
asking at the
gate of stone
none opens*

So then there is no speech that can resolve
Their texture to clear thought and enter them.

The Virgin of Chartres whose bleaching
    bones still wear
The sapphires of her glory knew a word—
That now is three round letters like the three
Round empty staring punctures in a skull.
And there were words in Rome once and
    one time
Words at Eleusis.

              Now there are no words
Nor names to name them and they will
    not speak

Einstein hearing behind the wall of the Grand Hôtel du Nord the stars discovers the Back Stair

But grope against his groping touch and
    throw
The long unmeaning shadows of themselves
Across his shadow and resist his sense.

Why then if they resist destroy them. Dumb
Yet speak them in their elements. Whole,
Break them to reason.

              He lies upon his bed
Exerting on Arcturus and the moon
Forces proportional inversely to
The squares of their remoteness, and conceives
The universe.

      Atomic.

             He can count
Ocean in atoms and weigh out the air
In multiples of one and subdivide
Light to its numbers.

            If they will not speak
Let them be silent in their particles.
Let them be dead and he will lie among
Their dust and cipher them,—undo the signs
Of their unreal identities and free
The pure and single factor of all sums,—
Solve them to unity.

Democritus
Scooped handfuls out of stones and like the sea
Let earth run through his fingers. Well, he too,
He can achieve obliquity and learn
The cold distortion of the winter's sun
That breaks the surfaces of summer.

Einstein on the terrasse of The Acacias forces the secret door

Stands
Facing the world upon a windy slope
And with his mind relaxes the stiff forms
Of all he sees so that the heavy hills
Impend like rushing water and the earth
Hangs on the steep and momentary crest
Of overflowing ruin.

Overflow!
Sweep over into movement and dissolve
All differences in the indifferent flux!
Crumble to eddyings of dust and drown
In change the thing that changes!

There begins
A vague unquiet in the fallow ground,
A seething in the grass, a bubbling swirl
Over the surface of the fields that spreads
Around him gathering until the green
Boils and beneath the frothy loam the rocks
Ferment and simmer and like thinning smoke
The trees melt into nothing.

Still he stands
Watching the vortex widen and involve
In swirling dissolution the whole earth
And circle through the skies till swaying time
Collapses crumpling into dark the stars
And motion ceases and the sifting world
Opens beneath.

When he shall feel infuse
His flesh with the rent body of all else
And spin within his opening brain the motes
Of suns and worlds and spaces.

                              Like a foam
His flesh is withered and his shrivelling
And ashy bones are scattered on the dark.
But still the dark denies him. Still withstands
The dust his penetration and flings back
Himself to answer him.

                              Which seems to keep
Something inviolate. A living something.

You, Andrew Marvell

AND here face down beneath the sun,
 And here upon earth's noonward height
To feel the always coming on,
The always rising of the night.

To feel creep up the curving east
The earthly chill of dusk and slow
Upon those under lands the vast
And ever-climbing shadow grow,

And strange at Ecbatan the trees
Take leaf by leaf the evening, strange,
The flooding dark about their knees,
The mountains over Persia change,

And now at Kermanshah the gate,
Dark, empty, and the withered grass,
And through the twilight now the late
Few travellers in the westward pass.

And Baghdad darken and the bridge
Across the silent river gone,
And through Arabia the edge
Of evening widen and steal on,

And deepen on Palmyra's street
The wheel rut in the ruined stone,
And Lebanon fade out and Crete
High through the clouds and overblown,

And over Sicily the air
Still flashing with the landward gulls,
And loom and slowly disappear
The sails above the shadowy hulls,

And Spain go under and the shore
Of Africa, the gilded sand,
And evening vanish and no more
The low pale light across that land,

Nor now the long light on the sea —

And here face downward in the sun
To feel how swift, how secretly,
The shadow of the night comes on. . . .

Memorial Rain

AMBASSADOR PUSER the ambassador
Reminds himself in French, the felicitous tongue,
What these (young men no longer) lie here for
In rows that once, and somewhere else, were young —

All night in Brussels the wind had tugged at my door:
I had heard the wind at my door and the trees strung
Taut, and to me who had never been before
In that country it was a strange wind blowing
Steadily, stiffening the walls, the floor,
The roof of my room. I had not slept for knowing
He too, dead, was a stranger in that land
And felt beneath the earth in the wind's flowing
A tightening of roots and would not understand,
Remembering lake winds in Illinois,
That strange wind. I had felt his bones in the sand
Listening.

— Reflects that these enjoy
Their country's gratitude, that deep repose,
That peace no pain can break, no hurt destroy,
That rest, that sleep —

                    At Ghent the wind rose.
There was a smell of rain and a heavy drag
Of wind in the hedges but not as the wind blows
Over fresh water when the waves lag
Foaming and the willows huddle and it will rain:
I felt him waiting.

                              —Indicates the flag
Which (may he say) enisles in Flanders' plain
This little field these happy, happy dead
Have made America—

                              In the ripe grain
The wind coiled glistening, darted, fled,
Dragging its heavy body: at Waereghem
The wind coiled in the grass above his head:
Waiting—listening—

                              —Dedicates to them
This earth their bones have hallowed, this last gift
A grateful country—

                              Under the dry grass stem
The words are blurred, are thickened, the words sift
Confused by the rasp of the wind, by the thin grating
Of ants under the grass, the minute shift
And tumble of dusty sand separating
From dusty sand. The roots of the grass strain,
Tighten, the earth is rigid, waits—he is waiting—
And suddenly, and all at once, the rain!

The people scatter, they run into houses, the wind
Is trampled under the rain, shakes free, is again
Trampled. The rain gathers, running in thinned
Spurts of water that ravel in the dry sand
Seeping into the sand under the grass roots, seeping
Between cracked boards to the bones of a clenched
        hand:
The earth relaxes, loosens; he is sleeping,
He rests, he is quiet, he sleeps in a strange land.

MARK VAN DOREN

No Faith

WHAT held the bones together? Not belief,
　　Not anything he could probe, no ligament god.
Why was the world so one for him yet many,
So woman and yet so speechless? Then the odd,
The furtive, ashamed security. We wondered.
But there was no faith in him that sang or thundered.

There was no understanding in this man
Of his own simplest secret: of the way
Earth's air kept warm for him, and how there shone
Always another light outdoors of day.
He would have chosen darkness; he denied
What was so strange, so palpable, inside;

He said he could be unhappy. But we knew.
There was this sweet continuum, this flesh;
There were these bones, articulated so—
A web they were, with music up the mesh,
A frame of hidden wires too deep for tone,
A skeleton wholeness, humming up to him alone.

He must have heard the harmony, but he swore
Time talked to him in separated sounds.
He took them as they came and loved them singly—
Each one, he parried, perfect within its bounds.
As for the burden's end, the tune's direction—
He smiled; he was content with disconnection.

Yet who could smile and mean it? Who could rest,
As this man did, midway the million things?

Who else could be serene at truth's circumference
When only the known center of it sings?
Who else but he? —submissive to each part
Till it became the all, the homeless heart.

His Trees

ONLY when he was old enough, and silent:
  Not breaking-old; time-coated; that was it;
Only when he was dry enough: but seasoned;
Time-guarded against all weather-warp and split;
Time-roughened, with years of ridges down his bark:
Then only grew he worthy of their remark.

They did not move; but watched him as he came,
Man-tired, and paused and peered among their shade.
No magical advancing; each emerged
Only as slow acquaintance thus was made:
The oaks and he confronted, that was all;
Save that his leaves of ignorance could fall.

They fell, and filled the temperate aging air
With a crisp rustle, flake on flake descending;
Till in some month it ceased, and trunk on trunk
Acknowledged him, in rows without an ending.
The lesser with the greater shadows wove:
He there with them, companions of the grove.

The ash was proud to show him in its side
How narrowly and coldly time had cut:
A flank of iron; and how its sharpened leaves
Stood out too stiff for any wind to shut:
Stubborn; yet some antiquity of grace
Still kept it king, still proved the priestly face.

That maple there, the old man of the wood:
Shaggy, with clefts of shadow in its rind;
Like a deep-bearded deity, becloaked,
Shed down upon him, slowly, what of its mind

Went floating: lightly, lightly; though of late
Time pressed it under centuries of weight.

He touched ┌hem all, and moved among their shapes
Like a blind child whom giants might despise.
Yet he was their true copy; so they leaned,
Indulgent to his autumn; met his eyes;
And uttered as much, responding to his hands,
As ever a second childhood understands.

Exaggerator

THE truth for him was like a tree,
　　Was like a funnel; like a fan;
Like any point from which a cone
Spreads upside down until the span
From base to base across the top
Cannot be guessed by any man.

The truth for him was not the seed,
Was not the apex, handle, spout;
Was not the particle or germ,
Or what grew thence so wild and stout;
Was not the great, the upper end.
It was the joy of starting out;

Of feeling something in him rise
And widen instantly—and swell,
As if the wind and he were one,
And blew upon each other well;
As if the sky and he were single:
Clapper there and flangèd bell.

The truth for him was hearing quick
The cordage whistle, and the whine
Of wakened metal; something bronze;
Something moaning thin and fine,
Something low; until it burst,
And all was plangent with word-shine.

The truth for him was leaving earth
Between two beams that sloped and rose;
And never joined—the angle's bound
Was all of distance at the close;
Whence he descended, narrowing down
And resting gently where he chose.

The Whisperer

BE extra careful by this door,
No least, least sound, she said.
It is my brother Oliver's,
And he would strike you dead.

Come on. It is the top step now,
And carpet all the way.
But wide enough for only one,
Unless you carry me.

I love your face as hot as this.
Put me down, though, and creep.
My father! He would strangle you,
I think, like any sheep.

Now take me up again, again;
We're at the landing post.
You hear her saying Hush, and Hush?
It is my mother's ghost.

She would have loved you, loving me.
She had a voice as fine—
I love you more for such a kiss,
And here is mine, is mine.

And one for her—Oh, quick, the door!
I cannot bear it so.
The vestibule, and out; for now
Who passes that would know?

Here we could stand all night and let
Strange people smile and stare.
But you must go, and I must lie
Alone up there, up there.

Remember? But I understand.
More with a kiss is said.
And do not mind it if I cry,
Passing my mother's bed.

E. E. CUMMINGS

Love Is More Thicker Than Forget

LOVE is more thicker than forget
more thinner than recall
more seldom than a wave is wet
more frequent than to fail

it is most mad and moonly
and less it shall unbe
than all the sea which only
is deeper than the sea

love is less always than to win
less never than alive
less bigger than the least begin
less littler than forgive

it is most sane and sunly
and more it cannot die
than all the sky which only
is higher than the sky

My Father Moved Through Dooms of Love

MY father moved through dooms of love
through sames of am through haves of give,
singing each morning out of each night
my father moved through depths of height

this motionless forgetful where
turned at his glance to shining here;
that if (so timid air is firm)
under his eyes would stir and squirm

newly as from unburied which
floats the first who, his april touch
drove sleeping selves to swarm their fates
woke dreamers to their ghostly roots

and should some why completely weep
my father's fingers brought her sleep:
vainly no smallest voice might cry
for he could feel the mountains grow.

Lifting the valleys of the sea
my father moved through griefs of joy;
praising a forehead called the moon
singing desire into begin

joy was his song and joy so pure
a heart of star by him could steer
and pure so now and now so yes
the wrists of twilight would rejoice

keen as midsummer's keen beyond
conceiving mind of sun will stand,
so strictly (over utmost him
so hugely) stood my father's dream

his flesh was flesh his blood was blood:
no hungry man but wished him food;

no cripple wouldn't creep one mile
uphill to only see him smile.

Scorning the pomp of must and shall
my father moved through dooms of feel;
his anger was as right as rain
his pity was as green as grain

septembering arms of year extend
less humbly wealth to foe and friend
than he to foolish and to wise
offered immeasurable is

proudly and (by octobering flame
beckoned) as earth will downward climb.
so naked for immortal work
his shoulders marched against the dark

his sorrow was as true as bread:
no liar looked him in the head;
if every friend became his foe
he'd laugh and build a world with snow.

My father moved through theys of we,
singing each new leaf out of each tree
(and every child was sure that spring
danced when she heard my father sing)

then let men kill which cannot share,
let blood and flesh be mud and mire,
scheming imagine, passion willed,
freedom a drug that's bought and sold

giving to steal and cruel kind,
a heart to fear, to doubt a mind,
to differ a disease of same,
conform the pinnacle of am

though dull were all we taste as bright,
bitter all utterly things sweet,

maggoty minus and dumb death
all we inherit, all bequeath

and nothing quite so least as truth
—i say though hate were why men breathe—
because my father lived his soul
love is the whole and more than all

As Freedom Is a Breakfastfood

AS freedom is a breakfastfood
   or truth can live with right and wrong
or molehills are from mountains made
—long enough and just so long
will being pay the rent of seem
and genius please the talentgang
and water most encourage flame

as hatracks into peachtrees grow
or hopes dance best on bald men's hair
and every finger is a toe
and any courage is a fear
—long enough and just so long
will the impure think all things pure
and hornets wail by children stung

or as the seeing are the blind
and robins never welcome spring
nor flatfolk prove their world is round
nor dingsters die at break of dong
and common's rare and millstones float
—long enough and just so long
tomorrow will not be too late

worms are the words but joy's the voice
down shall go which and up come who
breasts will be breasts thighs will be thighs
deeds cannot dream what dreams can do
—time is a tree (this life one leaf)
but love is the sky and i am for you
just so long and long enough

Always Before Your Voice My Soul

ALWAYS before your voice my soul
half-beautiful and wholly droll
is as some smooth and awkward foal,
whereof young moons begin
the newness of his skin,

so of my stupid sincere youth
the exquisite failure uncouth
discovers a trembling and smooth
Unstrength, against the strong
silences of your song;

or as a single lamb whose sheen
of full unsheared fleece is mean
beside its lovelier friends, between
your thoughts more white than wool
My thought is sorrowful:

but my heart smote in trembling thirds
of anguish quivers to your words,
As to a flight of thirty birds
shakes with a thickening fright
the sudden fooled light.

it is the autumn of a year:
When through the thin air stooped with fear,
across the harvest whitely peer
empty of surprise
death's faultless eyes

(whose hand my folded soul shall know
while on faint hills do frailly go
The peaceful terrors of the snow,
and before your dead face
which sleeps, a dream shall pass)

and these my days their sounds and flowers
Fall in a pride of petaled hours,
like flowers at the feet of mowers
whose bodies strong with love
through meadows hugely move.

yet what am i that such and such
mysteries very simply touch
me, whose heart-wholeness overmuch
Expects of your hair pale,
a terror musical?

while in an earthless hour my fond
soul seriously yearns beyond
this fern of sunset frond on frond
opening in a rare
Slowness of gloried air . . .

The flute of morning stilled in noon—
noon the implacable bassoon—
now Twilight seeks the thrill of moon,
washed with a wild and thin
despair of violin

H. PHELPS PUTNAM

Hasbrouck and the Rose

HASBROUCK was there and so were Bill
And Smollet Smith the poet, and Ames was there.
After his thirteenth drink, the burning Smith,
Raising his fourteenth trembling in the air,
Said, "Drink with me, Bill, drink up to the Rose."
But Hasbrouck laughed like old men in a myth,
Inquiring, "Smollet, are you drunk? What rose?"

And Smollet said, "I drunk? It may be so;
Which comes from brooding on the flower, the flower
I mean toward which mad hour by hour
I travel brokenly; and I shall know,
With Hermes and the alchemists—but, hell,
What use is it talking that way to you?
Hard-boiled, unbroken egg, what can you care
For the enfolded passion of the Rose?"
Then Hasbrouck's voice rang like an icy bell:

"Arcane romantic flower, meaning what?
Do you know what it meant? Do I?
We do not know.
Unfolding pungent rose, the glowing bath
Of ecstasy and clear forgetfulness;
Closing and secret bud one might achieve
By long debauchery—
Except that I have eaten it, and so
There is no call for further lunacy.
In Springfield, Massachusetts, I devoured
The mystic, the improbable, the Rose.
For two nights and a day, rose and rosette,
And petal after petal and the heart,
I had my banquet by the beams
Of four electric stars which shone
Weakly into my room, for there,
Drowning their light and gleaming at my side,
Was the incarnate star
Whose body bore the stigma of the Rose.
And that is all I know about the flower;
I have eaten it—it has disappeared.
There is no Rose."

Young Smollet Smith let fall his glass; he said
"Oh Jesus, Hasbrouck, am I drunk or dead?"

About Women

FAIR golden thoughts and lovely words
   Away, away from her they call,
For women are the silly birds,
And perching on a sunny wall
They chirp the answer and the all;
They hold for true all futile things—
Life, death, and even love—they fall
To dreaming over jeweled rings.

Their bodies are uncouthly made,
And heavy swollen like a pear,
And yet their conquered, undismayed
And childish lovers call them fair.
Their honor fills them full of care,
Their honor that is nothingness,
The mystery of empty air,
The veil of vain delightfulness.

Their subtleties are thin and pale,
Their hearts betray them in their eyes:
They are a simple flute, and frail,
With triple stops for playing lies.
These poor machines of life are wise
To scorn the metaphysic glow,
The careless game that laughs and dies,
The heady grace they cannot know.

Well, give them kisses, scatter flowers,
And whisper that you cannot stay;
We shall have clarity and hours
Which women shall not take away.

ROBERT HILLYER

Letter to a Teacher of English

JAMES B. MUNN

YOUR learning, James, in classics and romance,
Sits lightlier than most men's ignorance;
But often do I see in our profession
Learning a mere extraneous possession,
An undigested mass of dates and sources
Roll'd round in academe's diurnal courses,
Where scholars prepare scholars, not for life,
But gaudy footnotes and a threadbare wife,—
Keen eyes for errors in a worthless text,
But none at all for this world or the next.
Your modesty, that even tops your learning,
Forbids what I would say of you, so turning
Not, as I hope, from Ghibelline to Guelph,
I will discuss, as is the vogue, myself.

I fall between two stools—I can't say Chairs—
A bard too learn'd, a scholar in arrears.
The critical reviewers, week by week,
Damn poets who command their own technique.
Professor is a title that to them
Begins in laughter and concludes in phlegm.
A careful rhyme, a spondee nobly planned
Is academic, and the work unmanned.
Would that these critics lived in houses fashioned
By carpenters congenially impassioned.
I'd love to see the rooftree fall on . . . no,
The name is Legion; let us leave it so.
But as a teacher I have equal luck,—
In ponds a chicken and on shore a duck.

My wretched memory, for all my pains,
Drops tons for every ounce that it retains;
Far wiser now, I have less factual knowledge
At forty-one than when I was in college. . . .

Yet there is recompense for knowing well
One language, if it be incomparable.
Disdainful, the Athenian would speak
No other language than his native Greek.
Now his provincial literature is prized
In every barbarous tongue that he despised.
The learned Roman, who knew Greek by heart,
Had twice the scholarship, and half the art.
The great Elizabethans' education
Thrived less on lore than on superb translation.
Our scholars, to whom every root is known,
Command all languages, except their own.
For confirmation, but consult the theses
That year by year bankrupt the college presses.

When poets go, grammarians arrive.
Is Virgil dead? Let commentators thrive.
The gift of tongues without the Holy Ghost
Becomes a Babel, not a Pentecost.
In short, dear James, by now you plainly see
I find no virtue in philology;
At best a sterile hobby, often worse,
The plumes, when language dies, upon its hearse. . . .

Now, James, I stop complaining, I will plan
An education to produce a man.
Make no mistake, I do not want this done,—
My limitations are the cornerstone.
Plato's *Republic* may have served some use
In manuscript, but not in Syracuse,
So let my dream Academy remain
A dream;—I'm sure I do not ask in vain.
First would I have my scholar learn the tongue
He never learned to speak when he was young;
Then would I have him read therein, but merely

In the great books, to understand them clearly.
O that our living literature could be
Our sustenance, not archæology!
Time is the wisest judge, who folds away
The surplus of a too-abundant day.
My scholar shall be brilliantly forbidden
To dig old garbage from a kitchen midden.
Far better Alexandria in flames
Than buried beneath unimportant names,
And even Sappho, glory that was Greece's,
Lives best, I blasphemously think, in pieces.
Surely our sprite, who over Amherst hovered,
Would gain if no more poems were discovered.
That Chinese emperor who burned the books
Succumbed to madness shrewder than it looks;
The minor poets and the minor sages
Went up in smoke; the great shine down the ages.
The Harvard Library's ungainly porch
Has often made me hunger for a torch,
But this not more to simplify a lecture
Than to appease the Muse of architecture.

When music and sweet poetry agree,
Who would be thinking of a Ph.D.?
O who would Ablauts bear, when Brahms's First
Is soon to be performed or but rehearsed?
My scholar must have music in his heart,
Bach and Beethoven, Schumann and Mozart,
Franck and Sibelius, and more like these,
Their works, if not their names, sweet symphonies.
Ah, James, I missed my calling; I would turn
To that one art toward which the others yearn,—
But I observe my neighbor's cow, who leaves
Her fertile pasture for my barren sheaves.
The field next door, the next-door art, will thus
Always attract the mildly covetous.
Yet some day I will play you the main theme
Of the immortal counterpoint I dream:
Clear melody in fugue and canon rises
On strings, with many structural surprises.

No letter, but a prelude, for your sake
I would compose beside this tranquil lake.
Its line should rise toward heaven until it broke
Halfway between the sky and the great oak;
Then waver, like a flock of homing birds,
In slow descending flights of minor thirds.
Music alone can set the spirit free
From the dark past and darker things to be.
Could Man be judged by music, then the Lord
Would quench the angel of the flaming sword.
Alas, the final tones so soon disperse
Their echoes through the empty universe,
And hearers, weak from following Beethoven,
Relax with Gershwin, Herbert, and de Koven.

But to return to Polyhymnia,
And incidentally to my student. Ah,
Where is the creature? No, but is that he?
A saxophone is nuzzling on his knee!
His eyes pop out, his bellied cheeks expand,
His foot taps "Alexander's Ragtime Band."
Ungraceful and unpardonable wretch!
Was it for you my eager pen would sketch
A new, a sensible curriculum?
Burst with your Panpipes! and we'll both be dumb.
I was about to urge philosophy,
Especially the Greek, I was to be
Your godfather in recommending Faith
To you, fit godson for a Sigmund Spaeth!
Of history and time I was to tell,
Things visible and things invisible,
But what to you are echoes from Nicea,
Who never prayed nor cherished an idea?
And what have you to gain from education,
Blown bellows for unceasing syncopation?
Learning and life are too far wrenched apart,
I cannot reconcile, for all my art,
Studies that go one way and life another,
Tastes that demoralize, and tests that smother.

James, what is this I find? an angry scowl
Sits on my brow like a Palladian owl!
Let me erase it, lest it should transform
The soft horizon with a thunderstorm.
I would you were beside me now, to share
The sound of falling water, the sweet air.
Under the yew a vacant easy chair
Awaits your coming; and long-planted seeds
Begin to bloom amid the encircling weeds.
I bade my student an abrupt adieu
But find it harder to take leave of you.
May we not some day have a mild carouse
In Pontefract instead of Warren House?
The distance nothing,—in two hours' time
Another land where that word's but a rhyme.
Would I were Marvell, then you could not harden
Your heart against a visit to my garden.
I'd write those happy lines about the green
Annihilation, and you'd soon be seen
Hatless and coatless, bootless,—well, my soul!
He's in the lake with nothing on at all!
To sink, to swim, that is the only question:
Thus ends my treatise on—was it digestion?
Farewell, and yours sincerely, and yours ever,
The time has come for the initial shiver.
When into lakes, as into life, we dive,
We're fortunate if we come up alive.

---•·•·•---

EDMUND WILSON

---•·•·•---

Riverton

HERE am I among elms again—ah, look
How, high above low windows hung with white,
Dark on white dwellings, rooted among rock,

They rise like iron ribs that pillar night!
The stars are high again; the night is clear;
The bed rolls with the old uneven floor;
The air is still again—I lie and hear
The river always falling at the door.

—O elms! O river! aid me at this turn—
Their passing makes my late imperative:
They flicker now who frightfully did burn,
And I must tell their beauty while I live.
Changing their grace as water in its flight,
And gone like water; give me then the art,
Firm as night-frozen ice found silver-bright,
That holds the splendor though the days depart.

A House of the Eighties

NO more in dreams as once it draws me there,
All fungus-grown and sunken in damp ground—
No more as once when waking I gazed down
On elms like water-weeds in moonlit air
Or heard the August downpour with its dull full sound—
Drenched hedges and the hillside and the night,
The largest house in sight—
And thought it sunken out of time or drowned
As hulks in Newark Bay are soaked and slowly drown.

—The ugly stained-glass window on the stair,
Dark-panelled dining-room, the guinea fowl's fierce clack,
The great gray cat that on the oven slept—
My father's study with its books and birds,
His scornful tone, his eighteenth-century words,
His green door sealed with baize
—Today I travel back
To find again that one fixed point he kept
And left me for the day
In which this other world of theirs grows dank, decays,
And founders and goes down.

LOUISE BOGAN

Summer Wish

That cry's from the first cuckoo
of the year.
I wished before it ceased.

FIRST VOICE

WE call up the green to hide us
     This hardened month, by no means the beginning
Of the natural year, but of the shortened span
Of leaves upon the earth. We call upon
The weed as well as the flower: groundsel, stellaria.
It is the month to make the summer wish;
It is time to ask
The wish from summer as always: *It will be,*
It will be.
          That tool we have used
So that its haft is smooth; it knows the hand.
Again we lift the wish to its expert uses,
Tired of the bird that calls one long note downward,
And the forest in cast-iron. No longer, no longer,
The season of the lying equinox
Wherein false cock-crow sounds!

SECOND VOICE

In March the shadow
Already falls with a look of summer, fuller
Upon the snow, because the sun at last
Is almost centered. Later, the sprung moss
Is the tree's shadow; under the black spruces
It lies where lately snow lay, bred green from the cold
Cast down from melting branches.

FIRST VOICE

A wish like a hundred others.
You cannot, as once, yearn forward. The blood now never
Stirs hot to memory, or to the fantasy
Of love, with which, both early and late, one lies
As with a lover.
Now do you suddenly envy
Poor praise you told long since to keep its tongue,
Of pride's acquired accent,—pomposity, arrogance,
That trip in their latinity? With these at heart
You could make a wish, crammed with the nobility
Of error. It would be no use. You cannot
Take yourself in.

SECOND VOICE

Count over what these days have: lilies
Returned in little to an earth unready,
To the sun not accountable;
The hillside mazed and leafless, but through the ground
The leaf from the bulb, the unencouraged green
Heaving the metal earth, presage of thousand
Shapes of young leaves—lanceolate, trefoil,
Peach, willow, plum, the lilac like a heart.

FIRST VOICE

Memory long since put by,—to what end the dream
That drags back lived-out life with the wrong words,
The substitute meaning?
Those that you once knew there play out false time,
Elaborate yesterday's words, that they were deaf to,
Being dead ten years.—Call back in anguish
The anger in childhood that defiled the house
In walls and timber with its violence?
Now must you listen again
To your own tears, shed as a child, hold the bruise
With your hand, and weep, fallen against the wall,
And beg, *Don't, don't,* while the pitiful rage goes on
That cannot stem itself?
Or, having come into woman's full estate,

Enter the rich field, walk between the bitter
Bowed grain, being compelled to serve,
To heed unchecked in the heart the reckless fury
That tears fresh day from day, destroys its traces,—
Now bear the blow too young?

SECOND VOICE

In early April
At six o'clock the sun has not set; on the walls
It shines with scant light, pale, dilute, misplaced,
Light there's no use for. At overcast noon
The sun comes out in a flash, and is taken
Slowly back to the cloud.

FIRST VOICE

Not memory, and not the renewed conjecture
Of passion that opens the breast, the unguarded look
Flaying clean the raped defence of the body,
Breast, bowels, throat, now pulled to the use of the eyes
That see and are taken. The body that works and sleeps,
Made vulnerable, night and day, to delight that changes
Upon the lips that taste it, to the lash of jealousy
Struck on the face, so the betraying bed
Is gashed clear, cold on the mind, together with
Every embrace that agony dreads but sees
Open as the love of dogs.

SECOND VOICE

The cloud shadow flies up the bank, but does not
Blow off like smoke. It stops at the bank's edge.
In the field by trees two shadows come together.
The trees and the cloud throw down their shadow upon
The man who walks there. Dark flows up from his feet
To his shoulders and throat, then has his face in its mask,
Then lifts.

FIRST VOICE

Will you turn to yourself, proud breast,
Sink to yourself, to an ingrained, pitiless
Rejection of voice and touch not your own, press sight

Into a myth no eye can take the gist of;
Clot up the bone of phrase with the black conflict
That claws it back from sense?

> Go into the breast . . .

You have traced that lie, before this, out to its end,
Heard bright wit headstrong in the beautiful voice
Changed to a word mumbled across the shoulder
To one not there; the gentle self split up
Into a yelling fiend and a soft child.
You have seen the ingrown look
Come at last upon a vision too strong
Ever to turn away.

The breast's six madnesses repeat their dumb-show.

SECOND VOICE

In the bright twilight children call out in the fields.
The evening takes their cry. How late it is!
Around old weeds worn thin and bleached to their pith
The field has leaped to stalk and strawberry blossom.
The orchard by the road
Has the pear-tree full at once of flowers and leaves,
The cherry with flowers only.

FIRST VOICE

The mind for refuge, the grain of reason, the will,
Pulled by a wind it thinks to point and name?
Malicious symbol, key for rusty wards,
The crafty knight in the game, with its mixed move,
Prey to an end not evident to craft. . . .

SECOND VOICE

Fields are ploughed inward
From edge to center; furrows squaring off
Make dark lines far out in irregular fields,
On hills that are builded like great clouds that over them
Rise, to depart.
Furrow within furrow, square within a square,
Draw to the center where the team turns last.
Horses in half-ploughed fields
Make earth they walk upon a changing color.

FIRST VOICE

The year's begun; the share's again in the earth.

Speak out the wish like music, that has within it
The horn, the string, the drum pitched deep as grief.
Speak it like laughter, outward. O brave, O generous
Laughter that pours from the well of the body and draws
The bane that cheats the heart: aconite, nightshade,
Hellebore, hyssop, rue,—symbols and poisons
We drink, in fervor, thinking to gain thereby
Some difference, some distinction.
Speak it, as that man said, *as though the earth spoke,*
By the body of rock, shafts of heaved strata, separate,
Together.
           Though it be but for sleep at night,
Speak out the wish.
The vine we pitied is in leaf; the wild
Honeysuckle blows by the granite.

SECOND VOICE

See now
Open above the field, stilled in wing-stiffened flight,
The stretched hawk fly.

———— •◆•◆• ————

MALCOLM COWLEY

—— •◆•◆• ——

The Long Voyage

NOT that the pines were darker there,
nor mid-May dogwood brighter there,
nor swifts more swift in summer air;
    it was my own country,

having its thunderclap of spring,
its long midsummer ripening,

its corn hoar-stiff at harvesting,
    almost like any country.

yet being mine; its face, its speech,
its hills bent low within my reach,
its river birch and upland beech
    were mine, of my own country.

Now the dark waters at the bow
fold back, like earth against the plow;
foam brightens like the dogwood now
    at home, in my own country.

———•—•—•———

THEODORE SPENCER

———•—•—•———

Song

I WHO love you bring
  Against our cherishing
These faults I daren't deny
Lest love should prove a lie.
    But Oh, if you love me forgive me,
    And none of this is true.

A too resilient mind
That seeking fact, must find
Reasons on every side
Why fact should be denied.
    But Oh, if you love me forgive me,
    And none of this is true.

A body that has wooed
More pleasure than it should,
And for that pleasure sought
What it had thrived without.
    But Oh, if you love me, forgive me,
    And none of this is true.

And until now, a soul
That could find no goal
Beyond body and mind;
And so turned blind.
　　　But Oh, if you love me, forgive me,
　　　And none of this is true.

Spring Song

I have come again, gentlemen and ladies,
　Whatever you call me, ladies, gentlemen;
Dancing, dancing down, sweet ladies,
And up with a dance I come, kind gentlemen;
I am here; we are dancing again.

Brown leaf on a dust-hill, ladies, ladies;
A running ant from the dust-hill, gentlemen;
Look out of the window; here I am;
Look back to the bedroom; here I am.
Sleep; and we'll fall together, gentlemen—
Falling towers and crumpled gowns
To a dust, a most sleepy dust, ladies,
From towers and golden gowns. But sleep,
Oh sleep again, and I'll promise you green,
A green, shattering sun-blade green,
With a daffodil prance like forever, gentlemen,
Forever a tower of gold like a daffodil.

I have come again, gentlemen and ladies;
Whatever you call me, a leaf and a dust-hill;
Dancing up, gentlemen, sweet ladies;
And dancing down, ladies, kind gentlemen.
I am here; we are dancing again.

R. P. BLACKMUR

Half-Tide Ledge

SUNDAY the sea made morning worship, sang
Venite, Kyrie, and a long Amen,
over a flowing cassock did put on
glittering blindness, surplice of the sun.
Towards high noon her eldest, high-run tide
rebelled at formal song and in the Sanctus
made heavy mockery of God,
and I, almost before I knew it, saw
the altar ledges of the Lord awash.
These are the obsequies I think on most.

Scarabs for the Living

I

O sailor sailor tell me why
though in the seawine of your eye
I see nothing dead and nothing die
I know from the stillness seething there
my heart's hope is my soul's despair.

II

To meditate upon the tiger, turn
your human eyes from his past-human stare;
beyond his cage a pigeon tops an urn,
beyond the pigeon falls the twilight air,
and there, steadfast, he sees a viewless lair.

III

Lay down one hand before you like a tool
and let the other, in your mind, grow strange;
then let the strangers meet. Who but a fool

or a passionate man, thinks loss is blood-exchange,
if the cold hand should warm and the hot cool!

IV

Within this windless covert silence drops
leaf by leaf and birches make bare bones;
a startled woodcock's whistling flight new-stops
the wind beyond the woods, and I, alone,
feel my still flight trembling into stone.

V

There is, besides the warmth, in this new love—
besides the radiance, the spring—the chill
that in the old had seemed the slow, the still
amounting up of that indifferent will
in which we die. I keep last winter's glove.

VI

Oh, I was honest in the womb
where I had neither time nor room
nor any secret hope to hide.
Now there are love and work this side
of honesty, two hopes that lied.

VII

The chickadee-dee-dee is not a bird
like stilted heron fishing minnie pools
that in their fleeing shriek the sky like fools;
the chickadee (dee-dee) is most a word
to keep the thicket warm when summer cools.

VIII

It is the slow encroachment, word by word,
of sleep upon the wakened mind, the slow
manoeuvre of unseemly vertigo,
whereby disease in order is inferred;
and in the sleep a blotting fall of snow.

IX

Quiet the self, and silence brims like spring:
the soaking in of light, the gathering

of shadow up, after each passing cloud,
the green life eating into death aloud,
the hum of seasons; all on beating wing.

Sir Gawaine and the Green Knight

REPTILIAN green the wrinkled throat,
Green as a bough of yew the beard;
He bent his head, and so I smote;
Then for a thought my vision cleared.

The head dropped clean; he rose and walked;
He fixed his fingers in the hair;
The head was unabashed and talked;
I understood what I must dare.

His flesh, cut down, arose and grew.
He bade me wait the season's round,
And then, when he had strength anew,
To meet him on his native ground.

The year declined; and in his keep
I passed in joy a thriving yule;
And whether waking or in sleep,
I lived in riot like a fool.

He beat the woods to bring me meat.
His lady, like a forest vine,
Grew in my arms; the growth was sweet;
And yet what thoughtless force was mine!

By practice and conviction formed,
With ancient stubbornness ingrained,

Although her body clung and swarmed,
My own identity remained.

Her beauty, lithe, unholy, pure
Took shapes that I had never known;
And had I once been insecure,
Had grafted laurel in my bone.

And then, since I had kept the trust,
Had loved the lady, yet was true,
The knight withheld his giant thrust
And let me go with what I knew.

I left the green bark and the shade,
Where growth was rapid, thick, and still;
I found a road that men had made
And rested on a drying hill.

JOHN WHEELWRIGHT

Train Ride

AFTER rain, through afterglow, the unfolding fan
of railway landscape sidled on the pivot
of a larger arc into the green of evening;
I remembered that noon I saw a gradual bud
still white; though dead in its warm bloom; though dead in its warm bloom;
always the enemy is the foe at home.
    And I wondered what surgery could recover
our lost, long stride of indolence and leisure
which is labor in reverse; what physic recalls the smile
not of lips, but of eyes as of the sea bemused.
    We, when we disperse from common sleep to several
tasks, we gather to despair; we, who assembled
once for hopes from common toil to dreams
or sickish and hurting or triumphal rapture;

always the enemy is our foe at home.

We, deafened with far scattered city rattles
to the hubbub of forest birds (never having
'had time" to grieve or to hear through vivid sleep
the sea knock on its cracked and hollow stones)
so that the stars, almost, and birds comply,
and the garden-wet; the trees retire; We are
a scared patrol, fearing the guns behind;
always the enemy is the foe at home.

What wonder that we fear our own eyes' look
and fidget to be at home alone, and pitifully
put off age by some change in brushing the hair
and stumble to our ends like smothered runners at their
      tape;
      Then (as while the stars herd to the great trough
the blind, in the always-only-outward of their dismantled
archways, awake at the smell of warmed stone
or to the sound of reeds, lifting from the dim
into their segment of green dawn) *always
our enemy is our foe at home,* more
certainly than through spoken words or from grief-
twisted writing on paper, unblotted by tears
the thought came:
                There is no physic
for the world's ill, nor surgery; it must
(hot smell of tar on wet salt air)
burn in a fever forever, an incense pierced
with arrows, whose name is Love and another name
Rebellion (the twinge, the gulf, split seconds,
the very raindrop, render, and instancy
of Love).

All Poetry to this not-to-be-looked-upon sun
of Passion is the moon's cupped light; all
Politics to this moon, a moon's reflected
cupped light, like the moon of Rome, after
the deep wells of Grecian light sank low;
always the enemy is the foe at home.

But these three are friends whose arms twine
without words; as, in a still air,
the great grove leans to wind, past and to come.

Fish Food

An Obituary to Hart Crane

AS you drank deep as Thor, did you think of milk or wine?
Did you drink blood, while you drank the salt deep?
Or see through the film of light, that sharpened your rage with
　　its stare,
a shark, dolphin, turtle? Did you not see the Cat
who, when Thor lifted her, unbased the cubic ground?
You would drain fathomless flagons to be slaked with vacuum—
The sea's teats have suckled you, and you are sunk far
in bubble-dreams, under swaying translucent vines
of thundering interior wonder. Eagles can never now
carry parts of your body, over cupped mountains
as emblems of their anger, embers to fire self-hate
to other wonders, unfolding white flaming vistas.

Fishes now look upon you, with eyes which do not gossip.
Fishes are never shocked. Fishes will kiss you, each
fish tweak you; every kiss takes bits of you away,
till your bones alone will roll, with the Gulf Stream's swell.
So has it been already, so have the carpers and puffers
nibbled your carcass of fame, each to his liking. Now
in tides of noon, the bones of your thought-suspended structures
gleam as you intended. Noon pulled your eyes with small
magnetic headaches; the will seeped from your blood. Seeds
of meaning popped from the pods of thought. And you fall.
　　And the unseen
churn of Time changes the pearl-hued ocean;
like a pearl-shaped drop, in a huge water-clock
falling; from *came* to *go,* from *come* to *went.* And you fell.
Waters received you. Waters of our Birth in Death dissolve you.
Now you have willed it, may the Great Wash take you.
As the Mother-Lover takes your woe away, and cleansing
grief and you away, you sleep, you do not snore.
Lie still. Your rage is gone on a bright flood
away; as, when a bad friend held out his hand

you said, "Do not talk any more. I know you meant no harm."
What was the soil whence your anger sprang, who are deaf
as the stones to the whispering flight of the Mississippi's rivers?
What did you see as you fell? What did you hear as you sank?
Did it make you drunken with hearing?
I will not ask any more. You saw or heard no evil.

ALLEN TATE

Ode to the Confederate Dead

ROW after row with strict impunity
The headstones yield their names to the element,
The wind whirrs without recollection;
In the riven troughs the splayed leaves
Pile up, of nature the casual sacrament
To the seasonal eternity of death;
Then driven by the fierce scrutiny
Of heaven to their election in the vast breath,
They sough the rumor of mortality.

Autumn is desolation in the plot
Of a thousand acres where these memories grow
From the inexhaustible bodies that are not
Dead, but feed the grass row after rich row.
Think of the autumns that have come and gone!—
Ambitious November with the humors of the year,
With a particular zeal for every slab,
Staining the uncomfortable angels that rot
On the siabs, a wing chipped here, an arm there:
The brute curiosity of an angel's stare
Turns you, like them, to stone,
Transforms the heaving air

Till plunged to a heavier world below
You shift your sea-space blindly
Heaving, turning like the blind crab.

Dazed by the wind, only the wind
The leaves flying, plunge

You know who have waited by the wall
The twilight certainty of an animal,
Those midnight restitutions of the blood
You know—the immitigable pines, the smoky frieze
Of the sky, the sudden call: you know the rage,
The cold pool left by the mounting flood,
Of muted Zeno and Parmenides.
You who have waited for the angry resolution
Of those desires that should be yours tomorrow,

You know the unimportant shrift of death
And praise the vision
And praise the arrogant circumstance
Of those who fall
Rank upon rank, hurried beyond decision—
Here by the sagging gate, stopped by the wall.

Seeing, seeing only the leaves
Flying, plunge and expire

Turn your eyes to the immoderate past,
Turn to the inscrutable infantry rising
Demons out of the earth—they will not last.
Stonewall, Stonewall, and the sunken fields of hemp,
Shiloh, Antietam, Malvern Hill, Bull Run.
Lost in that orient of the thick and fast
You will curse the setting sun.

Cursing only the leaves crying
Like an old man in a storm

You hear the shout, the crazy hemlocks point
With troubled fingers to the silence which
Smothers you, a mummy, in time.

                           The hound bitch
Toothless and dying, in a musty cellar
Hears the wind only.

                     Now that the salt of their blood
Stiffens the saltier oblivion of the sea,
Seals the malignant purity of the flood,
What shall we who count our days and bow
Our heads with a commemorial woe
In the ribboned coats of grim felicity,
What shall we say of the bones, unclean,
Whose verdurous anonymity will grow?

The ragged arms, the ragged heads and eyes
Lost in these acres of the insane green?
The gray lean spiders come, they come and go;
In a tangle of willows without light
The singular screech-owl's tight
Invisible lyric seeds the mind
With the furious murmur of their chivalry.

    We shall say only the leaves
    Flying, plunge and expire

We shall say only the leaves whispering
In the improbable mist of nightfall
That flies on multiple wing:
Night is the beginning and the end
And in between the ends of distraction
Waits mute speculation, the patient curse
That stones the eyes, or like the jaguar leaps
For his own image in a jungle pool, his victim.

What shall we say who have knowledge
Carried to the heart? Shall we take the act
To the grave? Shall we, more hopeful, set up the grave
In the house? The ravenous grave?

Leave now
The shut gate and the decomposing wall:
The gentle serpent, green in the mulberry bush,
Riots with his tongue through the hush—
Sentinel of the grave who counts us all!

HART CRANE

VOYAGES: II

AND yet this great wing of eternity,
  Of rimless floods, unfettered leewardings,
Samite sheeted and processioned where
Her undinal vast belly moonward bends,
Laughing the wrapt inflections of our love;

Take this Sea, whose diapason knells
On scrolls of silver snowy sentences,
The sceptered terror of whose sessions rends
As her demeanors motion well or ill,
All but the pieties of lovers' hands.

And onward, as bells off San Salvador
Salute the crocus lusters of the stars,
In these poinsettia meadows of her tides,—
Adagios of islands, O my Prodigal,
Complete the dark confessions her veins spell.

Mark how her turning shoulders wind the hours,
And hasten while her penniless rich palms
Pass superscription of bent foam and wave,—
Hasten, while they are true,—sleep, death, desire,
Close round one instant in one floating flower.

Bind us in time, O seasons clear, and awe.
O minstrel galleons of Carib fire,

Bequeath us to no earthly shore until
Is answered in the vortex of our grave
The seal's wide spindthrift gaze toward paradise.

VOYAGES: VI

Where icy and bright dungeons lift
Of swimmers their lost morning eyes,
And ocean rivers, churning, shift
Green borders under stranger skies,

Steadily as a shell secretes
Its beating leagues of monotone,
Or as many waters trough the sun's
Red kelson past the cape's wet stone;

O rivers mingling toward the sky
And harbor of the phoenix' breast—
My eyes pressed black against the prow,
—Thy derelict and blinded guest

Waiting, afire, what name, unspoke,
I cannot claim: let thy waves rear
More savage than the death of kings,
Some splintered garland for the seer.

Beyond siroccos harvesting
The solstice thunders, crept away,
Like a cliff swinging or a sail
Flung into April's inmost day—

Creation's blithe and petaled word
To the lounged goddess when she rose
Conceding dialogue with eyes
That smile unsearchable repose—

Still fervid convenant, Belle Isle,
—Unfolded floating dais before
Which rainbows twine continual hair—
Belle Isle, white echo of the oar!

The imaged word, it is, that holds
Hushed willows anchored in its glow.
It is the unbetrayable reply
Whose accent no farewell can know.

Praise for an Urn

IT was a kind and northern face
That mingled in such exile guise
The everlasting eyes of Pierrot
And, of Gargantua, the laughter.

His thoughts, delivered to me
From the white coverlet and pillow,
I see now, were inheritances—
Delicate riders of the storm.

The slant moon on the slanting hill
Once moved us toward presentiments
Of what the dead keep, living still,
And such assessments of the soul

As, perched in the crematory lobby,
The insistent clock commented on,
Touching as well upon our praise
Of glories proper to the time.

Still, having in mind gold hair,
I cannot see that broken brow
And miss the dry sound of bees
Stretching across a lucid space.

Scatter these well-meant idioms
Into the smoky spring that fills
The suburbs, where they will be lost.
They are no trophies of the sun.

The River

(from "The Bridge")

S TICK your patent name on a signboard
brother—all over—going west—young man
Tintex—Japalac—Certain-teed Overalls ads
and lands sakes! under the new playbill ripped
in the guaranteed corner—see Bert Williams what?
Minstrels when you steal a chicken just
save me the wing, for if it isn't
Erie it ain't for miles around a
Mazda—and the telegraphic night coming on Thomas

a Ediford—and whistling down the tracks
a headlight rushing with the sound—can you
imagine—while an EXPRESS makes time like
SCIENCE—COMMERCE and the HOLYGHOST
RADIO ROARS IN EVERY HOME WE HAVE THE NORTHPOLE
WALLSTREET AND VIRGINBIRTH WITHOUT STONES OR
WIRES OR EVEN RUNNING brooks connecting ears
and no more sermons windows flashing roar
Breathtaking—as you like it . . . eh?

                              So the 20th Century—so
whizzed the Limited—roared by and left
three men, still hungry on the tracks, ploddingly
watching the tail lights wizen and converge, slip-
ping gimleted and neatly out of sight.
The last bear, shot drinking in the Dakotas,
Loped under wires that span the mountain stream.
Keen instruments, strung to a vast precision
Bind town to town and dream to ticking dream.
But some men take their liquor slow—and count
—Though they'll confess no rosary nor clue—
The river's minute by the far brook's year.
Under a world of whistles, wires and steam
Caboose-like they go ruminating through
Ohio, Indiana—blind baggage—
To Cheyenne tagging . . . Maybe Kalamazoo.

Time's renderings, time's blendings they construe
As final reckonings of fire and snow;
Strange bird-wit, like the elemental gist
Of unwalled winds they offer, singing low
My Old Kentucky Home and *Casey Jones,*
Some Sunny Day. I heard a road-gang chanting so.
And afterwards, who had a colt's eyes—one said,
"Jesus! Oh I remember watermelon days!" And sped
High in a cloud of merriment, recalled
"—And when my Aunt Sally Simpson smiled," he
    drawled—
"It was almost Louisiana, long ago."

"There's no place like Booneville though, Buddy,"
One said, excising a last burr from his vest,
"—For early trouting." Then peering in the can,
"—But I kept on the tracks." Possessed, resigned,
He trod the fire down pensively and grinned,
Spreading dry shingles of a beard. . . .

                         Behind
My father's cannery works I used to see
Rail-squatters ranged in nomad raillery,
The ancient men—wifeless or runaway
Hobo-trekkers that forever search
An empire wilderness of freight and rails.
Each seemed a child, like me, on a loose perch,
Holding to childhood like some termless play.
John, Jake, or Charley, hopping the slow freight
—Memphis to Tallahassee—riding the rods,
Blinding fists of nothing, humpty-dumpty clods.

Yet they touch something like a key perhaps.
From pole to pole across the hills, the states
—They know a body under the wide rain;
Youngsters with eyes like fjords, old reprobates
With racetrack jargon,—dotting immensity
They lurk across her, knowing her yonder breast
Snow-silvered, sumac-stained or smoky blue,
Is past the valley-sleepers, south or west.
—As I have trod the rumorous midnights, too.

And past the circuit of the lamp's thin flame
(O Nights that brought me to her body bare!)
Have dreamed beyond the print that bound her name.
Trains sounding the long blizzards out—I heard
Wail into distances I knew were hers.
Papooses crying on the wind's long mane
Screamed redskin dynasties that fled the brain,
—Dead echoes! But I knew her body there,
Time like a serpent down her shoulder, dark,
And space, an eaglet's wing, laid on her hair.

Under the Ozarks, domed by Iron Mountain,
The old gods of the rain lie wrapped in pools
Where eyeless fish curvet a sunken fountain
And re-descend with corn from querulous crows.
Such pilferings make up their timeless eatage,
Propitiate them for their timber torn
By iron, iron—always the iron dealt cleavage!
They doze now, below axe and powder horn.

And Pullman breakfasters glide glistening steel
From tunnel into field—iron strides the dew—
Straddles the hill, a dance of wheel on wheel.
You have a half-hour's wait at Siskiyou,
Or stay the night and take the next train through.
Southward, near Cairo passing, you can see
The Ohio merging,—borne down Tennessee;
And if it's summer and the sun's in dusk
Maybe the breeze will lift the River's musk
—As though the waters breathed that you might know
Memphis Johnny, Steamboat Bill, Missouri Joe.
Oh, lean from the window, if the train slows down,
As though you touched hands with some ancient clown,
—A little while gaze absently below
And hum *Deep River* with them while they go.

Yes, turn again and sniff once more—look see,
O Sheriff, Brakeman and Authority—
Hitch up your pants and crunch another quid,
For you, too, feed the River timelessly.

And few evade full measure of their fate;
Always they smile out eerily what they seem.
I could believe he joked at heaven's gate—
Dan Midland—jolted from the cold brake-beam.

Down, down—born pioneers in time's despite,
Grimed tributaries to an ancient flow—
They win no frontier by their wayward plight,
But drift in stillness, as from Jordan's brow.

You will not hear it as the sea; even stone
Is not more hushed by gravity . . . But slow,
As loth to take more tribute—sliding prone
Like one whose eyes were buried long ago

The River, spreading, flows—and spends your dream.
What are you, lost within this tideless spell?
You are your father's father, and the stream—
A liquid theme that floating niggers swell.

Damp tonnage and alluvial march of days—
Nights turbid, vascular with silted shale
And roots surrendered down of moraine clays:
The Mississippi drinks the farthest dale.

O quarrying passion, undertowed sunlight!
The basalt surface drags a jungle grace
Ochreous and lynx-barred in lengthening might;
Patience! and you shall reach the biding place!

Over De Soto's bones the freighted floors
Throb past the City storied of three thrones.
Down two more turns the Mississippi pours
(Anon tall ironsides up from salt lagoons)

And flows within itself, heaps itself free.
All fades but one thin skyline 'round . . . Ahead
No embrace opens but the stinging sea;
The River lifts itself from its long bed,

Poised wholly on its dream, a mustard glow,
Tortured with history, its one will—flow!
—The Passion spreads in wide tongues, choked and slow,
Meeting the Gulf, hosannas silently below.

The Dance

(from "The Bridge")

THE swift red flesh, a winter king— *A*
   Who squired the glacier woman down the sky? *B*
She ran the neighing canyons all the spring; *A*
She spouted arms; she rose with maize—to die. *B*

And in the autumn drouth, whose burnished hands *C*
With mineral wariness found out the stone *D*
Where prayers, forgotten, streamed the mesa sands? *C*
He holds the twilight's dim, perpetual throne. *D*

Mythical brows we saw retiring—loth, *E*
Disturbed and destined, into denser green. *F*
Greeting they sped us, on the arrow's oath: *E*
Now lie incorrigibly what years between. . . . *F*

There was a bed of leaves, and broken play; *G*
There was a veil upon you, Pocahontas, bride— *H*
O Princess whose brown lap was virgin May; *G*
And bridal flanks and eyes hid tawny pride. *H*

I left the village for dogwood. By the canoe *I*
Tugging below the mill-race, I could see *J*
Your hair's keen crescent running, and the blue *I*
First moth of evening take wing stealthily. *J*

What laughing chains the water wove and threw!
I learned to catch the trout's moon whisper; I
Drifted how many hours I never knew,
But, watching, saw that fleet young crescent die,—

And one star, swinging, take its place, alone,
Cupped in the larches of the mountain pass —
Until, immortally, it bled into the dawn.
I left my sleek boat nibbling margin grass. . . .

I took the portage climb, then chose
A further valley-shed; I could not stop.
Feet nozzled watery webs of upper flows;
One white veil gusted from the very top.

O Appalachian Spring! I gained the ledge;
Steep, inaccessible smile that eastward bends
And northward reaches in that violet wedge
Of Adirondack! — wisped of azure wands,

Over how many bluffs, tarns, streams I sped!
— And knew myself within some boding shade:
Grey tepees tufting the blue knolls ahead,
Smoke swirling through the yellow chestnut glade. . .

A distant cloud, a thunder bud — it grew,
That blanket of the skies: the padded foot
Within, — I hear it; 'til its rhythm drew,
— Siphoned the black pool from the heart's hot root.

A cyclone threshes in the turbine crest,
Swooping in eagle feathers down your back;
Know, Maquokeeta, greeting; know death's best,
— Fall, Sachem, strictly as the tamarack!

A birch kneels. All her whistling fingers fly.
The oak grove circles in a crash of leaves;
The long moan of a dance is in the sky.
Dance, Maquokeeta: Pocahontas grieves . . .

And every tendon scurries toward the twangs
Of lightning deltaed down your saber hair.
Now snaps the flint in every tooth; red fangs
And splay tongues thinly busy the blue air. . . .

Dance, Maquokeeta! snake that lives before,
That casts his pelt, and lives beyond! Sprout, horn!
Spark, tooth! Medicine-man, relent, restore—
Lie to us—dance us back the tribal morn!

Spears and assemblies: black drums thrusting on—
O yelling battlements,—I, too, was liege
To rainbows currying each pulsant bone:
Surpassed the circumstance, danced out the siege!

And buzzard-circleted, screamed from the stake;
I could not pick the arrows from my side.
Wrapped in that fire, I saw more escorts wake—
Flickering, sprint up the hill, groins like a tide.

I heard the hush of lava wrestling your arms,
And stag teeth foam about the raven throat;
Flame cataracts of heaven in seething swarms
Fed down your anklets to the sunset's moat.

Oh, like the lizard in the furious noon,
That drops his legs and colors in the sun,
—And laughs, pure serpent, Time itself, and moon
Of his own fate, I saw thy change begun!

And saw thee dive to kiss that destiny
Like one white meteor, sacrosanct and blent
At last with all that's consummate and free
There, where the first and last gods keep thy tent.

*   *   *

Thewed of the levin, thunder-shod and lean,
Lo, through what infinite seasons dost thou gaze—
Across what bivouacs of thine angered slain,
And see'st thy bride immortal in the maize!

Totem and fire-gall, slumbering pyramid—
Though other calendars now stack the sky,
Thy freedom is her largesse, Prince, and hid
On paths thou knewest best to claim her by.

High unto Labrador the sun strikes free
Her speechless dream of snow, and stirred **again,**
She is the torrent and the singing tree;
And she is virgin to the last of men. . . .

West, west and south! winds over Cumberland
And winds across the llano grass resume
Her hair's warm sibilance. Her breasts are fanned·—
O stream by slope and vineyard—into bloom!

And when the caribou slant down for salt
Do arrows thirst and leap? Do antlers shine
Alert, star-triggered in the listening vault
Of dusk?—And are her perfect brows to thine?

We danced, O Brave, we danced beyond their farms,
In cobalt desert closures made our vows . . .
Now is the strong prayer folded in thine arms,
The serpent with the eagle in the boughs.

Indiana

(from "The Bridge")

. . . and read her in a mother's farewell gaze.

THE morning-glory, climbing the morning long
    Over the lintel on its wiry vine,
Closes before the dusk, furls in its song
    As I close mine . . .

And bison thunder rends my dreams no more
    As once my womb was torn, my boy, when you
Yielded your first cry at the prairie's door . . .
    Your father knew

Then, though we'd buried him behind us, far
    Back on the gold trail—then his lost bones stirred . . .
But you who drop the scythe to grasp the oar
    Knew not, nor heard.

How we, too, Prodigal, once rode off, too—
  Waved Seminary Hill a gay good-bye . . .
We found God lavish there in Colorado
      But passing sly.

The pebbles sang, the firecat slunk away
  And glistening through the sluggard freshets came
In golden syllables loosed from the clay
      His gleaming name.

A dream called Eldorado was his town,
  It rose up shambling in the nuggets' wake,
It had no charter but a promised crown
      Of claims to stake.

But we,—too late, too early, howsoever—
  Won nothing out of fifty-nine—those years—
But gilded promise, yielded to us never,
      And barren tears . . .

The long trail back! I huddled in the shade
  Of wagon-tenting looked out once and saw
Bent westward, passing on a stumbling jade
      A homeless squaw—

Perhaps a halfbreed. On her slender back
  She cradled a babe's body, riding without rein.
Her eyes, strange for an Indian's, were not black
      But sharp with pain

And like twin stars. They seemed to shun the gaze
  Of all our silent men—the long team line—
Until she saw me—when their violet haze
      Lit with love shine . . .

I held you up—I suddenly the bolder,
  Knew that mere words could not have brought
      us nearer.
She nodded—and that smile across her shoulder
      Will still endear her

As long as Jim, your father's memory, is warm.
　　Yes, Larry, now you're going to sea, remember
You were the first—before Ned and this farm,—
　　　　First-born, remember—

And since then—all that's left to me of Jim
　　Whose folks, like mine, came out of Arrowhead.
And you're the only one with eyes like him—
　　　　Kentucky bred!

I'm standing still, I'm old, I'm half of stone!
　　Oh, hold me in those eyes' engaging blue;
There's where the stubborn years gleam and atone,—
　　　　Where gold is true!

Down the dim turnpike to the river's edge—
　　Perhaps I'll hear the mare's hoofs to the ford . . .
Write me from Rio . . . and you'll keep your pledge;
　　　　I know your word!

Come back to Indiana—not too late!
　　(Or will you be a ranger to the end?)
Good-bye . . . Good-bye . . . oh, I shall always wait
　　You, Larry, traveller—
　　　　　　　　stranger,
　　　　　　　　　　son,
　　　　　　　　　　　　—my friend—

Atlantis

(from "The Bridge")

Music is then the knowledge of that which relates to
love in harmony and system.
　　　　　　　　　　　　—*Plato*

THROUGH the bound cable strands, the arching path
　Upward, veering with light, the flight of strings,—
Taut miles of shuttling moonlight syncopate
The whispered rush, telepathy of wires.
Up the index of night, granite and steel—

Transparent meshes—fleckless the gleaming staves—
Sibylline voices flicker, waveringly stream
As though a god were issue of the strings. . . .

And through that cordage, threading with its call
One arc synoptic of all tides below—
Their labyrinthine mouths of history
Pouring reply as though all ships at sea
Complighted in one vibrant breath made cry,—
"Make thy love sure—to weave whose song we ply!"
—From black embankments, moveless soundings hailed,
So seven oceans answer from their dream.

And on, obliquely up bright carrier bars
New octaves trestle the twin monoliths
Beyond whose frosted capes the moon bequeaths
Two worlds of sleep (O arching strands of song!)—
Onward and up the crystal-flooded aisle
White tempest nets file upward, upward ring
With silver terraces the humming spars,
The loft of vision, palladium helm of stars.

Sheerly the eyes, like seagulls stung with rime—
Slit and propelled by glistening fins of light—
Pick biting way up towering looms that press
Sidelong with flight of blade on tendon blade
—Tomorrows into yesteryear—and link
What cipher-script of time no traveller reads
But who, through smoking pyres of love and death,
Searches the timeless laugh of mythic spears.

Like hails, farewells—up planet-sequined heights
Some trillion whispering hammers glimmer Tyre:
Serenely, sharply up the long anvil cry
Of inchling æons silence rivets Troy.
And you, aloft there—Jason! hesting Shout!
Still wrapping harness to the swarming air!
Silvery the rushing wake, surpassing call,
Beams yelling Æolus! splintered in the straits!

From gulfs unfolding, terrible of drums.
Tall Vision-of-the-Voyage, tensely spare—
Bridge, lifting night to cycloramic crest
Of deepest day—O choir, translating time
Into what multitudinous Verb the suns
And synergy of waters ever fuse, recast
In myriad syllables,—Psalm of Cathay!
O Love, thy white, pervasive Paradigm . . . !

We left the haven hanging in the night—
Sheened harbor lanterns backward fled the keel.
Pacific here at time's end, bearing corn,—
Eyes stammer through the pangs of dust and steel.
And still the circular, indubitable frieze
Of heaven's meditation, yoking wave
To kneeling wave, one song devoutly binds—
The vernal strophe chimes from deathless strings!

O Thou steeled Cognizance whose leap commits
The agile precincts of the lark's return;
Within whose lariat sweep encinctured sing
In single chrysalis the many twain,—
Of stars Thou art the stitch and stallion glow
And like an organ, Thou, with sound of doom—
Sight, sound and flesh Thou leadest from time's realm
As love strikes clear direction for the helm.

Swift peal of secular light, intrinsic Myth
Whose fell unshadow is death's utter wound,—
O River-throated—iridescently upborne
Through the bright drench and fabric of our veins;
With white escarpments swinging into light,
Sustained in tears the cities are endowed
And justified conclamant with ripe fields
Revolving through their harvests in sweet torment.
Forever Deity's glittering Pledge, O Thou

Whose canticle fresh chemistry assigns
To rapt inception and beatitude,—
Always through blinding cables, to our joy,
Of thy white seizure springs the prophecy:

Always through spiring cordage, pyramids
Of silver sequel, Deity's young name
Kinetic of white choiring wings . . . ascends.

Migrations that must needs void memory,
Inventions that cobblestone the heart,—
Unspeakable Thou Bridge to Thee, O Love.
Thy pardon for this history, whitest Flower,
O Answerer of all,—Anemone,—
Now while thy petals spend the suns about us, hold—
(O Thou whose radiance doth inherit me)
Atlantis,—hold thy floating singer late!

So to thine Everpresence, beyond time,
Like spears ensanguined of one tolling star
That bleeds infinity—the orphic strings,
Sidereal phalanxes, leap and converge:
—One Song, one Bridge of Fire! Is it Cathay,
Now pity steeps the grass and rainbows ring
The serpent with the eagle in the leaves . . . ?
Whispers antiphonal in azure swing.

OSCAR WILLIAMS

The Man Coming Toward You

THE man coming toward you is falling forward on all
    fronts:
He has just come in from the summer hot box of circumstance,
His obedient arm pulls a ticket from the ticket machine,
A bell announces to the long tables his presence on the scene;
The room is crowded with Last Suppers and the air is angry;
The halleluiahs lift listless heads; the man is hungry.

He looks at the people, the rings of lights, the aisles, the chairs,
They mass and attack his eyes and they take him unawares,

But in a moment it is over and the immense hippopotamus
    cries
And swims away to safety in the vast past of his eyes;
The weeks recoil before the days, the years before the months;
The man is hungry and keeps moving forward on all fronts.

His hair is loosening, his teeth are at bay, he breathes fear,
His nails send futile tendrils into the belly of the atmosphere;
Every drop of his blood is hanging loose in the universe;
His children's faces everywhere bring down the college doors;
He is growing old on all fronts; his foes and his friends
Are bleeding behind invisible walls bedecked with dividends;

His wife is aging, and his skin puts on its anonymous gloves;
The man is helpless, surrounded by two billion hates and loves;
Look at him squirm inside his clothes, the harpies around
    his ears,
In just one minute his brothers will have aged four thousand
    years.
Who records his stupendous step on the delicate eardrum
    of Chance?
The man coming toward you is marching forward on all fronts.

The Leg in the Subway

WHEN I saw the woman's leg on the floor of the
    subway train,
Protrude beyond the panel (while her body overflowed my
    mind's eye),
When I saw the pink stocking, black shoe, curve bulging with
    warmth,
The delicate etching of the hair behind the flesh-colored gauze,
When I saw the ankle of Mrs. Nobody going nowhere for a
    nickel,
When I saw this foot motionless on the moving motionless
    floor,
My mind caught on a nail of a distant star, I was wrenched out
Of the reality of the subway ride, I hung in a socket of distance,
And this is what I saw:

The long tongue of the earth's speed was licking the leg,
Upward and under and around went the long tongue of speed:
It was made of a flesh invisible, it dripped the saliva of miles:
It drank moment, lit shivers of insecurity in niches between
      bones:
It was full of eyes, it stopped licking to look at the passengers
It was as alive as a worm, and busier than anybody in the train:

It spoke saying: To whom does this leg belong? Is it a bonus leg
For the rush hour? Is it a forgotten leg? Among the many
Myriads of legs did an extra leg fall in from the Out There?
O Woman, sliced off bodily by the line of the panel, shall I roll
Your leg into the abdominal nothing, among the digestive
      teeth?
Or shall I fit it in with the pillars that hold up the headlines?
But nobody spoke, though all the faces were talking silently,
As the train zoomed, a zipper closing up swiftly the seam of
      time.

Alas, said the long tongue of the speed of the earth quite
      faintly,
What is one to do with an incorrigible leg that will not melt—
But everybody stopped to listen to the train vomiting cauldrons
Of silence, while somebody's jolted-out afterthought trickled
      down
The blazing shirt-front solid with light bulbs, and just then
The planetary approach of the next station exploded atoms of
      light,
And when the train stopped, the leg had grown a surprising
      mate,
And the long tongue had slipped hurriedly out through a
      window:

I perceived through the hole left by the nail of the star in my
      mind
How civilization was as dark as a wood and dimensional
      with things
And how birds dipped in chromium sang in the crevices of
      our deeds.

ROBERT PENN WARREN

Bearded Oaks

THE oaks, how subtle and marine,
Bearded, and all the layered light
Above them swims; and thus the scene,
Recessed, awaits the positive night.

So, waiting, we in the grass now lie
Beneath the langorous tread of light:
The grasses, kelp-like, satisfy
The nameless motions of the air.

Upon the floor of light, and time,
Unmurmuring, of polyp made
We rest; we are, as light withdraws,
Twin atolls on a shelf of shade.

Ages to our construction went,
Dim architecture, hour by hour:
And violence, forgot now, lent
The present stillness all its power.

The storm of noon above us rolled,
Of light the fury, furious gold,
The long drag troubling us, the depth:
Dark is unrocking, unrippling, still.

Passion and slaughter, ruth, decay
Descend, minutely whispering down,
Silted down swaying streams, to lay
Foundation for our voicelessness.

All our debate is voiceless here,
As all our rage, the rage of stone;
If hope is hopeless, then fearless fear,
And history is thus undone.

Our feet once wrought the hollow street
With echo when the lamps were dead
At windows, once our headlight glare
Disturbed the doe that, leaping, fled.

I do not love you less that now
The caged heart makes iron stroke,
Or less that all that light once gave
The graduate dark should now revoke.

We live in time so little time
And we learn all so painfully,
That we may spare this hour's term
To practice for eternity.

Revelation

BECAUSE he had spoken harshly to his mother,
The day became astonishingly bright,
The enormity of distance crept to him like a dog now,
And earth's own luminescence seemed to repel the night

Roof was rent like the loud paper tearing to admit
Sun-sulphurous splendor where had been before
But the submarine glimmer by kindly countenances lit,
As slow, phosphorescent dignities light the ocean floor.

By walls, by walks, chrysanthemum and aster,
All hairy, fat-petalled species, lean, confer,
And his ears, and heart, should burn at that insidious
    whisper
Which concerns him so, he knows; but he cannot make
    out the words.

The peacock screamed, and his feathered fury made
Legend shake, all day, while the sky ran pale as milk;

That night, all night, the buck rabbit stamped in the
 moonlit glade,
And the owl's brain glowed like a coal in the grove's
 combustible dark.

When Sulla smote and Rome was rent, Augustine
Recalled how Nature, shuddering, tore her gown,
And kind changed kind, and the blunt herbivorous
 tooth dripped blood;
At Duncan's death, at Dunsinane, chimneys blew down.

But, oh! his mother was kinder than ever Rome,
Dearer than Duncan—no wonder, then, Nature's frame
Thrilled in voluptuous hemispheres far off from his home;
But not in terror: only as the bride, as the bride.

In separateness only does love learn definition,
Though Brahma smiles beneath the dappled shade,
Though tears, that night, wet the pillow where the boy's
 head was laid
Dreamless of splendid antipodal agitation;

And though across what tide and tooth Time is,
He was to lean back toward that recalcitrant face,
He would think, than Sulla more fortunate, how once
 he had learned
Something important about love, and about love's grace.

———— • ————

KENNETH PATCHEN

———— • ————

At the New Year

IN the shape of this night, in the still fall of snow, Father
In all that is cold and tiny, these little birds and children
In everything that moves tonight, the trolleys and the lovers,
 Father
In the great hush of country, in the ugly noise of our cities

In this deep throw of stars, in those trenches where the dead
    are, Father
In all the wide land waiting, and in the liners out on the black
    water
In all that has been said bravely, in all that is mean anywhere
    in the world, Father
In all that is good and lovely, in every house where sham and
    hatred are
In the name of those who wait, in the sound of angry voices,
    Father
Before the bells ring, before this little point in time has rushed
    us on
Before this clean moment has gone, before this night turns to
    face tomorrow, Father
There is this high singing in the air
Forever this sorrowful human face in eternity's window
And there are other bells that we would ring, Father
Other bells that we would ring.

DELMORE SCHWARTZ

"*Mentrechè il Vento, Come Fa, Si Tace*"

WILL you perhaps consent to be
    Now that a little while is still
(Ruth of sweet wind) now that a little while
My mind's continuing and unreleasing wind
Touches this single of your flowers, this one only,
Will you perhaps consent to be
My many-branchéd, small and dearest tree?

My mind's continuing and unreleasing wind
—The wind which is wild and restless, tired and asleep,
The wind which is tired, wild and still continuing,
The wind which is chill, and warm, wet, soft, in every
    influence.

Lusts for Paris, Crete and Pergamus,
Is suddenly off for Paris and Chicago,
Judaea, San Francisco, the Midi,
—May I perhaps return to you
Wet with an Attic dust and chill from Norway
My dear, so-many-branchéd smallest tree?

Would you perhaps consent to be
The very rack and crucifix of winter, winter's wild
Knife-edged, continuing and unreleasing,
Intent and stripping, ice-caressing wind?
My dear, most dear, so-many-branchéd smallest tree
My mind's continuing and unreleasing wind
Touches this single of your flowers, faith in me,
Wide as the—sky!—accepting as the (air)!
—Consent, consent, consent to be
My many-branchéd, small and dearest tree.

Socrates' Ghost Must Haunt Me Now

SOCRATES' ghost must haunt me now,
Notorious death has let him go,
He comes to me with a clumsy bow,
Saying in his disuséd voice,
That I do not know I do not know,
The mechanical whims of appetite
Are all that I have of conscious choice,
The butterfly caged in electric light
Is my only day in the world's great night,
Love is not love, it is a child
Sucking his thumb and biting his lip,
But grasp it all, there may be more!
From the topless sky to the bottomless floor
With the heavy head and the finger tip:
All is not blind, obscene, and poor.
Socrates stands by me stockstill,
Teaching hope to my flickering will,
Pointing to the sky's inexorable blue
—Old Noumenon, come true, come true!

RICHARD EBERHART

The Groundhog

IN June, amid the golden fields,
I saw a groundhog lying dead.
Dead lay he; my senses shook,
And mind outshot our naked frailty.
There lowly in the vigorous summer
His form began its senseless change,
And made my senses waver dim
Seeing nature ferocious in him.
Inspecting close his maggots' might
And seething cauldron of his being,
Half with loathing, half with a strange love,
I poked him with an angry stick.
The fever arose, became a flame
And Vigour circumscribed the skies,
Immense energy in the sun,
And through my frame a sunless trembling.
My stick had done nor good nor harm.
Then stood I silent in the day
Watching the object, as before;
And kept my reverence for knowledge
Trying for control, to be still,
To quell the passion of the blood;
Until I had bent down on my knees
Praying for joy in the sight of decay.
And so I left; and I returned
In Autumn strict of eye, to see
The sap gone out of the groundhog,
But the bony sodden hulk remained.
But the year had lost its meaning,
And in intellectual chains
I lost both love and loathing,

Mured up in the wall of wisdom.
Another summer took the fields again
Massive and burning, full of life,
But when I chanced upon the spot
There was only a little hair left,
And bones bleaching in the sunlight
Beautiful as architecture;
I watched them like a geometer,
And cut a walking stick from a birch.
It has been three years, now.
There is no sign of the groundhog.
I stood there in the whirling summer,
My hand capped a withered heart,
And thought of China and of Greece,
Of Alexander in his tent;
Of Montaigne in his tower,
Of Saint Theresa in her wild lament.

KARL JAY SHAPIRO

Poet

Il arrive que l'esprit demande la poesie

LEFT leg flung out, head cocked to the right,
Tweed coat or army uniform, with book,
Beautiful eyes, who is this walking down?
Who, glancing at the pane of glass looks sharp
And thinks it is not he—as when a poet
Comes swiftly on some half-forgotten poem
And loosely holds the page, steady of mind,
        Thinking it is not his?

And when will *you* exist?—Oh, it is I,
Incredibly skinny, stooped, and neat as pie,
Ignorant as dirt, erotic as an ape,

Dreamy as puberty—with dirty hair!
Into the room like kangaroo he bounds,
Ears flopping like the most expensive hound's;
His chin received all questions as he bows
    Mouthing a green bon-bon.

Has no more memory than rubber. Stands
Waist-deep in heavy mud of thought and broods
At his own wetness. When he would get out,
To his surprise he lifts in air a phrase
As whole and clean and silvery as a fish.
Which jumps and dangles on his damned hooked grin,
But like a name-card on a man's lapel
    Calls him a conscious fool.

And childlike he remembers all his life
And cannily constructs it, fact by fact,
As boys paste postage stamps in careful books,
Denoting pence and legends and profiles,
Nothing more valuable.—And like a thief,
His eyes glassed over and concealed with guilt,
Fondles his secrets like a case of tools,
    And waits in empty doors.

By men despised for knowing what he is,
And by himself. But he exists for women.
As dolls to girls, as perfect wives to men,
So he to women. And to himself a thing,
All ages, epicene, without a trade.
To girls and wives always alive and fated;
To men and scholars always dead like Greek
    And always mistranslated.

Towards exile and towards shame he lures himself,
Tongue winding on his arm, and thinks like Eve
By biting apple will become most wise.
Sentio ergo sum: he feels his way
And words themselves stand up for him like Braille
And punch and perforate his parchment ear.
All language falls like Chinese on his soul,
    Image of song unsounded.

This is the coward's coward that in his dreams
Sees shapes of pain grow tall. Awake at night
He peers at sounds and stumbles at a breeze.
And none holds life less dear. For as a youth
Who by some accident observes his love
Naked and in some natural ugly act,
He turns with loathing and with flaming hands,
  Seared and betrayed by sight.

He is the business man, on beauty trades,
Dealer in arts and thoughts who, like the Jew,
Shall rise from slums and hated dialects
A tower of bitterness. Shall be always strange,
Hunted and then sought after. Shall be sat
Like an ambassador from another race
At tables rich with music. He shall eat flowers,
Chew honey and spit out gall. They shall all smile
  And love and pity him.

His death shall be by drowning. In that hour
When the last bubble of pure heaven's air
Hovers within his throat, safe on his bed,
A small eternal figurehead in terror,
He shall cry out and clutch his days of straw
Before the blackest wave. Lastly, his tomb
Shall list and founder in the troughs of grass.
  And none shall speak his name.

The Twins

LIKENESS has made them animal and shy.
 See how they turn their full gaze left and right,
Seeking the other, yet not moving close;
Nothing in their relationship is gross,
But soft, conspicuous, like giraffes. And why
Do they not speak except by sudden sight?

Sisters kiss freely and unsubtle friends
Wrestle like lovers; brothers loudly laugh:

These in a dreamier bondage dare not touch.
Each is the other's soul and hears too much
The heartbeat of the other; each apprehends
The sad duality and the imperfect half.

The one lay sick, the other wandered free,
But like a child to a small plot confined
Walked a short way and dumbly reappeared.
Is it not all-in-all of what they feared,
The single death, the obvious destiny
That maims the miracle their will designed?

For they go emptily from face to face,
Keeping the instinctive partnership of birth
A ponderous marriage and a sacred name;
Theirs is the pride of shouldering each the same
The old indignity of Esau's race
And Dromio's denouement of tragic mirth.

Travelogue for Exiles

LOOK and remember. Look upon this sky;
    Look deep and deep into the sea-clean air,
The unconfined, the terminus of prayer.
Speak now and speak into the hallowed dome.
What do you hear? What does the sky reply?
The heavens are taken: this is not your home.

Look and remember. Look upon this sea;
Look down and down into the tireless tide.
What of a life below, a life inside,
A tomb, a cradle in the curly foam?
The waves arise; sea-wind and sea agree
The waters are taken: this is not your home.

Look and remember. Look upon this land,
Far, far across the factories and the grass.
Surely, there, surely, they will let you pass.
Speak then and ask the forest and the loam.
What do you hear? What does the land command?
The earth is taken: this is not your home.

Nostalgia

MY soul stands at the window of my room,
    And I ten thousand miles away;
My days are filled with Ocean's sound of doom,
    Salt and cloud and the bitter spray.
Let the wind blow, for many a man shall die.

My selfish youth, my books with gilded edge,
    Knowledge and all gaze down the street;
The potted plants upon the window ledge
    Gaze down with selfish lives and sweet,
Let the wind blow, for many a man shall die.

My night is now her day, my day her night,
    So I lie down, and so I rise;
The sun burns close, the star is losing height,
    The clock is hunted down the skies.
Let the wind blow, for many a man shall die.

Truly a pin can make the memory bleed,
    A world explode the inward mind
And turn the skulls and flowers never freed
    Into the air, no longer blind.
Let the wind blow, for many a man shall die.

Laughter and grief join hands. Always the heart
    Clumps in the breast with heavy stride;
The face grows lined and wrinkled like a chart,
    The eyes bloodshot with tears and tide.
Let the wind blow, for many a man shall die.

JOHN MALCOLM BRINNIN

Islands: A Song

ISLANDS are subtle places, still,
Lonely and shining;
Islands of grief refuse to tell
Their separating difference ever;
Feudally they stand, nor cry
"I wait for your discovery!"
Breakers go over,
Sympathy never.

Furious my island city,
Treeless and steepled,
Ample its flashing pity,
Touchable, eager, sweet to wear;
Come, lover, to your radio,
Put fingers to your wrist-veins, so:
Sea-parted, share
This quickening fear.

LLOYD FRANKENBERG

The Sea

IN the midmost of ocean
the water lifts its arms dreaming of spars;
the world is very round, projects its roundness
past all the poles, beyond the one horizon

on that bald ocean overhead, the sky
where swim the worlds like fish in soundless waters.

Imposing its single structure on the sky
and drawing thence its variable mood
of bright confusion, gloom and equable
conformity, the ocean goes scotfree
of other obligation but to pay
the moon its due respects, discharged like spouse.

Left to its own enormous devices the sea
in timeless reverie conceives of life,
being itself the world in pantomime.

Predicting past and future in one long
drawn breath it blends its tides with dawn,
rolls in panoramic sleight-of-hand
creation out of chaos endlessly;

all forms revealed in fluid architecture
flowing like time as if time were turned back:
undreamed-of wars all happening at once
(what rage pent up in atoms: do the drops
take toll of one another? no the sea
had not dreamed this)

                              but like a savage plays
archaic symmetries and simple shapes:
builds promontories, houses lakes, holds out
mirages of itself, erects straw cliffs
hurdled with ease;

                              or lolling all its length
coiled and Niled, in coat of mail tilts evil
complete with scale and hiss, smitten to sculpture,
to iron leaves, to flame, to birds flying
in and out of fluted, spandreled, spired
buildings out of all time swaying, crumpling
in scaffoldings of spray.

                              And then the flowers
all petal and no stem: then finned and ferned,
the leaping swordfish an effrontery
to all its backs, all life presumptuous

and those looking too long upon its wake
who thought to make themselves immortal too,
taking it at its word, instruct it now

(old moonface cratered and sunksocketed,
seamywrinkled, picked and pocked with waves,
the waves all faces lifted looking around,
hair dripping across their foreheads or flung back
for a last despairing gasp before they drown)

for now the last least vestige of the air
that gave the ocean its free hand with space,
gave fins wings roots and legs to walk the sky,
withdraws and leaves it still.

                        Now on its sleeve
it wears the heart that every shipwreck finds;
lies flat, unworked by other element

and in this state of utter unbelief
that keeps it what it is, like nothing else,
smoother than glass, stiller than the dead,
its natural supine and spineless self
that never will arise but from without
(yet even now protests the least intrusion)

believing not that all its mimicry
has ever come to pass, how perfectly
mirrors God's face, the workings of his mind.

Hide in the Heart

I

HERE is no shadow but cloudshadow and
      nightshadow
Moving across and rolling away and leaving
Only the purple avenues the ant
Drags his weight across from here to there
Between the leaning towers of his town.

Here are no voices but the gull's hard lot
Easing his discontent with all the beach,
Abusive tongues of terns, rheumatic crows'
Dry commentaries concerning tomorrow's weather
And pipers fleeing the sound of their own lament.

And the wind's singing is before all music
Picking the strings of grass and thumping the roof
And all the stops of the ocean to be pulled out
When anger is the howling of the wind
And all armies the marches of the sea.

And mornings bringing the white lies of peace,
The rags of truce upon the sea and sky,
Ambassadorial breeze from cloud to wave,
All solved and settled under a smiling sun
Blandly agreeing his hands to everything.

Until the fog with sidelong stratagem
Confers in huddled whispers with the earth—
And ships and birds are asking their way about
Of the whistling buoy that keeps its courage up
Through the long dark and vistas of the mist—

Then lifts again, its mission otherwhere
And leaves us this again our isle of quiet:
Surrounded with seas of grass and the glassy sea
Here in the sweet unreasonable weather
We think us safe, we think us housed in peace.

II

All day the storm stood off from about our door.
The tongues of sand lay panting in the sun,
We listening to the sounds of listless water
With wisps of ragtime over the dunes from town
And scraps of headline: BOMBING ALMERIA.

Who brought this newspaper in like contraband
To poison the horizons of our minds?
All day the sun was stored serenity

Before the cloud fulfilled its promised rain.
Now seeing the fire-edged cloud our thought is of war.

Our sea was water where we drowned our thoughts.
We plunged and lay like time—not like this time.
Our sea was not an endless belt of bullets
Round after round transmitted to the breech
To riddle time to tatters and red teeth.

Now more than ever we do not know how long
This little space of peace will be our own.
The nations run like nightmare toward the repeated
Dream's end and beyond the end and beyond,
Toward the waking up screaming and it's true! it's true!

III

Nations perpetuate the fatal motion
Letting their anger go from them with no
Power to retract, to make amends and an end.
The people standing under the balconies
Look up and become part of what they see.

The cannon standing at stiff-armed salute
Discharge their duties in the innocent air.
The bleak and bankrupt bones are all there is
To pay revenge its dividend and hate
Its pebble dropped, its circle widening.

IV

There is no hiding in these island seas.
The air is full of forebodings of disaster
The gulls come up dead on the tide. It is one to them
Whether the world hold fish. The sandfleas dance
Burning alive on the phosphorescent beach.

The stars are a regiment of fixed bayonets;
The steelgrey seas a rank upon rank of helmets.
Clouds march and countermarch. Winds marshal them;
Roll on their spokes guncarriages of thunder.
The army of grass is led in all directions.

A large drop falls and that is all. The storm
Wheels to the skyline; leaves a sunspace; waits.
These little silly bombardments are but a device
To larger ends; rally the peace-protectors
About false standards, his eye upon another.

V

All day the storm stood off in a rift of cloud.
We thought us safe, we thought us housed in peace.
Ringed in by sun, chalked off by grass, passed by
In a lull of the storm, in a quiet isle. Till night
Darkened our door and the storm broke and the sea

Moving in fury upon the enduring beach
We put our windows against the rain, we drew
Bolts on the wind and shuttered out the storm.
At night the four walls shook like a heart in the gale
Shedding a light like blood on the troubled darkness.

Four walls in the wind are the wind's mouse and we
The heart in the mouse. The lightning lifts a paw,
Purrs in its throat and lets the paw fall slack.
The tail of the wind stirs lazily, shakes the floor
And we are alone with the taste of mouth on mouth.

VI

Hide in the heart. There is no help without.
The strong winds ramp about the world tonight.
The heart is wide enough to move about.
The heart is tall. In a world too small for flight
This is the only border out of doubt.

The light comes in as through the hand's devotion.
The world is held in the hollow of this hand.
Its own sea with its own moon-made motion
Rolls upon the shores of its own land.
Before all singing is the music of this ocean.

Find out this music pounding through the wrists.
Stop out the sounds of the feet tramping the roof.
Let the rain beat with all its mailed fists.

The heart is the only timber to be proof
Against all thunderclaps and lightningtwists.

Hide in this roof until the storm has been;
Till fear leaves us under the eaves of the blood
And one by one arising let them in
Disarming at the door the roaring flood,
The infantry of rain and the strong wind.

JOSÉ GARCIA VILLA

Be Beautiful, Noble, Like the Antique Ant

BE beautiful, noble, like the antique ant,
Who bore the storms as he bore the sun,
Wearing neither gown nor helmet,
Though he was archbishop and soldier:
Wore only his own flesh.

Salute characters with gracious dignity:
Though what these are is left to
Your own terms. Exact: the universe is
Not so small but these will be found
Somewhere. Exact: they will be found.

Speak with great moderation: but think
With great fierceness, burning passion:
Though what the ant thought
No annals reveal, nor his descendants
Break the seal.

Trace the tracelessness of the ant,
Every ant has reached this perfection.
As he comes, so he goes,
Flowing as water flows,
Essential but secret like a rose.

God Said, "I Made a Man"

GOD said, "I made a man
Out of clay—
    But so bright he, he spun
Himself to brightest Day

Till he was all shining gold,
And oh,
    He was lovely to behold!
But in his hands held he a bow

Aimed at me who created
Him. And I said,
    'Wouldst murder me
Who am thy Fountainhead!'

Then spoke he the man of gold:
'I will not
    Murder thee: I do but
Measure thee. Hold

Thy peace!' And this I did.
But I was curious
    Of this so regal head.
'Give thy name!'—'Sir! Genius.'"

Now, If You Will Look in My Brain

NOW, if you will look in my brain
You will see not Because
But Cause—
The strict Rose whose clean
Light utters all my pain.
Dwelleth there my God
With a strict Rod
And a most luminous mien.

And He whippeth! lo how
He whippeth! O see
The rod's velocity
In utterest unmercy
Carve, inflict upon this brow
The majesty of its doomèd Now

My Mouth Is Very Quiet

MY mouth is very quiet
Reverencing the luminance of my brain:
If words must find an outlet
They must work with jewelled pain.

They must cut a way immaculate
To leave the brain incorrupt:
They must repay their Debt
Like archangels undropt.

The miracle of a word is to my mouth
The miracle of God in my brain:
Archangels holding to His North and South,
His East and West by an inviolable chain.

An archangel upon my mouth
May blow his silver trumpet:
But he holds to his North or South,
Blows—and again is quiet.

The Way My Ideas Think Me

THE way my ideas think me
Is the way I unthink God.
As in the name of heaven I make hell
That is the way the Lord says me.

And all is adventure and danger
And I roll Him off cliffs and mountains
But fast as I am to push Him off
Fast am I to reach Him below.

And it may be then His turn to push me off,
I wait breathless for that terrible second:
And if He push me not, I turn around in anger:
"O art thou the God I would have!"

Then He pushes me and I plunge down, down!
And when He comes to help me up
I put my arms around Him, saying, "Brother,
Brother." . . . This is the way we are.

Saw God Dead but Laughing

SAW God dead but laughing.
Uttered the laugh for Him.
Heard my skull crack with doom
Tragedian laughing!

Peered into the cracked skull—
Saw the tragic monkhood
In the shape of God's deathhead
Laughter upon its mouth a jewel.

Jewel bright, O Jewel bright,
Laughter of the Lord.
Laughter with eternity immured
O laugh bright, laugh bright.

Then did the Lord laugh louder
I laughing for Him,
I from the heart's honeycomb
Feeding braver, braver,

Till all the universe was Laughter
But the Laughter of the Lord
O the Laughter of His Word
That could laugh only—after His murder.

INDEX OF POETS

INDEX OF FIRST LINES

Conrad Aiken was guided in his selections for this volume by the principle that American poetry has reached the maturity and dignity of the poetry of older countries. With this conviction firmly in mind, he could afford to eliminate some of the stodgy old bards and make place for the refreshing and vital work of the poets who have arisen during the last quarter-century. Besides being representative, this anthology has the merit of being always on the side of excellence as against sentimentality and mediocrity.